URBAN PROBLEMS

AND PROSPECTS

URBAN PROBLEMS

AND PROSPECTS

Anthony Downs

Senior Vice President
Real Estate Research Corporation

MARKHAM PUBLISHING COMPANY / Chicago

MARKHAM SERIES IN PUBLIC POLICY ANALYSIS
Julius Margolis and Aaron Wildavsky, Editors

Bish, *The Public Economy of Metropolitan Areas*

Bogart, ed., *Social Research and the Desegregation of the U.S. Army*

Davis and Dolbeare, *Little Groups of Neighbors: The Selective Service System*

Downs, *Urban Problems and Prospects*

Feldstein, *Economic Analysis for Health Service Efficiency*

Hansen and Weisbrod, *Benefits, Costs, and Finance of Public Higher Education*

Kershaw, *Government Against Poverty*

Leites and Wolf, *Rebellion and Authority: An Analytic Essay on Insurgent Conflicts*

Wagner, *Fiscal Organization of American Federalism*

Contents

Introduction

Nearly all aspects of urban life in America are changing faster than ever before, but not with equal speed. Technical and economic factors, plus cultural and spiritual ones, are shifting much more rapidly than our legal and social institutions. The result is an escalation of general tensions and conflicts, and great pressure for major alterations in even the most basic institutions.

This book is about how our society might cope with such pressures by altering some of its existing urban policies and programs. It contains eleven articles concerning urban growth in general, race relations, housing, transportation, government administration, and education. Nearly all focus upon how to change the key institutions in these fields. By *institutions*, I mean established laws and organizational structures, their rules, their interrelations, and the entrenched patterns of behavior built around them.

This emphasis results from my belief that significant progress towards curing our most serious urban ills—including pollution, high crime rates, hunger, poverty, racism, poor housing, and poor education—cannot be made without major changes in existing institutions. True, marginal alterations in present institutional policies can help alleviate a few symptoms. Moreover, attacking symptoms is frequently both effective and worthwhile. But it is not enough to accommodate the pressures for change generated by our media-saturated culture. President Nixon recognized this in his State of the Union Message in January, 1970, when he said, "As we enter the seventies, we should enter also a great age of reform of the institutions of American government."

Unfortunately, in recent decades, social scientists have not devoted much of their attention to urban institutions. A few excellent studies have been made. But there is a serious dearth of knowledge about the way new concepts and ideas get translated— or fail to get translated—into working policies and programs through institutional change. Institutions have not been studied enough partly because it is so easy to take them for granted. They appear so well-established, so much a part of the landscape, that they become almost invisible even to professional analysts. Yet I believe it is vital for social scientists in general, and social policy designers in particular, to start reexamining this institutional background. In working on a particular problem, they should challenge the "conventional wisdom," and take very little of the relevant institutional structure as "given" or unchangeable. The traumatic history of the twentieth century proves beyond doubt that even the most fundamental assumptions about society do not always hold true. The average citizen usually assumes—and should assume—that the basic fabric of society is stable and can be relied upon from day to day. But policy analysts should not.

Yet this conclusion does not imply that every analyst must consider the entire universe in every policy study. True, the complex interdependencies inherent in our society mean that "everything depends upon everything else" to an important degree. This "wholeness" has been emphasized recently by ecologists in their attacks upon pollution. But it is both naive and false to leap from this true insight to the false assertion that no specialized or particular analyses can be valid or meaningful. On the contrary, thorough, highly specialized knowledge, analysis, and action are among the keystones of western civilization, and will remain so. Our world is vastly too complicated to allow everyone grappling with a particular issue or problem to reexamine every facet of life, or to eschew specialized concentration upon a relatively narrow subject. Thus, in the jargon of economics, suboptimization is inescapable.

Yet my initial emphasis upon not taking institutions for granted is perfectly consistent with focusing upon particular problems or areas of activity in policy studies. I hope this is demonstrated by the articles in this book. All of them are specialized in subject matter, but some propose rather sweeping changes in existing institutions.

However, I have deliberately avoided presenting any single all-encompassing or overarching theme or theory of urban development, urban problems, or urban growth. The main reason is simple: I do not have one. Other analysts have developed excellent fragments of such a theme or theory—even large-sized fragments. And every competent urban analyst has some unconscious or partly-formed "images" or "models" of how the larger context of urban society works. But formulating those fragments into a unified, coherent theory that might be useful (comparable in scope to my theories of democracy and bureaucracy in earlier works) is beyond my own present capabilities for three reasons. First, the urban world is too complex. Even the most highly sophisticated, computerized models cannot yet encompass most of its significant subtleties, in my opinion. Second, the pace of change is too fast.

Today's brilliant global generalization about urban affairs is tomorrow's laughable blunder, outmoded by some unpredictable change in behavior, or new empirical finding. Third, I am paid to think about specific problems, though in a broad context; so that is what I have concentrated my energies upon.

In doing so, I have employed certain specific techniques embodied in these studies. None are original with me, but I believe all are worth using in analyzing urban affairs. They are:

1. Clearly defining, in operational terms, basic concepts that are widely used but normally considered so "obvious" their meanings are rarely spelled out. Consequently, different people use them to denote very different ideas, conditions or policies. The resulting ambiguities often generate confusion and needless controversies. Examples treated in this book are *new cities* and *racism.*

2. Using simple and straightforward language instead of technical or professional jargon. Policy ideas are useless unless they can be easily understood by those who can translate them into action.

3. Carefully evaluating all widely quoted bits of "conventional wisdom" that derive their authority from repetition, familiarity, or association with high officialdom. Such wisdom often consists of sheer myths based upon erroneous analysis or data. Examples discussed herein include the Census Bureau's population projections, and the belief that a great deal of future urban growth will—or should—occur in "new cities."

4. Formulating several alternative courses of future action, rather than just one preferred course. One of the alternatives should usually describe what will happen if present policies are continued unchanged. This "alternative futures" technique forces people to confront the consequences of their own actions—or inactions—by comparing them with the consequences of those policies the analyst really prefers. Thus, it denies potential critics the intellectual luxury of attacking the analyst's preferred course without offering any alternatives of their own. It also provides them with the basis for selecting different policies in case their preferences are not the same as the analyst's. This method is best illustrated in my study of possible policies towards American ghettos.

5. Using an "all feasible combinations" approach in designing multiple future alternatives. This consists of the following steps: (a) Selecting those specific traits or variables which are most significant in regard to a given problem; (b) Estimating a few alternative possible future values for each variable; (c) Calculating the

total number of possible combinations of these values, taking all the key variables into account (this may be in the millions); (d) Designing criteria for eliminating most of these combinations; and (e) Narrowing down the number to a manageable few for more detailed analysis. This technique is employed in considering alternative forms of future urban growth and alternative ghetto futures.

6. Using arbitrary, but bold and imaginative, judgments and assumptions in analyzing behavior patterns and formulating policies. I believe that extremely arbitrary—even ridiculous—simplifying judgments are often useful in advancing perception, analysis or prescription. For example, I divide all expressway commuters into two categories: explorers and sheep. Similarly, there are hundreds of conceivable futures for ghettos, but important insights can be gained by assuming only five are possible. Another application of this approach is assuming that seemingly permanent conditions can be changed by deliberate policies. Examples are achieving greater suburban dispersal of the U.S. Negro population, and lowering quality standards for new housing.

7. Making very rough calculations in order to gain some quantitative insights into various policy alternatives. In countless policy decisions, the *magnitude* of a proposed change, rather than its *direction*, is the critical factor. Whenever this is true, even crude calculations are vastly superior to none. An example herein is the treatment of uncompensated costs imposed upon urban households by highways and urban renewal.

8. Taking explicit account of redistribution effects in evaluating policy alternatives. I reject the common assumption that all the costs and benefits of any policy are borne by the same people; so redistribution effects can be ignored. Economists in particular are fond of isolating the so-called "efficiency implications" of a policy from its "income redistribution implications." They often make policy recommendations based solely upon the former, while assuming the latter can be handled through a set of taxes and payments treated somewhere else in society. In my opinion, this procedure is both totally unrealistic and harmful. True, efficiency and redistribution effects should often be separated analytically. But they must both be considered in designing policy recommendations, because congressmen and other real actors do not separate them when adopting policies. Moreover, in most cases, the redistribution impacts of a policy are vitally important in determining its desirability. This means most public policy decisions are strongly political in nature, and cannot be treated as purely economic or

scientific. But I believe we should face this fact squarely, rather than ignoring it so as to arrive at less ambiguous policy recommendations.

The eleven essays in this book were written over eight years under many different circumstances. Some were purely academic in origin; others were prepared as parts of assignments for various clients; and some combine these elements. This diversity makes it impossible for me to acknowledge all the many others who contributed ideas to these essays, or otherwise aided in their creation. I wish I could claim that any errors are due to those others, while I am solely responsible for everything either original or valuable. However, honesty forbids such immodesty. It also requires me to single out two people who made major contributions for which I am especially grateful. They are John McKnight, whose ideas comprise much of the essay on racism, and Kay Mulligan, whose constant secretarial efficiency enables me to multiply the results of my labors. Finally, I dedicate this book to my many past and present colleagues at Real Estate Research Corporation. Their efforts, inspiration, and patience have been the *sine qua non* of the many challenging and tremendously varied activities we have undertaken together in the past decade.

1

Alternative Forms of Future Urban Growth in the United States

The prospect of further large-scale urban growth in the United States has evoked cries of alarm from many observers. One such cry (the "Columbus Challenge") warns that we will have to build as many new homes, roads, schools, shopping centers, and the like, from 1960 to 2000 as we did from the time of Columbus up to 1960. A second demands that we build a large number of completely new, freestanding cities to cope with population growth and avoid continuing the supposedly chaotic horrors of urban sprawl. Another commonly heard exhortation urges the U.S. to develop a "national urban policy" or a "national land policy" before we become submerged in "megalopolis."

In my opinion, these and other similar views lack an adequate framework for viewing future urban growth and development as a whole. Such a framework should allow us to explore alternative ways in which future growth might occur and to design one or more effective strategies for shaping it.

This article sets forth a classification of alternative future forms of urban growth, some factors relevant to deciding which are most likely and which are most desirable, and some policy implications for influencing this growth. Limited space permits me to present only an overview and basic conclusions, rather than any detailed analysis justifying the many admittedly arbitrary judgments involved.

Classification of Growth Forms

Defining the most likely forms of future urban growth requires an inherently subjective and arbitrary selection of a few combinations of key factors out of thousands of possibilities. Urban development

Reprinted from the *Journal of the American Institute of Planners*, Vol. 36, No. 1 (January, 1970), pp. 3-11, by permission of the American Institute of Planners.

involves dozens of important variables, each of which could reasonably take on several different future values. Some of these variables are:

1. Location of new growth in relation to existing metropolitan areas.

2. Contiguity of new growth to smaller existing communities located beyond the continuously built-up portions of metropolitan areas (including outside such areas).

3. Type of planning control (such as unplanned and highly fragmented, planned-unit development, or citywide).

4. Level of quality standards required in new construction.

5. Degree of public control over new urban development.

6. Degree of public subsidy for new urban development.

7. Distribution of housing subsidies among various income groups.

8. Degree of social class integration.

9. Degree and nature of racial integration.

10. Mixture of transportation modes.

Just considering these ten variables, and several arbitrarily chosen values for each one, yields at least 93,312 logically possible combinations—each representing a potential form of future urban growth! Clearly, it is impossible to formulate practical policy analysis on the basis of so many alternatives; drastic narrowing down must occur.

I accomplished this by using only variables 1, 2, and 3 to form possible future growth alternatives, thereby shifting consideration of the remaining seven to other parts of the analysis. I further reduced the many possible combinations of values for these three variables by eliminating those which seemed either internally inconsistent, or unlikely to accommodate large-scale new growth. The remaining ten combinations form my candidates for a standard classification of alternative forms of future urban growth in the United States:

1. *Redevelopment* of older neighborhoods in central cities or older suburbs through clearance and rebuilding. It has two forms:

    a. *Unplanned redevelopment* (by individual parcel-owners at a highly-fragmented scale of control).

    b. *Planned redevelopment* (at the planned-unit-development scale of control).

2. *Peripheral sprawl* with unplanned development control, either on the edges of the continuously built-up portions of metro-

politan areas, or beyond those edges but still within commuting range.[1]

3. *Planned peripheral growth* on the edges of the continuously built-up portions of existing metropolitan areas. It has two forms:

    a. *Peripheral planned-unit-development* (under planned-unit-development type of control).

    b. *Peripheral new cities* (under comprehensively planned, citywide type of control).

4. *Satellite growth* beyond the continuously built-up portions of existing metropolitan areas but within commuting range of them. It has three forms:

    a. *Scattered satellites* (under planned-unit-development type of control).

    b. *Satellite new cities* (under citywide type of control but not contiguous to existing smaller communities).

    c. *Satellite expanded cities* (under citywide type of control but contiguous to existing smaller communities).

5. *Nonmetropolitan growth* beyond commuting range from any existing metropolitan areas. It has two forms:

    a. *Nonmetropolitan new cities* (under citywide type of control and not contiguous to any existing communities).

    b. *Expanded nonmetropolitan communities* under citywide scale of control but contiguous to existing communities.

Admittedly, it might be desirable to modify this scheme under some circumstances. For example, scattered development along interstate highways outside of metropolitan areas might be considered "nonmetropolitan sprawl." However, I believe the ten basic forms of urban growth set forth above will form an adequate framework for most analyses of future urban development.

Two important aspects of these alternatives should be emphasized. First, they are not mutually exclusive. All of them could occur simultaneously within a single state, and the first eight could even occur simultaneously within a single metropolitan area. Second, these alternatives are not equally probable. In fact, far more future urban growth is likely to be peripheral sprawl than all the others combined. Public policies can influence the relative likelihood of these alternatives, but they hardly start with even odds.

Key Factors for Urban Growth

Before any policy conclusions can be drawn concerning these alternative forms of future urban growth, it is necessary to understand certain key factors related to such growth. Brief discussion of these factors will form the basis for the policy implications set forth later in this article.

THE SIZE OF THE "URBAN" EXPLOSION

Among urban futurists, a prevalent cause of alarm is the "explosion" of urban population they foresee. Extreme estimates indicate that total U.S. population will *double* from 1960 to 2000, rising from 180.7 million to 361.4 million. This gain of 180.7 million in forty years is derived from the U.S. Census Bureau's highest-fertility projection (Series A), which assumes fertility rates typical of the peak postwar years.[2] But, since 1957, U.S. fertility rates have plummeted 30 percent. Hence, they are already down to the level assumed by the Census Bureau's lowest-fertility projection (Series D), which indicates a gain of 101.9 million from 1960 to 2000.[3] If fertility rates keep on falling (as I believe they will), then even this projection may be too high.

For comparison, I have made a crude calculation based upon the assumption that fertility rates will continue to fall steeply for another decade, then level off until 2000. My rough approximation shows this would reduce the total population gain between 1960 to 2000 to 68.8 million. This would result in a total U.S. population in the year 2000 of about 250 million. Lacking a really precise cohort analysis, I do not contend my estimate is terribly reliable, but it certainly convinces me that most current estimates of future U.S. population are far too high.[4] This error has caused most urban observers to grossly exaggerate the magnitude, or at least the rate, of future urban population growth.

Another consideration centers on the definition of "urban." The Census Bureau officially considers any place containing 2,500 or more inhabitants as "urban." I believe the word "urban" as used in popular and expert parlance really should be defined as "pertaining to metropolitan areas." In 1960, about 63 percent of all Americans lived in metropolitan areas. However, those areas captured about 80 percent of total U.S. population growth from 1950 to 1960, 83 percent from 1960 to 1966, and somewhat less than that from 1966 to 1969. Assuming that such areas receive about 80 percent of future U.S. population growth, Table 1 indicates future "urban" growth defined in terms of these metropolitan areas.

Table 1

"Urban" Growth, 1960-2000

U.S. Population Projection Used	Millions	As Percent Gain Over 1960
My estimate	55.0	49.2%
Census Series D	80.5	71.7
HUD estimate	96.4	85.8
Census Series A	144.6	128.8

The table shows why believers in Census Series A are still reciting the "Columbus Challenge." According to their estimate, metropolitan areas will more than double in population from 1970 to 2000. However, I think they are wrong—and by a huge amount. Even so, future urban growth will hardly be trivial. A gain of 55 million people in metropolitan areas is just about *double* the gain experienced from 1950 to 1960—the great decade of suburbanization. And future growth after the year 2000 will probably make even the Series A projection for 2000 come true several decades later. But the *rate* of such growth will clearly slow down. That fact has critical implications for the strain on our economy likely to result from meeting urban expansion needs.

LINKING THE TWO "URBAN FRONTIERS"

It is useful to simplify the incredibly complex welter of urban problems by viewing them as clustered around what I call two "urban frontiers." One is the *Frontier of Deterioration* in older central cities and suburbs, especially in ghetto areas. The other is the *Frontier of Growth* on the periphery of built-up portions of our metropolitan areas.

At present, most public policies treat these frontiers as completely separate from and totally unrelated to each other. One set of policies focuses almost entirely on improving central cities and ghettos as if they were hermetically sealed off from the suburbs. This includes most public housing, most urban anti-poverty programs, most urban job training programs, most housing code enforcement programs, a great deal of the urban Aid-to-Families-with-Dependent-Children, and even many mass transit grants. The one apparent exception is the federal highway-aid program. Yet even its effect has been mainly to link downtowns and suburbs more closely, thereby making it even easier to bypass deteriorating areas within central cities.

On the other hand, plans for further suburban development deliberately exclude ways to use such expansion to help solve inner-city problems. Low-income housing is systematically blocked out of growth areas, even though suburban industrial firms are desperately short of unskilled labor. Only token efforts are made to introduce minority group workers into suburban building trades, in spite of critical shortages of construction workers in many areas. Thus, "natural" ways to simultaneously alleviate inner-city unemployment and suburban labor shortages are ignored. Metropolitan-wide plans drawn up by federally supported regional planning agencies almost never contain any explicit consideration of where minority group members—especially Negroes—will live in the future. Yet the expansion of such groups provides the single most important dynamic force in many big central city housing markets. But it is "too hot to handle" for politically powerless metropolitan planning agencies, who are often fearful of their segregationist suburban constituencies.

We continue to ignore the need to use the dynamic economic expansion of suburban growth as a major input to solving inner-city problems. This bifurcation can only perpetuate the two racially separate societies properly condemned by the Kerner Commission, and the myriad fiscally separate communities rightly criticized by the Douglas Commission. I realize that the present institutional structure of metropolitan areas makes linking these two frontiers extremely difficult in practice. Yet some movements toward significant institutional change have already begun. The Department of Housing and Urban Development is beginning to push for regional housing strategies and programs run by state agencies, and the President has proposed a revenue sharing plan that could ultimately overcome the key fiscal barriers to "opening up the suburbs" for low-income housing. These efforts and other attempts to link the two urban frontiers so they can reinforce each other must be a vital part of any policies concerning future U.S. urban growth.

"EXTRA" COSTS IN NEW CITIES

Accommodating future urban growth in new cities involves several real costs larger than the costs of alternative forms of development. These "extra" costs result from the following key characteristics which differentiate new cities from other forms of urban growth.

Comprehensive Planning at a Citywide Scale

This requires centralized control over land use and development in a very large area *before* anything is created on that land, so it generates the following added costs (as compared to growth at lesser scales of planning control):

a.   The added costs of assembling a large enough site to accommodate 100,000 people (or whatever number is considered to be "city-sized"), and holding parts of that site vacant during the first stages of development—which may last years.

b.   The cost of developing and operating new institutions for centralized planning and control of such a large-scale activity.

c.   The cost of overcoming the obstacles to new city development created by existing fragmented landownership and government institutions. A great deal of extra lobbying skill, waiting time, and money is needed to wrest comprehensive planning opportunities from them.

Distance from Existing Metropolitan Facilities

In nonmetropolitan new cities or expanded cities, where residents are beyond range of existing facilities, the following extra costs arise:

a.   The *initial* loss of return on, or initially inefficient operation of, facilities which must be built immediately with a capacity to handle a large population long before that population itself arrives. These facilities include public infrastructure (such as roads, sewer and water facilities, high schools, and public buildings) and private enterprises (such as shopping centers and industrial plants).

b.   The *total* costs of duplicating elements of existing metropolitan areas that now have enough excess capacity to serve many more people. Examples are some museums, universities, libraries, concert halls, public buildings, theaters, and business firms. No new facilities like these would be required if growth occurred peripherally or in satellites not too far from existing central cities.

Housing Everyone and Everything in Brandnew Quarters   Not all households, business firms, or other institutions can afford brandnew quarters. But in a new city, everything is brandnew. Yet society cannot operate a large community without the services of many low-income households and many low-cost business firms. To enable these entities to survive in a new city, some form of public subsidy must be extended to cover the higher cost of their occupying new structures. This subsidy would not be required by peripheral growth. Then, such households and firms could occupy older quarters in the existing inventory of structures in each metropolitan area. Some subsidy for such entities might be required by satellite growth, but then many low-income workers could commute from lower cost housing existing elsewhere. Moreover, these are not trivial costs. New housing is so expensive that over one-half the households in the U.S. cannot afford even to *rent* newly-built, modestly designed, appropriately sized apartments without spending an inordinate fraction of their incomes on housing. So unless almost all residents of a new city are relatively affluent—which is impossible if the city is to operate efficiently—a large fraction of its residents will need subsidies to live there. The same is true of many businesses.

Some proponents of new cities argue that these costs should not be considered "extra." Either they are offset by extra benefits (such as lower air pollution), or we "ought to" bear them in *any* future growth (in particular, we "ought to" replace substandard housing with new units). Hence, they regard paying for these extra costs as a form of *social investment* that will pay off handsomely in the long run.

Measuring the net total costs of alternative ways to accommodate future urban growth is an extremely complex task beyond the scope of this article. Nevertheless, I believe there are three reasons why building new cities—especially nonmetropolitan ones— would definitely require extra public subsidies unnecessary if future growth occurred through peripheral or even satellite expansion. First, some of the extra costs cited above produce no offsetting benefits or reductions in other costs. This is true of duplicating existing facilities that now have excess capacity. Second, most of the benefits resulting from the extra costs cited above would be of the type for which no direct revenues could be collected. They are what economists call "external benefits" or "public goods." Hence, they are received directly by consumers without going through any market; so no prices can be charged for their use. Examples are reduced air pollution, lower traffic congestion, and improved aesthetic conditions. The private sector—including the beneficiaries themselves—will not voluntarily pay the extra costs of producing these benefits; therefore, the government would have to incur much larger expenditures for urban growth in new cities—especially nonmetropolitan ones—than in other forms. Third, it is not true that society would have to pay for upgrading many low-income households or businesses into brand new quarters if peripheral urban growth occurred. We could continue our traditional strategy of upgrading the poor by building new housing at the high-cost end of the market and relying on "filtering down" to open up adequate quarters for the poor in the older existing inventory. In part, this strategy has failed in the past because we did not build enough new units of any kind; but even if we decided to use large-scale housing subsidies to overcome this failure, the per unit subsidy cost would be lower if we still focused new subsidized construction on middle-income and upper-income households, rather than requiring *all* households to pay the high costs of new quarters—as in nonmetropolitan new cities.

Thus, to the extent that any future urban growth strategy emphasizes new cities, it compels society, early in the development process, to pay extra public expenditures as compared to peripheral or satellite growth. True, if those extra public expenditures are eventually offset by extra benefits and if public authorities own most of the land in new cities, then they may eventually recapture enough profits and land value appreciation to repay this large initial investment. This appears to be happening in Great Britain. Nevertheless, public authorities will still have to make some arrangements to pay the extra initial costs of new cities in order to bring them into being.

LESSONS FROM EUROPEAN EXPERIENCE WITH GROWTH CONTROLS

For several decades, many European nations have been exerting significant controls of various types over their own urban growth. In my opinion, their experience indicates the following significant conclusions relevant to future policies affecting U.S. urban growth.

Any attempt to exert significant public influence over the nature, location, magnitude, or physical form of urban growth requires public ownership or other direct control of a significant part of the land in major metropolitan areas, especially on their growth peripheries. Leaving most of the control over land use in private hands, especially where private ownership is fragmented into thousands of small parcels, as in the U.S., makes it impossible to impose any real guided development policy on even one metropolitan area. This conclusion implies that creation of any overall "urban growth strategy" or "urban land policy" would involve radical *restructuring* of traditional land ownership and control arrangements in the U.S. Also, development of any significant number of nonmetropolitan new cities, or even peripheral or satellite new cities, will require *public* ownership of much of the land in those cities.

Creation of relatively independent nonmetropolitan new cities is an extraordinarily difficult achievement of dubious long-run value. In Great Britain, public agencies promoting new town development have for decades exercised financial and administrative powers vastly greater than any currently contemplated in the U.S. Yet after over 20 years of effort, only about 2.5 percent of all new housing construction in Britain occurs in new towns. Moreover, British government planners have virtually abandoned formation of additional nonmetropolitan new cities. They now favor peripheral new cities adjoining middle-sized metropolitan areas beyond commuting range from London or the big Midlands industrial centers. This policy shift is essentially an attempt to escape many of the extra costs of nonmetropolitan new city development described above. To the best of my knowledge, in Sweden and the biggest Soviet cities, all so-called new cities are either peripheral or satellite in nature.

A crucial determinant of the physical form which publicly controlled urban growth takes is the type of transportation serving new growth areas. The decision to plan such areas around public mass transit (as in Sweden and the Soviet Union) influences the physical form, density, and structure of the communities concerned—as does the universal decision to build them around automobiles in the United States. Swedish peripheral new cities linked to downtown Stockholm by subway feature very high-density residential areas clustered around each subway stop so that thousands of people can live within walking distance of transportation facilities. Huge shopping centers are built over each subway stop for the convenience of these pedestrian residents. This is in striking contrast to our own shopping centers built near expressway interchanges for the convenience of auto-driving residents scattered across low-density neighborhoods. Thus, public decisions about what kind of transportation systems should serve new growth areas exert profound influence over every facet of their development. Any decision to shift major emphasis to mass transit in U.S. urban growth areas would cause radical transformations in the patterns of development typical of such areas during the past twenty-five years.

Rapid construction of new urban facilities to accommodate large-scale growth cannot be achieved through clearance and redevelopment; it must be done on initially vacant land. Even in the Soviet Union, clearance and redevelopment of built-up areas takes much longer than construction on peripheral vacant land. In Paris, the huge *La Defense* urban redevelopment project had finished only 600 net new housing units (in addition to those needed for relocation) after ten years; whereas a single public housing project on suburban vacant land housed over 40,000 residents eight years after its inception. These facts simply reemphasize a conclusion long established by U.S. urban renewal experience; the average redevelopment project takes from six to nine years.

Deliberately slowing down the growth of major urban centers —especially the national capital—is extremely difficult. With all their powers, Soviet urban authorities have been unable to prevent the Moscow area from continuing to grow rapidly. Although British authorities have had some success in shifting growth out of the center of London, there is still pressure to locate more activities within the London metropolitan region. The economic, political, cultural, and psychological advantages of being "where the action is," or at least within easy range, strongly favor peripheral or satellite expansion, rather than nonmetropolitan growth.

Undoubtedly, many other significant lessons could be drawn from European experience in trying to impose a "national strategy" upon urban growth. I think they point to two basic conclusions. *First, the focal point of public concern should be urban growth in general, not just nonmetropolitan new cities.* In fact, the latter invariably encompass only a small fraction of total urban expansion. *Second, public policies regarding urban growth are severely constrained by many forces over which public authorities concerned with urban development have little effective control.* Achieving an "optimal" pattern of urban development is almost everywhere subordinated to other public policy objectives. The latter create formidable obstacles to formation and execution of rational urban growth strategies. This suggests that changes in long-established institutional structures or behavior patterns needed to improve urban development are not likely to be undertaken solely for that purpose. The more radical such changes are, the more they need to be linked with other public policy purposes, or with powerful forces unrelated to urban development, in order to be enacted.

Specific Policy Implications for the United States

In our diffused political system, creating a rational urban development strategy is extraordinarily difficult, even within a single metropolitan area. My own experience on the National Commission on Urban Problems convinces me that certain specific policy objectives must be attained before we can create any such strategies. These objectives are aimed at expanding the possible forms of future urban development beyond peripheral sprawl, which now encompasses almost all urban growth. They do not form a single urban development strategy in themselves; rather, they are the foundations on which several such strategies might be built. Each of these objectives can be achieved through one or more tactics.

INCREASING THE QUANTITY OF NEW HOUSING BUILT

The first key objective is *building much more new housing each year than in the recent past, and subsidizing much of it so as to improve housing conditions among the poorest and most ill-housed citizens.* I do not believe that the U.S. will come very close to the ten-year "target" of twenty-six million new units (including six million subsidized units) set forth in the Housing and Urban Development Act of 1968.[5] Nevertheless, it is clear that we must build more units than in the recent past if we are to prevent a worsening housing shortage. Also, since many of the households in the worst housing are very poor, they cannot possibly afford to rent or buy new units.

Several specific tactics are necessary to move toward this objective. The first is creation of an *economic climate* conducive to much larger housing production than in the past. Such a climate would be marked by low interest rates, a somewhat slack economy with relatively high unemployment, and much more spending than in the past for all aspects of housing, including planning and data gathering. Thus, there is a fundamental conflict between sustained large-scale housing production and sustained high-level prosperity. When the economy is booming, demands for capital surge upward. But many alternative uses of capital have traditionally paid much higher returns than investment in housing. Housing production tends to be choked off—or at least fails to rise very high. The only way to counteract this relationship would be to raise housing to a much higher level of national priority. This would justify using various subsidies to increase the rate of return on housing invest-ment. I believe such a shift in national priorities will occur only if the emerging housing shortage becomes bad enough to incon-venience large numbers of middle- and upper-income households.

The second tactic necessary to generate large-scale housing production aiding the poor is *using much greater housing subsidies* than ever before. Such subsidies would have two effects: increasing total housing production (as noted above), and making new units directly available to low-income households who otherwise could not afford them. Traditionally, we have concentrated our housing subsidies on middle-income and upper-income households by allow-ing them to deduct mortgage interest payments and local property taxes from their federally taxable incomes. This has stimulated total housing production, but has aided low-income households only indirectly, and often ineffectively, through acceleration of the "filtering-down" process. Really improving access of the ill-housed poor to good housing would require providing them with direct housing subsidies. Although Congress authorized this in the 1968 Housing Act, it has never provided large-scale appropriations for low-income housing subsidies. Nor does the present political climate indicate that it soon will do so.

Yet almost all forms of urban growth would benefit from placing at least some low- and moderate-income households in brand new housing. This is necessary in order to avoid continued spatial segregation of poor and low-middle-income groups from wealthier Americans. The vast majority of all new housing is built on vacant land, which is normally at the edges of existing built-up areas. If only upper-middle-income and upper-income households can afford to live in newly built units (as is now the case), then growth areas will always be occupied only by such households. This would lead to economically and socially "unbalanced" new communities, especially if new growth took the form of peripheral new cities, or satellites of any type. It would be extremely expensive to house *all* the low-income households related to a new community in brand new quarters, as in nonmetropolitan new cities. Yet, for several reasons, at least *some* low- and moderate-income households ought to live in new-growth areas. First, they perform vital roles in the local labor force, so if they live in the new growth areas where they work, total commuting time and traffic congestion are reduced. Second, they provide class diversity in local schools and other cultural institutions, hopefully enriching the experiences of everyone and stimulating their own upward mobility. Third, this gives them a much wider set of housing options. Thus, *the degree to which Congress provides direct housing subsidies to low- and moderate-income households has crucial implications for the particular forms of urban growth likely to occur in the future.* The less such subsidies are provided, the more future growth will be "locked in" to peripheral or satellite forms that will perpetuate economic class segregation. The more such subsidies are provided, the greater freedom we will have to use other forms, especially new cities and nonmetropolitan forms.

OPENING UP THE SUBURBS

The second key objective needed to widen our choice among future forms of urban development is *opening up the suburbs and outlying portions of central cities to new low- and moderate-income housing.* This is desirable not only for all the reasons cited above, but also because we cannot build large numbers of housing units for such groups within central cities. There is not enough vacant land there, and that which exists is needed for nonresidential uses. Creating new housing through relocation and clearance is impractical. It is time consuming, expensive, and simply defers the problem by compelling poor people to move somewhere else. Further, most new jobs are being created in the suburbs. So it makes sense to put housing for low- and moderate-income households there.

As noted above, this would require large-scale direct subsidies so that such households could live in newly built housing. Some of these subsidies would probably take the form of a "writedown" of land costs similar to that under urban renewal, but applied to vacant land. In addition, four other tactics would help attain this

objective. The first is weakening the power of small local governments to block federally assisted housing of all kinds. This could
be done by eliminating the present workable program requirement
for federal-aid eligibility, and empowering central city and county-
wide housing authorities to operate outside central cities and inside
suburbs.

A second tactic consists of escalating land use control powers
to areas of wider jurisdiction. This would prevent small communities from blocking the entry of low-income households through
large-lot zoning and other manipulations of local ordinances. It
could be accomplished by shifting all zoning powers to large bodies
such as counties or cities with 50,000 or more population, providing review and alteration powers over small town zoning decisions
to such larger bodies or to the state itself, or having the state
require all communities to zone a certain amount of their buildable
land so it could contain low- and moderate-income housing.

A third tactic for opening up suburbs is increasing the ability
of state governments to create low- and moderate-income housing.
They could do so by means of state housing authorities and other
organizations provided with federally financed incentives. A fourth
tactic is tying many forms of federal aid to the prior provision of
low-income housing by local communities. Such aid might include
sewer and water assistance, highway funds, aid to education, and
funds distributed under the proposed federal revenue sharing plan.

ESCALATING THE LEVEL OF PLANNING

A third key objective relevant to future urban development is
*escalation of the level of planning so that "spillover effects," now
ignored by most developers, will be effectively taken into account.*
Most building is now done by owners of relatively small parcels.
They do not, and cannot, pay much attention to how their own
behavior affects their neighbors. They have very little control over
their neighbors' projects except for that provided by zoning
ordinances, which are vulnerable to court overthrow. This fragmentalized approach to new growth leads to "hodgepodge" development that is aesthetically disastrous and often inefficient. In
order to achieve more fully integrated planning of urban growth, it
is necessary to escalate the level of planning control to larger areas.

Several tactics would accomplish this. The first has already
been discussed: shifting zoning and other land use control powers

away from smaller communities to larger ones. No one in our fragmentalized system of local government simultaneously has both the overall interest of the entire metropolitan area at heart, and sufficient power to influence critical decisions about the area's urban growth. But this tactic would widen the parochial legal and geographic horizons of planning bodies so that their actions would exhibit far more comprehensive scope.

A second possible tactic would be forcing developers in at least some parts of each metropolitan area to undertake action only at a certain minimum geographic scale. This is a means of "internalizing" within a single plan certain land use relationships which would be "external"—and therefore largely ignored—under our present fragmented land development. If development occurred mainly in large chunks, such relations could be fully taken into account by the one plan covering everything within the boundaries of each chunk. For example, assume that in some high-growth part of a metropolitan area, the state passed a law that no urban development could occur at a scale less than 1,500 acres, or under a single plan encompassing such an area. This would compel individual owners to get together somehow in a cooperative plan, or to sell out to larger developers. In order to avoid injustice, the state would have to develop some procedure for buying and holding the individual parcels of those owners who wanted to sell before any overall plan was developed. Such sales would occur at the price of the land before development, so this practice would not allow such owners to capture speculative land value gains.

A third tactic for escalating the scale of planning is bolstering state planning powers and creating new institutions to carry out urban development at a citywide scale. This would involve three different kinds of institutions. The first would be a *national framework organization* charged with creating and administering national policies toward urban development. It could be part of the Department of Housing and Urban Development or an offshoot of the new Council of Urban Affairs. Its functions might include (1) developing national migration and population-growth policies; (2) coordinating all federal programs relevant to new cities; (3) coordinating land acquisition and disposition policies of all federal and some state agencies; (4) administering direct financial assistance to both state enabling organizations and actual developers of new cities; and (5) forming other national policies toward urban growth.

The second type of new institution would be *state or regional enabling organizations.* They would make it easier for private or public developers to overcome existing institutional obstacles to large-scale urban development. Possible functions for them include (1) creating statewide plans for shaping future urban growth (including selecting sites for new cities if any are built); (2) controlling the location of major public investments such as universities and highways; (3) granting franchises to developers to build new cities on specific sites; (4) establishing multi-purpose taxing districts to help finance public improvements needed in urban growth; (5) using powers of eminent domain to assemble large-scale sites or create land banks or buffer zones; (6) "writing down" the cost of assembled land with federal funds so some housing on it could be occupied by low-income households; and (7) suggesting needed changes in existing regulations concerning zoning, subdivision, building codes, and the like to improve urban growth patterns.

The third type of new institution would be *operating development organizations,* created to plan and build large-scale new developments. These could be fully public corporations (like New York's Urban Development Corporation), quasi-public organizations, or fully private organizations benefiting from special powers exercised by the state (as private developers benefit from the eminent domain powers of local urban renewal agencies). They would carry out most of the initial planning, land assembly, public infrastructure construction, and some residential and other construction required for large-scale new developments. Since it is impossible to select from the menu of different possible organizations for such development any one best way applicable everywhere, national legislation should be designed to encourage formation of many different kinds of enabling and operating development organizations.

BROADER FINANCING OF LOCAL GOVERNMENTS

A fourth objective critical to expanding our choices among forms of future urban growth is *widening the financial base of most local governments.* We cannot expect narrowminded thinking to disappear from most small communities as long as existing local government financial structures provide strong incentives for parochialism. Suburban resistance to the entry of low-income residents is partly—perhaps even mainly—a matter of fiscal self-defense.

When low-income residents move into a wealthier community, they generally bring many children. The added cost of educating them is larger than the added tax revenues produced by the housing in which the low-income families live. Thus, every new low-income family represents an instant deficit to the local government and instantly higher taxes on all existing residents. We can hardly expect rational citizens to disregard these conditions by welcoming more low-income neighbors at their own expense. Americans have also traditionally resisted mixing with "lower-class elements" after having escaped from those same elements themselves, so not all suburban hostility to low-income residents is fiscally motivated. Yet, we will never reduce that hostility unless we first remove its economic causes. I believe we must shift a large part of the financial burden for key local government activities—particularly schools and welfare—away from local property taxes to a much broader base. That base could either be much larger property taxing districts encompassing whole metropolitan areas, state funds, federal funds, or federal funds channeled through the states (as President Nixon recently proposed).

OTHER OBJECTIVES

Other key objectives that would expand our future choices among forms of urban growth include *reducing the diversity of existing building codes, zoning rules, and other local regulations, and reducing the cost of producing housing.* These are the focal points of OPERATION BREAKTHROUGH now being carried out by the Department of Housing and Urban Development. The first is necessary so that builders can capture more of the economies of large-scale production and marketing than in the past. At present, more than 8,000 legal entities in the United States issue building and/or housing codes. Almost all these codes are significantly different from each other. It is nearly impossible for housing developers of truly nationwide scope to come into being, since they must tailor their products to these immense local variations in requirements. We do not know what kinds of economies might possibly be achieved through mass production, and through creation of nationwide market acceptance for a single type of housing unit, or a small number of such types. If each state adopted a single building and housing code applicable everywhere within its boundaries, then there would be sufficient uniformity to encourage mass production, but sufficient diversity to test a variety of code elements. States will probably not do this unless strong federal financial incentives are available, and a single national testing facility exists to verify particular building technology innovations.

Reducing housing costs significantly would surely be desirable, but I doubt if it will happen. Most of the cost of occupying housing pays for land and financing, rather than for building the unit. In fact, technical innovations in construction will have to be incredibly significant just to keep the cost of housing from continuing to rise, given the acute shortage of skilled construction labor, rising land costs, and zooming interest rates. In my opinion, unless we drastically reduce the size and quality we require in newly-built units, we will never have truly *low-cost* new housing. Hence new units for low- and moderate-income households will still require major subsidies.

Conclusions

The following conclusions represent what I believe are the most important implications of the foregoing analysis:

1. Future urban growth in the United States through 2000 will be much smaller than most official projections indicate, though it will still represent significant expansion of existing metropolitan areas.

2. Peripheral sprawl will undoubtedly be the dominant form of future urban growth throughout the United States. Whether it will be almost totally dominant, or just largely dominant, will depend upon the extent to which the key policy objectives set forth here are actually achieved.

3. Nonmetropolitan new cities or expanded communities are not likely to capture any significant fraction of the nation's future urban growth, in spite of their current vogue in planning literature. The extra costs of these forms of urban growth mean that peripheral or satellite alternatives to peripheral sprawl are far more likely to occur.

4. Formulation of any one "national urban strategy" or "national land policy" is neither likely nor desirable. It is not likely both because of our diffused decision-making structure and because the necessary pre-conditions for real alternatives to peripheral sprawl do not yet exist. It is not desirable because diversity

both within and among metropolitan areas makes a multiplicity of "urban strategies" better than just one.

5. State governments are the best focal points for development of any overall strategies controlling future urban growth or even for increasing our choices among forms of future urban growth. They are the only institutions that combine metropolitan-wide perspective, decisive powers to override local governments, and sufficient local knowledge and local political roots to make use of such powers acceptable.

6. The proper federal role in shaping future urban growth should probably be one of structuring effective financial incentives for state governments to assume major policy responsibilities, financing subsidies needed for socially and economically "balanced" new development, and continuing to sponsor innovative approaches to key urban problems.

7. Developing effective alternatives to peripheral sprawl, or even mitigating some of its socially segregating effects, will require major changes in deeply-rooted existing political and other institutions. These include local control over land use and zoning, local financing for schools, fragmented planning of new development, and the ability of individual landowners to engage in real estate speculation. The traumatic nature of these changes to many citizens can hardly be overestimated. In fact, they are likely to occur only if the failings of existing arrangements become far more pressing and obvious than they are now in most areas.

8. The choices Americans make among alternative forms of future urban growth will ultimately depend upon the way they resolve certain key ambiguities among their own desires. On one hand is a widespread feeling that future urban growth could be improved through more comprehensive planning and less haphazard decision making. On the other hand is the traditional desire of individual Americans to control their own small parcels of land and their own small local governments, and to gain from speculating in land values. But more comprehensive planning and continued fragmentalized control over development are mutually exclusive; we cannot enjoy the benefits of both simultaneously. As Pogo said about racism, "We have met the enemy, and he is us."

Notes

¹The second form of growth I have called *peripheral sprawl* includes another form that might be more logically called *satellite sprawl*. It is not on the edge of existing cities (hence peripheral) but away from that edge (hence satellite). Yet the term *satellite* implies a cluster of some type, rather than more scattered development. Moreover, *peripheral sprawl* is used by many observers to refer to *all* scattered development outside existing built-up areas, both on the edge and farther out but within commuting range. Thus, I have adopted this dual definition.

²All data on official population projections are derived from U.S. Bureau of the Census, *Statistical Abstract of the United States: 1968* (89th Edition, Washington D.C.: GPO 1968), pp. 7-9.

³*Ibid.*

⁴This also means that many *local* estimates of future population growth are far too high. A common technique for making local estimates (such as for a given metropolitan area) is to estimate what percentage of the future total U.S. population the local area will contain as of a given date. This percentage is derived from past proportions of the U.S. population (or its growth) located in the local area. Hence, if the future estimate used for the entire nation is way too high, then any area estimates derived from it will likewise be too high.

⁵A detailed explanation of this belief is presented in, "Moving Toward Realistic Housing Goals," Kermit Gordon, Editor, *An Agenda for the Nation* (Washington, D.C.: The Brookings Institution, 1968), pp. 141-78. (Also reprinted in this volume, pp. 115-55.)

2

Alternative Futures for the American Ghetto

In the past few years, the so-called "ghetto" areas of large American cities have emerged as one of the major focal points of national and local concern. Yet there have been very few attempts to develop a comprehensive, long-run strategy for dealing with the complex forces that have created our explosive ghetto problems.

Historically, the word "ghetto" meant an area in which a certain identifiable group was compelled to live. The word retains this meaning of geographic constraint, but now refers to two different kinds of constraining forces. In its *racial* sense, a ghetto is an area to which members of an ethnic minority, particularly Negroes, are residentially restricted by social, economic, and physical pressures from the rest of society. In this meaning, a ghetto can contain wealthy and middle-income residents as well as poor ones. In its *economic* sense, a ghetto is an area in which poor people are compelled to live because they cannot afford better accommodations. In this meaning, a ghetto contains mainly poor people, regardless of race or color.

Considerable confusion arises from failure to distinguish clearly between these different meanings of the word "ghetto." In the remainder of this analysis, I will use the word in its racial sense unless otherwise noted.[1]

The Population of Ghettos

In March 1966, there were 12.5 million nonwhites living in all U.S. central cities, of whom 12.1 million were Negroes. Since the Negroes were highly segregated residentially, this number serves as a good estimate of the 1966 ghetto population in the racial sense. Approximately 39 per cent of these racial ghetto residents had

Reprinted from *Daedalus*, Vol. 97, No. 4 (Fall, 1968), pp. 1331–78, by permission of the American Academy of Arts and Sciences. Footnotes have been renumbered.

incomes below the "poverty level" (the equivalent of $3,300 per year for a four-person household), based upon data for 1964 (the latest available).[2]

On the other hand, in 1964 the total number of persons with incomes below the "poverty level" in all U.S. central cities was about 10.1 million. Approximately 56 per cent of these persons were white and 44 per cent were nonwhite.[3] Since there were about 11.3 million nonwhites altogether in central cities in 1964, the ghetto in its purely economic sense contained about 11 per cent fewer people than in its racial sense. Moreover, about 4.4 million persons were doubly ghetto residents in 1964—they were central-city citizens who were both poor and nonwhite.[4]

No matter which ghetto definition is used, it is clear that the population of ghettos is a small fraction of total U.S. population—less than 7 per cent. Moreover, future growth in the ghetto population will be dwarfed by future growth in the suburbs of metropolitan areas, which are predominantly white. From 1960 through 1980, those suburbs will gain about 40.9 million persons.[5] Thus the *growth* of suburban population in this period will be almost twice as large as the *total size* of all U.S. ghettos by 1980.

Any policies designed to cope with the ghetto must recognize that the concentrations of Negro population in our central cities are growing rapidly. In 1950, there were 6.5 million Negroes in central cities. In 1960, there were 9.7 million. This represents an increase of 49.2 per cent, or an average of 320,000 persons per year. In the same decade, the white population of central cities went from 45.5 million to 47.7 million, an increase of 2.2 million, or 4.8 per cent. However, in the largest central cities, the white population actually declined while the Negro population rose sharply.[6]

Since 1960, the growth of nonwhite population in central cities has continued unabated. White population growth in all those cities taken together has, however, ceased entirely. In 1966 the total Negro population of all central cities was about 12.1 million. This is a gain of 2.4 million since 1960, or about 400,000 persons per year. Thus the *absolute* rate of growth of ghettos per year has gone up to its highest level in history. In contrast, the white population of central cities in 1965 was 46.4 million, or 1.3 million *less* than in 1960. So for all 224 central cities considered as a whole, all population growth now consists of gains in Negro population.[7]

Moreover, nearly all Negro population growth is now occurring in ghettos, rather than in suburbs or rural areas. From 1960 to 1966, 89 per cent of all nonwhite population growth was in central cities, and 11 per cent was in suburbs. Nonmetropolitan areas (including the rural South) actually *lost* nonwhite population. This indicates that heavy out-migration from rural areas to cities is still going on.[8]

Future Ghetto Growth If Present Policies Continue

All evidence points to the conclusion that future nonwhite population growth will continue to be concentrated in central cities unless major changes in public policies are made. Not one single significant program of any federal, state, or local government is aimed at altering this tendency or is likely to have the unintended effect of doing so.[9] Moreover, although nonwhite fertility rates have declined since 1957 along with white fertility rates, ghetto growth is likely to remain rapid because of continued in-migration, as well as natural increase.

Recent estimates made by the National Advisory Commission on Civil Disorders indicate that the central-city Negro population for the whole U.S. will be about 13.6 million in 1970 and could rise to as high as 20.3 million by 1985. These estimates assume continued nonwhite in-migration at about the same rate as prevailed from 1960 to 1966. But even if net in-migration is reduced to zero, the 1985 central-city Negro population would be about 17.3 million.[10]

Within individual cities, rapid expansion of segregated ghetto areas will undoubtedly continue. Our 1967 field surveys in Chicago show that about 2.9 city blocks *per week* are shifting from predominantly white to nonwhite occupancy, mainly on the edge of already nonwhite areas. This is somewhat lower than the 3.5 blocks-per-week average from 1960 to 1966, but above the average of 2.6 from 1950 to 1960.[11] If such "peripheral spread" of central-city ghettos continues at nearly the same rate—and there is no present reason to believe it will not—then a number of major central cities will become over 50 per cent Negro in total population by 1985. These cities include Chicago, Philadelphia, St. Louis, Detroit, Cleveland, Oakland, Baltimore, New Orleans,

Richmond, and Jacksonville. Washington, D.C., Newark, and Gary are already over 50 per cent Negro. The proportion of nonwhites in the public school systems in most of these cities now exceeds 50 per cent. It will probably be approaching 90 per cent by 1985—unless major changes in school programs and districting are adopted before then.[1][2]

This future growth has critical implications for a great many policy objectives connected with ghettos. For example, it has been suggested that school district boundaries within central cities should be manipulated so as to counteract *de facto* segregation by creating districts in which many Negroes and many whites will jointly reside. This solution is practical over the long run only when there is reasonable stability in the total size of these two groups. But when one group is rapidly expanding in a city where there is no vacant land to build additional housing, then the other group must contract. The only alternative is sharp rises in density which are not occurring. Therefore, as the Negro population expands in such cities, the white population inevitably falls. So possibilities for ending *de facto* segregation in this manner inexorably shrink as time passes. For this and other reasons, no policy toward ghettos can afford to ignore this rapid expansion of the Negro population.

The Complexity of the Ghetto Population and Ghetto Problems

To be accurate, every analysis of ghettos and their problems must avoid two tempting oversimplifications. The first is conceiving of the ghetto population as a single homogeneous group, all of whose members have similar characteristics, attitudes, and desires.Thus, because many ghetto residents are unemployed or "under-employed" in low-paying, transient jobs, it is easy—but false—to think of all ghetto households as plagued by unemployment. Similarly, because some ghetto residents have carried out riots and looting, whites frequently talk as though *all* ghetto dwellers hate whites, are prone to violence, or are likely to behave irresponsibly. Yet all careful studies of recent riots show that only a small minority of ghetto residents participated in any way, a majority disapprove of such activity, and most would like to have more contact with whites and more integration.[1][3]

In reality, each racial ghetto contains a tremendous variety of persons who exhibit widely differing attitudes toward almost every question. Many are very poor, but just as many are not. Many have radical views—especially young people; many others are quite conservative—especially the older people. Many are "on welfare," but many more are steadily employed.

This diversity means that public policy concerning any given ghetto problem cannot be successful if it is aimed at or based upon the attitudes and desires of only one group of persons affected by that problem. For example, take unemployment. Programs providing job training for young people could, if expanded enough, affect a large proportion of ghetto dwellers. But the inability of many adult ghetto men to obtain and keep steady, well-paying jobs is also a critical ghetto problem.[14] Also, many women with children cannot work because no adequate day-care facilities are available. Thus, public policy concerning every ghetto problem must have many complex facets in order to work well.

A second widely prevalent oversimplification of ghetto problems is concentration of remedial action upon a single substandard condition. For instance, improving the deplorable housing conditions in many slums would not in itself eliminate most of the de-humanizing forces which operate there. In fact, no single category of programs can possibly be adequate to cope with the tangled problems that exist in ghettos. Any effective ghetto-improvement strategy must concern itself with at least jobs and employment, education, housing, health, personal safety, crime prevention, and income maintenance for dependent persons. A number of other programs could be added, but I believe these are the most critical.[15]

The Location of New Jobs

Most new employment opportunities are being created in the suburban portions of our metropolitan areas, not anywhere near central-city ghettos.[16] Furthermore, this trend is likely to continue indefinitely into the future. It is true that downtown office-space concentrations in a few large cities have created additional jobs near ghettos. But the out-flow of manufacturing and retailing jobs has normally offset this addition significantly—and in many cases has caused a net loss of jobs in central cities.

If we are going to provide jobs for the rapidly expanding ghetto population, particularly jobs that do not call for high levels of skills, we must somehow bring these potential workers closer to the locations of new employment opportunities. This can be done in three ways: by moving job locations so new jobs are created in the ghetto, by moving ghetto residents so they live nearer the new jobs, or by creating better transportation between the ghetto and the locations of new jobs. The first alternative—creating new jobs in the ghetto—will not occur in the future under normal free-market conditions, in my opinion.

That nearly all *new* job opportunities will be located in suburbs does not mean that central cities cannot provide *any* employment to their Negro residents. There are still millions of jobs located in central cities. Just the turnover in workers regarding those jobs will open up a great many potential positions for Negro central-city residents in the future—if employers and other workers cease racial discrimination in their hiring and promotion practices. Nevertheless, as the total number of Negro central-city job-seekers steadily rises, the need to link them with emerging sources of new employment in the suburbs will become more and more urgent as a means of reducing unemployment in Negro neighborhoods.

Recently, a number of proposals have been advanced to create public subsidies or guaranteed profits encouraging free enterprise to locate new jobs in ghettos.[17] It is possible that they might work to some extent if the promised profits are high enough to offset the risks and disadvantages involved. Any ghetto improvement strategy must, however, face the problem of linking up persons who need employment with those firms which can provide it or those public agencies assigned to create it.

The Future "Cost Squeeze" on Local Governments

Traditionally, individual productivity has risen faster in the manufacturing, mining, construction, and agricultural sectors of our economy than in sectors where personal services are dominant—such as finance, insurance, and real estate; retailing; services; and government. The ability to employ larger amounts of capital per worker, coupled with technological change, has caused much larger increases in hourly output-per-worker in the former sectors than in the latter.

All sectors compete with one another for talent and personnel, and all use many of the same products as basic inputs. This means that wages and salaries in the service-dominated sectors must generally keep up with those in the capital-dominated sectors. This tends to place a "squeeze" on the cost of those activities for which individual productivity is hard to increase.

A recent analysis of the performing arts by economists William Baumol and William Bowen highlighted this type of "cost squeeze" as the major reason why it is so difficult to sustain theaters, opera, symphonies, and ballet companies on a self-supporting basis.[18] A pianist cannot perform Chopin's Minute Waltz in 30 seconds, or spend half as much time learning how to play it, to improve efficiency. Yet his salary and the salaries of all the electricians, accompanists, administrators, and others needed for the performing arts are constantly raised to keep their living standards comparable with those of people in the sectors where wage gains can be offset by productivity increases.

Baumol has argued that a similar "cost squeeze" is one of the reasons why state and local expenditures have risen so fast in the postwar period. They increased 257 per cent from 1950 to 1966, as compared to 159 per cent for Gross National Product and 206 per cent for federal expenditures.[19] Moreover, Baumol believes that this pressure to increase service-oriented wages and salaries faster than real output-per-man-hour in the service-oriented sectors will generate an even bigger "explosion" of local and state government costs in the future. For one thing, a higher fraction of society is now and will be employed in public activities than ever before. So there is a steady increase in the proportion of persons whose compensation tends to rise faster than their real output. This reflects both rapid automation in non-service-oriented sectors and an increasing shift of consumer demand toward such services as education, entertainment, and government activities of all types.

The resulting upward pressure on local and state government costs—and tax needs—will undoubtedly be offset to some extent by two forces. The first is greater automation of services themselves through use of computers, closed-circuit TV, duplicating machines, and other devices. The second is the partial substitution of semiskilled and low-skilled assistants for highly-skilled professionals. For example, teachers' aids could relieve professional teachers of immense amounts of administration and paperwork, thereby freeing the latter for more effective use of their time.

Nevertheless, the huge future growth of suburban population will almost certainly force a continuance of the trend toward rising local and state taxes that has now gone on for twenty years. Similar upward pressure on revenue needs will be felt even more strongly by central-city governments. Central cities will contain ever higher proportions of low-income residents who need more services per capita than wealthier suburbanites.

This future "cost squeeze" is important to our analysis because of its impact upon the willingness of suburban taxpayers to help finance any large-scale programs aimed at improving ghetto conditions. Such programs would almost certainly require significant income redistribution from the relatively wealthy suburban population to the relatively poor central-city population. Yet suburbanites will be experiencing steadily rising local and state tax burdens to pay for the services they need themselves.

The "Law of Dominance"

The achievement of stable racial integration of both whites and nonwhites in housing or public schools is a rare phenomenon in large American cities. Contrary to the views of many, this is *not* because whites are unwilling to share schools or residential neighborhoods with nonwhites. A vast majority of whites of all income groups would be willing to send their children to integrated schools or live in integrated neighborhoods, *as long as they were sure that the white group concerned would remain in the majority* in those facilities or areas.

The residential and educational objectives of these whites are not dependent upon their maintaining any kind of "ethnic purity" in their neighborhoods or schools. Rather, those objectives depend upon their maintaining a certain degree of "cultural dominance" therein.[20] These whites—like most other middle-class citizens of any race—want to be sure that the social, cultural, and economic milieu and values of their own group dominate their own residential environment and the educational environment of their children. This desire in turn springs from the typical middle-class belief of all racial groups that everyday life should be primarily a *value-reinforcing* experience for both adults and children, rather than primarily a *value-altering* one. The best way to insure that this will happen is to isolate somewhat oneself and one's children in an everyday environment dominated by—but not necessarily exclusively comprised of—other families and children whose social, economic, cultural, and even religious views and attitudes are approximately the same as one's own.

There is no intrinsic reason why race or color should be perceived as a factor relevant to attaining such relative homogeneity. Clearly, race and color have no necessary linkage with the kinds of social, cultural, economic, or religious characteristics and values that can have a true functional impact upon adults and children. Yet I believe a majority of middle-class white Americans still perceive race and color as relevant factors in their assessment of the kind of homogeneity they seek to attain. Moreover, this false perception is reinforced by their lack of everyday experience and contact with Negroes who are, in fact, like them in all important respects. Therefore, in deciding whether a given neighborhood or a given school exhibits the kind of environment in which "their own" traits are and will remain dominant, they consider Negroes as members of "another" group.

It is true that some people want themselves and their children to be immersed in a wide variety of viewpoints, values, and types of people, rather than a relatively homogeneous group.[21] This desire is particularly strong among the intellectuals who dominate the urban planning profession. They are also the strongest supporters of big-city life and the most vitriolic critics of suburbia. Yet I believe their viewpoint—though dominant in recent public discussions of urban problems—is actually shared by only a tiny minority of Americans of any racial group. Almost everyone favors at least some exposure to a wide variety of viewpoints. But experience in our own society and most others shows that the overwhelming majority of middle-class families choose residential locations and schools precisely in order to provide the kind of value-reinforcing experience described above. This is why most Jews live in predominantly Jewish neighborhoods, even in suburbs; why Catholic parents continue to support separate school systems; and partly why so few middle-class Negro families have been willing to risk moving to all-white suburbs even where there is almost no threat of any harassment.

However demeaning this phenomenon may be to Negroes, it must be recognized if we are to understand why residential segregation has persisted so strongly in the United States, and what conditions are necessary to create viable racial integration. The expansion of nonwhite residential areas has led to "massive transition" from white to nonwhite occupancy mainly because there has been no mechanism that could assure the whites in any given area that they would remain in the majority after nonwhites once began entering. Normal population turnover causes about 20 per cent of the residents of the average U.S. neighborhood to move out every year because of income changes, job transfers, shifts in life-cycle position, or deaths. In order for a neighborhood to retain any given character, the persons who move in to occupy the resulting vacancies must be similar to those who have departed.

But once Negroes begin entering an all-white neighborhood near the ghetto, most other white families become convinced that the area will eventually become all Negro, mainly because this has happened so often before. Hence it is difficult to persuade whites not now living there to move in and occupy vacancies. They are only willing to move into neighborhoods where whites are now the dominant majority and seem likely to remain so. Hence the whites who would otherwise have moved in from elsewhere stop doing so.[22] This means that almost all vacancies are eventually occupied by nonwhites, and the neighborhood inexorably shifts toward a heavy nonwhite majority. Once this happens, the remaining whites also seek to leave, since they do not wish to remain in an area where they have lost their culturally dominant position.

As a result, whites who would be quite satisfied—even delighted—to live in an integrated neighborhood *as members of the majority* are never given the opportunity to do so. Instead, for reasons beyond the control of each individual, they are forced to choose between complete segregation or living in an area heavily dominated by members of what they consider "another group." Given their values, they choose the former.

Many—especially Negroes—may deplore the racially prejudiced desire of most white middle-class citizens to live in neighborhoods and use schools where other white middle-class households are dominant. Nevertheless, this desire seems to be firmly entrenched among most whites at present. Hence public policy cannot ignore this desire if it hopes to be effective. Moreover, this attitude does not preclude the development of racial integration, as long as whites are in the majority and believe they will remain so. The problem is convincing them that their majority status will persist in mixed areas in the face of past experience to the contrary.[23] Even more difficult, the people who must be persuaded are not those now living in a mixed area, but those who must keep moving in from elsewhere to maintain racial balance as vacancies occur through normal population turnover.

Clearly, the dynamic processes related to this "Law of Dominance" are critical to any strategy concerning the future of American ghettos. They are especially relevant to strategies which seek to achieve stable residential or educational integration of whites and nonwhites, instead of the "massive transition" and "massive segregation" which have dominated the spatial patterns of nonwhite population growth in the past twenty years. Such stable integration will occur in most areas only if there is some way to guarantee the white majority that it will remain the "dominant" majority. This implies some form of "quotas" concerning the proportion of nonwhites in the facility or area concerned—even legally supported "quotas."

Unless some such "balancing devices" are *explicitly* used and reinforced by public policies and laws to establish their credibility, whites will continue to withdraw from—or, more crucially, fail to keep entering—any facility or area into which significant numbers of nonwhites are entering. This means a continuation of *de facto* segregation and a reinforcement of the white belief that any nonwhite entry inevitably leads to "massive transition." Even more importantly, it means continued failure to eliminate white perception of race as a critical factor by encouraging whites and nonwhites to live together in conditions of stability. Thus, in my opinion, the only way to destroy the racial prejudice at the root of the "Law of Cultural Dominance" is to shape current public policy in recognition of that "Law" so as to encourage widespread experience that will undermine it.[24]

The Concept of Social Strategy

Americans typically do not attempt to solve problems by means of behavior patterns that could reasonably be considered "strategies." The concept of strategy implies development of a single comprehensive, long-range plan to cope with some significant social problem. But U.S. decision-making concerning domestic issues is too fragmented and diffused to permit the formulation of any such long-range plan regarding a given problem. Instead, we approach most social problems through a process which has been aptly labeled "disjointed incrementalism."[25] Each decision-maker or actor makes whatever choices seem to him to be most appropriate at that moment, in light of his own interests and his own view of the public welfare. For two reasons, he pays little attention to most of the consequences of his action upon others—especially the long-run consequences. First, no one has the detailed knowledge and foresight necessary to comprehend all those consequences. Second, no one has the time nor the energy to negotiate in advance with all others likely to be affected by his actions. So instead he acts "blindly" and waits for those who are hurt to complain or those who are benefited to applaud.

A process of mutual adjustment ensues. Those who are unduly harmed by each decision supposedly recoup their losses by exercising whatever economic, moral, or political powers are available to them. Those who benefit use their powers to encourage more of the same. Presiding over this melee is a set of mainly "reactive" governments and other public agencies. They keep altering the "rules of the game" and their own programs and behavior so as to correct any grievous imbalances that appear.

There is no guarantee that the checks and balances built into this uncoordinated process will effectively counteract every destructive condition or trend that emerges from it. It is certainly possible that each individual will be motivated by the incentives facing him to take actions that, when combined with those taken by others acting in a similar individualistic fashion, will lead to collective disaster.

So far in history, the system has been remarkably effective at avoiding such outcomes. Part of this success undoubtedly results from society's ability to generate in most of its citizens a single set of basic values and even broad policy objectives that exert a cohesive influence on their supposedly individualistic decisions. But another important ingredient in the system's success is the ability of enough significant actors in it to perceive threatening trends in time to formulate and carry out ameliorating policies.

This means they must accurately forecast any potentially dire outcome of current trends. They must also visualize alternative outcomes that would be preferable and are within the capabilities of society. Finally, they must devise policies and programs that will shift individual incentives so one of those alternatives will occur. In some cases, the ongoing trends that threaten society are strongly entrenched in its institutional structure. If so, alternatives that avoid the pending threats may not be attainable without fundamental changes in institutions. Those changes in turn may be possible only if a preponderance of powerful people in society share at least a broad concept of the need for change and the kinds of objectives motivating it. This concept closely resembles a social strategy. It visualizes a certain desired outcome, implies a wide range of policies by various actors necessary to attain that outcome, and serves as a "hidden coordinator" of seemingly individualistic behavior.

The above reasoning implies two conclusions crucial to this analysis. First, strategic thinking about social problems can play a vital role in stimulating social change even where decision-making is dominated by disjointed incrementalism. Second, the alternative outcomes conceived in such thinking can usefully include some which could not be achieved without major changes in existing institutions or values. For example, some of the strategies discussed herein require a highly coordinated set of policy decisions. Such coordination is unlikely to occur in the presently fragmentalized governmental structures of our metropolitan areas unless major changes in the incentives facing these governments are created.

I will therefore formulate several alternative strategies for coping with the problems posed by future ghetto growth, even though carrying out some of them would require a far more consciously coordinated development of social change than has been typical of America in the past.

Formulation of Major Alternative Strategies

Because of the immense complexity of our society, an infinite number of alternative future strategies regarding ghettos could conceivably be designed. But for purposes of practical consideration, this number must be narrowed drastically to a few that highlight the major choices facing us. Selecting these few is inescapably arbitrary—there is no "scientific" way to do it. I believe, however, that the narrowing of alternative ghetto futures can best be accomplished by focusing upon the major choices relating to the following three questions:

To what extent should future nonwhite population growth be concentrated within the central cities, as it has been in the past twenty years?

To what extent should our white and nonwhite populations be residentially segregated from each other in the future?

To what extent should society redistribute income to relatively depressed urban areas or population groups in society in a process of "enrichment"?

Each of these questions can be answered with any one of a whole spectrum of responses from one extreme to the other. But for purposes of analysis, I believe we can usefully narrow these answers down to just two points on the spectrum for each question. This allows us to reduce the alternatives to the following:

Degree-of-Concentration Alternatives
    1. Continue to concentrate nonwhite population growth in central cities or perhaps in a few older suburbs next to central cities *(Concentration)*
    2. Disperse nonwhite population growth widely throughout all parts of metropolitan areas. *(Dispersal)*

Degree-of-Segregation Alternatives
    1. Continue to cluster whites and nonwhites in residentially segregated neighborhoods, regardless of where they are within the metropolitan area. *(Segregation)*
    2. Scatter the nonwhite population, or at least a significant fraction of it, "randomly" among white residential areas to achieve at least partial residential integration. *(Integration)*

Degree-of-Enrichment Alternatives
    1. Continue to provide relatively low-level welfare, educational, housing, job training, and other support to the most deprived groups in the population—both those who are incapable of working, such as the vast majority of public-aid recipients, and those who might possibly work, but are unemployed because of lack of skills, discrimination, lack of desire, or any other reason. *(Non-enrichment)*
    2. Greatly raise the level of support to welfare, educational, housing, job-training, and other programs for the most deprived groups, largely through federally aided programs. *(Enrichment)*

Even narrowing the alternatives in this fashion leaves a logical possibility of eight different combinations. A number of these can, however, be ruled out as internally inconsistent in practice. For example, I believe it is extremely unlikely that any strategy of dispersing the nonwhite population throughout metropolitan areas could be accomplished without provision of substantially greater incentives to both nonwhites (to get them to move) and whites (to increase their willingness to accept large numbers of nonwhite in-migrants without strong resistance). Thus no combination of both dispersal and non-enrichment need be considered.

Similarly, in the very long run, concentration of future nonwhite population growth within central cities is probably inconsistent with integration. Many of those cities will become so preponderantly nonwhite that integration within their borders will be impossible. Admittedly, it may take two or more decades for this to occur in some central cities, and it might never occur in others. Nevertheless, some types of integration (such as in the public schools) will become impossible long before that if a concentration policy is followed. For these reasons, I will consider only one special combination containing both concentration and integration. This consists of continued concentration, but a build-up of a gradually expanding inner-city core of fully integrated housing and public facilities created through massive urban renewal. For reasons explained below, this strategy would require a significant enrichment program too.

This whole process of elimination leaves five basic alternative strategies relevant to future development of ghettos. For convenience, each has been assigned a short name to be used throughout the remainder of this article. These strategies can be summarized as follows:

1. *Present Policies:* concentration, segregation, and non-enrichment.

2. *Enrichment Only:* concentration, segregation, enrichment.

3. *Integrated Core:* concentration, integration (in the center only), enrichment.

4. *Segregated Dispersal:* dispersal, segregation, enrichment.

5. *Integrated Dispersal:* dispersal, integration, enrichment.

Before these strategies are examined in detail, two things about them should be emphasized.

First, they apply to individual metropolitan areas. Therefore, it would be at least theoretically possible to adopt different strategies toward the ghetto in different metropolitan areas. There are, in fact, some convincing reasons why this would be an excellent idea.

Second, these strategies are formed from relatively extreme points on the relevant ranges of possibilities. Hence they could actually be adopted in various mixtures, rather than in the "pure" forms set forth above. This further strengthens the case for using a variety of approaches across the country. For purposes of analysis, however, it is fruitful to examine each of these strategies initially as though it were to be the sole instrument for coping with ghetto problems in all metropolitan areas.

The Present-Policies Strategy

In order to carry out this strategy, we need merely do nothing more than we do now. Even existing federal programs aimed at aiding cities—such as the Model Cities Program—will continue or accelerate concentration, segregation, and non-enrichment, unless those programs are colossally expanded.

I do not wish to imply that present federal and local efforts in the anti-poverty program, the public housing program, the urban renewal program, health programs, educational programs, and many others are not of significant benefit to residents of ghettos. They are. Nevertheless, as both recent investigations and recent violence have emphasized, existing programs have succeeded neither in stemming the various adverse trends operating in ghetto areas nor in substantially eliminating the deplorable conditions there. Therefore, the strategy of continuing our present policies and our present level of effort is essentially not going to alter current conditions in ghettos.

This may make it seem silly to label continuation of present policies as a specific anti-ghetto strategy. Yet failure to adopt effective policies is still a strategy. It may not be a successful one, but it nevertheless is an expression of society's current commitment and attitude toward the ghetto.

Thus, if we maintain our current programs and policies, segregated areas of residence in our central cities will continue to expand rapidly and to suffer from all the difficult problems inherent in both racial and economic ghettos.

The Enrichment-Only Strategy

The second fundamental ghetto future strategy I call "enrichment only." This approach is aimed at dramatically improving the quality of life within the confines of present ghetto areas and those nearby areas into which ghettos will expand in the future if concentration continues. I presume that any such policy would apply to the poverty meaning of ghetto more than the racial one—that is, any enrichment strategy would aim at upgrading the lowest-income and most disadvantaged citizens of our central cities, regardless of race. Nevertheless, a sizable proportion of such persons are nonwhites. Moreover, programs aimed at reducing racial discrimination in employment and in the quality of public services would form an important part of any strategy aimed at upgrading the most deprived groups. So the enrichment-only strategy would still concentrate upon the same areas as if it were to follow a racial policy.

The basic idea underlying the enrichment-only strategy (and part of every other strategy involving enrichment) is to develop federally financed programs that would greatly improve the education, housing, incomes, employment and job-training, and social services received by ghetto residents. This would involve vastly expanding the scale of present programs, changing the nature of many of them because they are now ineffective or would be if operated at a much larger scale, and creating incentives for a much greater participation of private capital in ghetto activities. Such incentives could include tax credits for investments made in designated ghetto areas, wage subsidies (connected with on-the-job training but lasting longer than such training so as to induce employers to hire unskilled ghetto residents), rent or ownership supplements for poor families, enabling them to rent or buy housing created by private capital, and others.[26]

It is important to realize that the enrichment-only strategy would end neither racial segregation nor the concentration of nonwhites in central cities (and some older adjoining suburbs). It would help many Negroes attain middle-class status and thus make it easier for them to leave the ghetto if they wanted to. Undoubtedly many would. But, by making life in central-city ghettos more attractive without creating any strong pressures for integration or dispersal of the nonwhite population, such a policy would increase the in-migration of nonwhites into central cities. This would speed up the expansion of racially segregated areas in central cities, thereby accelerating the process of "massive transition" of whole neighborhoods from white to nonwhite occupancy.

The Integrated-Core Strategy

This strategy is similar to the enrichment-only strategy because both would attempt to upgrade the quality of life in central-city ghettos through massive federally assisted programs. The integrated-core strategy would also seek, however, to eliminate racial segregation in an ever expanding core of the city by creating a socially, economically, and racially integrated community there. This integrated core would be built up through large-scale urban renewal programs, with the land re-uses including scattered-site public housing, middle-income housing suitable for families with children, and high-quality public services—especially schools.

All of these re-uses would be based upon "managed integration"—that is, deliberate achievement of a racial balance containing a majority of whites but a significant minority of Negroes. Thus, the integrated-core stategy could be carried out only if deliberate racial discrimination aimed at avoiding *de facto* segregation becomes recognized by the Supreme Court as a legitimate tactic for public agencies. In fact, such recognition will probably be a necessity for any strategy involving a significant degree of integration in public schools, public housing, or even private residential areas. This conclusion was recently recognized by the Chicago Board of Education, its staff, and its consultants, who all recommended the use of quotas in schools located in racially changing neighborhoods to promote stable integration.[27]

The integrated-core strategy essentially represents a compromise between an ideal condition and two harsh realities. The ideal condition is development of a fully integrated society in which whites and Negroes live together harmoniously and the race of each individual is not recognized by anyone as a significant factor in any public or private decisions.

The first harsh reality is that the present desire of most whites to dominate their own environment means that integration can only be achieved through deliberate management and through the willingness of some Negroes to share schools and residences as a minority. The second harsh reality is the assumption that it will be impossible to disperse the massive Negro ghettos of major central cities fast enough to prevent many of those cities from eventually becoming predominantly, or even almost exclusively, Negro in population. The development of predominantly Negro central cities, with high proportions of low-income residents, ringed by predominantly white suburbs with much wealthier residents, might lead to a shattering polarization that would split society along both racial and spatial lines.

This strategy seeks to avoid any such polarization by building an integrated core of whites and nonwhites in central cities, including many leaders of both races in politics, business, and civic affairs. Negro leadership will properly assume the dominant position in central-city politics in many major cities after Negroes have become a majority of the municipal electorates there. By that time, integration of leadership within those cities will, it is to be hoped, have become a sufficient reality so that leaders of both races can work together in utilizing the central city's great economic assets, rather than fighting one another for control over them.

Thus, the integrated-core strategy postulates that a significant movement toward racial integration is essential to keep American society from "exploding" as a result of a combined racial-spatial confrontation of central cities vs. suburbs in many large metropolitan areas. It also postulates that development of integration in the suburbs through massive dispersal cannot occur fast enough to avoid such a confrontation. Therefore, integration must be developed on an "inside-out" basis, starting in the core of the central city, rather than in the suburbs.

The Concept of Dispersal

The two dispersal strategies concerning the future of ghettos are both based upon a single key assumption: that the problems of ghettos cannot be solved so long as millions of Negroes, particularly those with low incomes and other significant disadvantages, are required or persuaded to live together in segregated ghetto areas within our central cities. These strategies contend that large numbers of Negroes should be given strong incentives to move voluntarily from central cities into suburban areas, including those in which no Negroes presently reside.

To illustrate what "large numbers" really means, let us postulate one version of dispersal which I call the "constant-size ghetto strategy." This strictly hypothetical strategy aims at stopping the growth of existing central-city ghettos by dispersing enough Negroes from central cities to the suburbs (or to peripheral central-city areas) to offset potential future increases in that growth. Taking the period from 1970 through 1975, estimates made by the National Advisory Commission on Civil Disorders show that the nonwhite population of all U.S. central cities taken as a whole would, in the absence of any dispersal strategy, expand from about 13.6 million to about 15.5 million.[28] Thus, if dispersal of nonwhites were to take place at a scale large enough to keep central-city racial ghettos at their 1970 level during the five subsequent years, there would have to be an out-movement of 1.9 million Negroes into the suburbs. This amounts to 380,000 per year.

From 1950 to 1960, the suburban Negro population of all U.S. metropolitan areas grew a total of only 60,000 per year. In that decade, the white population of suburban portions of our metropolitan areas (the so-called "urban fringe") increased by about 1,720,000 persons per year. Thus, 96.6 per cent of all suburban population growth consisted of whites. From 1960 to 1966, the Negro population growth in all suburban areas declined sharply to a rate of 33,300 per year. In fact, there was actually in-migration of Negroes from suburbs to central cities. But the white population in all suburbs went up an average of 1,750,000 per year. Thus the proportion of suburban growth made up of whites climbed to 98.1 per cent—an even higher fraction than in the decade from 1950 to 1960.[29] Undoubtedly, some of this white population increase was caused by an exodus of whites from central cities in response to Negro growth therein. If future Negro population growth in central cities were stopped by a large-scale dispersion policy, then white population growth in the suburbs would be definitely smaller than it was from 1950 through 1966. The size of the resulting decline would depend upon the fraction of white exodus from central cities that occurs in response to Negro growth, as opposed to such other factors as rising incomes, the aging central-city housing stock, and shifts in life-cycle position. If whites leave central cities in a one-to-one ratio with the expansion of Negro population therein, then a cessation of Negro ghetto growth would result in a large drop in white suburban growth. In that case, future suburban population increases would consist of about 23 per cent Negroes (based on very rough calculations). This contrasts with proportions of less than 5 per cent from 1950 through 1960 and less than 3 per cent from 1960 through 1966.

Clearly, such dispersal would represent a radical change in existing trends. Not only would it stop the expansion of Negro ghettos in central cities, but it would also inject a significant Negro population into many presently all-white suburban areas. It is true that policies of dispersal would not necessarily have to be at this large a scale. Dispersal aimed not at stopping ghetto growth, but merely at slowing it down somewhat could be carried out at a much lower scale. Yet even such policies would represent a marked departure from past U.S. practice.

Such a sharp break with the past would be necessary for any significant dispersal of Negroes. Merely providing the *opportunity* for Negroes to move out of ghettos would, at least in the short run, not result in many moving. Even adoption of a vigorously enforced nationwide open-occupancy law applying to *all* residences would not greatly speed up the present snail's-pace rate of dispersion. Experience in those states that have open-occupancy ordinances decisively proves this conclusion.

Hence, positive incentives for dispersion would have to be created in order to speed up the rate at which Negroes voluntarily move from central cities and settle in suburban areas. (Certainly no policy involving *involuntary* movement of either whites or Negroes should ever be considered.) Such incentives could include rent supplements, ownership supplements, special school-support bonus payments linked to the education of children moving out from ghettos, and other devices which essentially attach a subsidy to a person. Then, when the person moves, he and the community into which he goes get credit for that subsidy. This creates incentives both for him to move and for the community to accept him gladly. Both of the strategies involving dispersal would thus represent radical changes in existing practices.

Segregated vs. Integrated Dispersal

One of the fundamental purposes of any dispersal strategy is providing Negro Americans with real freedom of choice concerning housing and school accommodations. The experience of other ethnic groups indicates that Negroes would exercise that choice in suburban areas in a combination of two ways. Some individual Negro households would become scattered "randomly" in largely white residential areas. But other Negro households—probably a larger number—would voluntarily cluster together. This would create primarily Negro neighborhoods, or even primarily Negro suburban communities. Such a combination of both *scattering* and *clustering* would occur even if Negro households had absolutely no fears of hostility or antagonism from white neighbors. It is unrealistic to suppose, however, that *all* prejudice against Negro neighbors can be eliminated from presently all-white suburbs in the immediate future. As a result, even if a dispersal strategy is carried out, there will still be some external pressure against Negro newcomers. This will encourage an even higher proportion of in-coming Negro households to cluster together than would do so in the absence of all fears and antagonism. Moreover, public policies to accomplish dispersion might include deliberate creation of some moderate-sized clusters of Negro families, as in scattered-site public housing developments.

Once all-Negro clusters appear in previously all-white suburbs, there is a high probability that they will turn into "ghetto-lets" or "mini-ghettos." The same forces that produced ghettos in central cities are likely to repeat themselves in suburbs, though in a much less pathological form. Those pressures are a rapidly expanding Negro population, the "Law of Cultural Dominance" among whites, and at least some restriction of Negro choice in areas far removed from existing all-Negro neighborhoods. Therefore, once a Negro cluster becomes large enough so that Negro children dominate a local elementary school, the typical phenomenon of white withdrawal from the local residential real-estate market is likely to occur. This has already taken place regarding Jews and gentiles in many suburban areas. Thus, any dispersal strategy that does not explicitly aim at preventing segregation, too, will probably create new segregated neighborhoods in the suburbs.

This new form of *de facto* segregation will, however, have far less damaging effects upon Negroes than existing segregation concentrated in central cities. In the first place, if Negro clusters are deliberately created in almost all parts of the metropolitan area at once, whites will be unable to flee to "completely safe" suburbs without accepting impractically long commuting journeys. This will strongly reduce the white propensity to abandon an area after Negroes begin entering it. Moreover, the presence of some Negroes in all parts of suburbia will also make it far easier for individual Negro families to move into all-white neighborhoods on a scattered basis. Thus any dispersal policy that really disperses Negroes in the suburbs will immediately create an enormous improvement in the real freedom of residential choice enjoyed by individual Negro families. This will be true even if most of those families actually choose to remain in Negro clusters.

Second, any dispersal strategy would presumably be accompanied by strongly enforced open-occupancy laws applying to all housing. At present, these laws do not lead to scattering, but they would in the climate of a dispersal strategy. Then Negro willingness to move into all-white areas would rise sharply, and white antagonism toward such move-ins would drop.

Third, *de facto* residential segregation need not lead to segregated suburban schools. In relatively small communities, such as most suburbs, it is easy to bus students to achieve stable racial balance. Thus, the formation of clustered Negro housing would not have to cause the quality-of-education problems that now exist in central-city ghettos. True, if a given suburb became predominantly Negro, its schools might become quite segregated. In that case, school systems in adjoining suburbs might have to merge or at least work out student exchange procedures with the segregated community in order to counteract segregation. This may be difficult to accomplish (though in the climate of a dispersal strategy, it would be at least thinkable). Hence it is possible that some segregated school systems might appear in suburban areas. But Negro families would still have far more opportunities than they do now to move to areas with integrated schools.

A dispersal strategy that did not succeed in initially placing Negro households in almost all parts of the metropolitan area would be more likely to generate "ghetto-lets." Hence, if dispersal tactics call for initially concentrating on dispersion only to a few suburbs, it is quite possible that segregated dispersal would result. This implies that integrated dispersal could be attained in only two ways. Either the initial dispersal strategy must place Negroes in almost all suburban communities, or specific integration-furthering mechanisms—such as school and residential quotas—must be adopted.

The speculative nature of the above discussion illustrates that society needs to do much more thinking about what dispersal really means, how it might be achieved, what alternative forms it might take, and what its consequences would be.

In an article of this length, it is impossible to present an adequate analysis of each of the strategies described above. Certain factors will, however, have a crucial influence on which strategy actually prevails. These factors should be at least briefly mentioned here.

The Possibility of a Spatial-Racial "Confrontation"

Society's existing policies toward the ghetto are, by definition, those called for by the present-policies strategy. Yet there are strong reasons to believe that maintenance of these policies in ghettos is not possible. The striking increase in violence in big-city ghettos is probably related to a combination of higher aspirations, reduced sanctions against the use of violence, and continued deplorable slum conditions. If so, persistence of the present-policies strategy may continue to spawn incidents, riots, and perhaps guerrilla warfare. Then existing local police forces might have to be supplemented with para-military forces on continuous alert. Thus, the present-policies strategy might lead to further polarization of whites and Negroes and even to the creation of semi-martial law in big cities.

Moreover, when Negroes become the dominant political force in many large central cities, they may understandably demand radical changes in present policies. At the same time, major private capital investment in those cities might virtually cease if white-dominated firms and industries decided the risks of involvement there were too great. In light of recent disorders, this seems very likely. Such withdrawal of private capital has already occurred in almost every single ghetto area in the U.S. Even if private investment continues, big cities containing high proportions of low-income Negroes would need substantial income transfers from the federal government to meet the demands of their electorates for improved services and living conditions.

But by that time, Congress will be more heavily influenced by representatives of the suburban electorate. The suburbs will comprise 41 per cent of our total population by 1985, as opposed to 33 per cent in 1960. Central cities will decline from 31 per cent to 27 per cent.[30] Under a present-policies strategy, this influential suburban electorate will be over 95 per cent white, whereas the central-city population in all metropolitan areas together will be slightly over 60 per cent white. The suburban electorate will be much wealthier than the central-city population, which will consist mainly of Negroes and older whites. Yet even the suburbs will be feeling the squeeze of higher local government costs generated by rising service salaries. Hence the federal government may refuse to approve the massive income transfers from suburbs to central cities that the mayors of the latter will desperately need in order to placate their relatively deprived electorates. After all, many big-city mayors are already beseeching the federal government for massive aid—including Republicans like John Lindsay—and their electorates are not yet dominated by low-income Negroes.

Thus the present-policies strategy, if pursued for any long period of time, might lead to a simultaneous political and economic "confrontation" in many metropolitan areas. Such a "confrontation" would involve mainly Negro, mainly poor, and fiscally bankrupt larger central cities on the one hand, and mainly white, much wealthier, but highly taxed suburbs on the other hand. Some older suburbs will also have become Negro by that time, but the vast majority of suburbs will still be "lily white." A few metropolitan areas may seek to avoid the political aspects of such a confrontation by shifting to some form of metropolitan government designed to prevent Negroes from gaining political control of central cities. Yet such a move will hardly eliminate the basic segregation and relative poverty generating hostility in the urban Negro population. In fact, it might increase that population's sense of frustration and alienation.

In my opinion, there is a serious question whether American society in its present form could survive such a confrontation. If the Negro population felt itself wrongly "penned in" and discriminated against, as seems likely, many of its members might be driven to supporting the kind of irrational rebellion now being preached by a tiny minority. Considering the level of violence we have encountered already, it is hard to believe that the conditions that might emanate from a prolonged present-policies strategy would not generate much more. Yet the Negro community cannot hope to defeat the white community in a pitched battle. It is outnumbered 9 to 1 in population and vastly more than that in resources. Thus any massive resort to violence by Negroes would probably bring even more massive retaliation by whites. This could lead to a kind of urban *apartheid*, with martial law in cities, enforced residence of Negroes in segregated areas, and a drastic reduction in personal freedom for both groups, especially Negroes.

Such an outcome would obviously violate all American traditions of individual liberty and Constitutional law. It would destroy "the American dream" of freedom and equal opportunity for all. Therefore, to many observers this result is unthinkable. They believe that we would somehow "change things" before they occurred. This must mean that either the present-policies strategy would not lead to the kind of confrontation I have described, or we would abandon that strategy before the confrontation occurred.

Can the Present-Policies Strategy Avoid "Confrontation"?

What outcomes from a present-policies strategy might prevent this kind of confrontation? For one thing, if incomes in the Negro community rise rapidly without any additional programs, the Negro population of central cities may enter the middle class at a fast rate. If so, the Negro electorate that comes to dominate many major central cities politically by 1985 under the present-policies strategy may consist largely of stable, well-to-do citizens capable of supporting an effective local government.

To test this possibility, we have done some projections of incomes in the nonwhite population on a rough basis through 1983, assuming a present-policies strategy. These indicate that about two thirds of the nonwhite population at that time will have incomes *above* the existing poverty level—about the same fraction as at present. Since nonwhites will then form a much larger share of total central-city population, however, the percentage of *total* central-city population below the present poverty level might actually *rise* slightly. It is possible that nonwhite incomes might increase faster than in this forecast. Yet it is almost certain that the substitution of a relatively poor nonwhite group for a middle-income white group in central cities under a status-quo strategy will counterbalance likely increases in the incomes of nonwhites.

As a result, the electorate that will exist in major cities when Negroes become a majority will probably be just as poor as it is now (in real income terms). In contrast, the population in surrounding suburbs will be much wealthier than it is now. Thus, even if nonwhite incomes rise rapidly, there is still likely to be a significant "gap" between central-city and suburban income levels at that time—probably larger than at present.

Yet even under *present* conditions, many large central cities are critically short of revenue. Furthermore, in a generally wealthier society, it is highly probable that most central-city electorates will demand higher-than-existing levels of public service. Finally, the general cost of all government services will have risen sharply because of the productivity trends explained earlier. Hence, future central-city governments will have much higher costs, but not much greater resources than they do now. So rising incomes among nonwhites will not remove the fiscal pressure on central-city governments that is a key ingredient in the "confrontation" described above.

Moreover, the population group most responsible for violence and disturbances in central cities appears to consist of young Negro men between fifteen and twenty-four years of age. A high proportion of these people are unemployed because they lack skills (many are high school dropouts) and elementary training and motivation. This group will undoubtedly grow larger through natural increase and in-migration. Its problems are not likely to be solved under a status-quo strategy. Hence, even if the vast majority of nonwhites in central cities have increasing reason to abhor violence and riots, the *absolute size* of this more alienated group in 1975 will be 40 per cent larger than in 1966, and even larger by 1985.[31] This implies that at least part of this group might start actions forcing the kind of "confrontation" I have described.

Most of the other possible developments under a non-enrichment strategy that would avoid any major "confrontation" involve abandoning concentration of Negroes in central cities. Thus, some observers argue that members of the Negro middle class will increasingly move out to suburban communities as their incomes rise with no further encouragement from public programs. In this way, Negroes would be following the precedent of other ethnic groups. Up to now, there is no evidence that this has started to occur, even though a large Negro middle class already exists. But if such a pattern did evolve, it would amount to dispersal rather than the concentration implicit in the present-policies strategy.

Can Present Policies Be Sustained?

In any event, there appears to be significant probability—which I subjectively judge to be at least 25 per cent and perhaps as high as 75 per cent—that the present-policies strategy will prove unsustainable. If adopted, it would probably generate major repercussions that would force it to be abandoned. Society would be compelled either to suspend traditional individual rights and adopt martial law in cities or to institute major programs to improve ghetto conditions or to move toward wider dispersal of the Negro population, or some combination of these. Admittedly, there is no certainty that the present-policies strategy will lead to these outcomes. Nevertheless, I believe the probability that it will is high enough to make this strategy essentially self-defeating. Modern life is too dynamic for the status quo to be preserved for long.

Yet the present-policies strategy is the one society has so far chosen. Almost all current public policies tend to further concentration, segregation, and non-enrichment, as mentioned earlier. The few supposedly anti-concentration devices adopted, such as open-occupancy laws, have proved almost totally ineffective. All we have to do to confirm our choice of this strategy is to continue existing policies. In fact, avoiding this strategy will be difficult, because doing so will require major changes in present attitudes as well as in existing resource allocations.

The "Black Power" Case for the Enrichment-Only Strategy

The enrichment-only stategy is consistent with a current ideology that has come to be called the "Black Power" viewpoint. This viewpoint has been criticized by many, and some of its proponents have misused it to incite violence. Yet it is certainly an intellectually respectable and defensible position containing some persuasive elements.

The "Black Power" argument states that the Negro American population needs to overcome its feelings of powerlessness and lack of self-respect before it can assume its proper role in society. It can do so only by exerting power over the decisions that directly affect its own members. According to this view, a fully integrated society is not really possible until the Negro minority has developed its own internal strength. Therefore, the ideal society in which race itself is not an important factor can only come much later. It could exist only after Negroes had gained power and self-respect by remaining in concentrated areas over which they could assume political and economic control and direction. Hence this view contends that a future in which central cities become primarily Negro and suburbs almost entirely white would be an advantage rather than a disadvantage.

The "Black Power" view has several notable strong points. First, such assumption of local power would be fully consistent with the behavior of previous nationality groups, such as the Irish in New York and Boston. They, too, came up from the bottom of the social and economic ladder, where they had been insulted and discriminated against. And they did it by gaining political and economic control over the areas in which they lived.

Second, it is unquestionably true that one of the two most important factors providing Negroes with all their recent gains in legal rights and actual welfare has been their own forceful presentation of grievances and demands. (The other factor has been high-level prosperity in the economy in general.) Negro-originated marches, demonstrations, protests, and even riots have had immensely more impact in improving their actual power, income, and opportunities than all the "purely voluntary" actions of whites combined—including those of white liberals.

Third, time is on the side of the "Black Power" argument if current population growth and location trends continue. As pointed out earlier, Negroes are likely to become a majority of the electorate in many large American cities within the next fifteen years, unless radically new policies are adopted. By giving Negroes political control over these cities, this trend would provide them with a powerful bargaining position in dealing with the rest of society—a tool they now sorely lack.

Fourth, the "Black Power" viewpoint provides many key ideological supports for Negro self-development. It stresses the need for Negroes to become proud of their color and their history, more conscious of their own strengths. Is also focuses their attention on the need for organizing themselves economically and politically. Hence it could provide a focal point for arousing and channeling the largely untapped self-development energies of the Negro American population. One of the greatest difficulties in improving ghettos is discovering effective ways in which the lowest-income and most deprived residents can develop their own capabilities by participating more fully in the decisions and activities that affect them. Such "learning by doing" is, in my opinion, a vital part of the process of bringing deprived people into the main stream of American society. Insofar as "Black Power" proponents could develop such mechanisms, they would immensely benefit American society.

There are, however, also significant flaws in the "Black Power" argument. First, Negroes do not in fact have much power in the U.S. Nor is it clear just how they can obtain power solely through their own efforts, particularly in the near future. "Black Power" advocates constantly talk about "taking what is rightfully theirs" because they are dissatisfied with what "whitey" is willing to turn over to them voluntarily. They also reject the condescension inherent in whites' "giving" Negroes anything, including more power. But what bargaining power can Negroes use to compel whites to yield greater control over the economic and political decisions that affect them?

There are two possible answers. First, they could organize themselves so cohesively that they would become a potent political and economic force through highly disciplined but fully legal action. Examples would be block voting and economic boycotts. So far, nearly all efforts at such internal organization have foundered on the solid rocks of apathy, lack of funds, internal dissension, and disbelief that anything could be accomplished.

Second, Negroes could launch direct action—such as demonstrations and marches—that would morally, economically, or physically threaten the white community. This approach has so far proved to be the most successful. But many Negroes believe it has not improved their situation as fast as is necessary. Hence, there is a tendency to shift the form of threat employed to more and more violent action in order to get faster and more profound results. This tendency need only influence a small minority of Negroes in order to cause a significant escalation of violence. Yet such an escalation might result in massive retaliation by the white community that would worsen the Negroes' position. What is needed is enough of a threat to cause the white community to start changing its own attitudes and allocation of resources in ways far more favorable to Negroes, but not so much of a threat as to cause withdrawal of all white cooperation and sympathy.

This conclusion points up the second flaw in the "Black Power" case: Ultimately, U.S. Negroes cannot solve their own problems in isolation, because they are fully enmeshed in a society dominated by whites. The solution of Negro problems lies as much in the white community as in the Negro community. This is especially true because whites control the economic resources needed to provide Negroes with meaningful equality of opportunity. Hence, any strategy of action by Negro leaders that totally alienates the white community is doomed to failure.

Yet "Black Power" advocates are probably correct in arguing that Negroes must develop an ideology that focuses upon self-determination and therefore has some "anti-white" tinges. They need an "enemy" against which to organize the Negro community. History proves that organization *against* a concrete opponent is far more effective than one *for* some abstract goal. They also need an abrasive ideology that threatens whites enough to open their eyes to the Negroes' plight and their own need to do something significant to improve it. The question is how they can accomplish these goals without going too far and thereby creating violent anti-white hostility among Negroes and equally violent anti-Negro sentiment among whites.

In the past few years, many Negro Americans—including prominent community leaders—have shifted their sights away from direct racial integration as a goal. Instead they have focused upon other goals more consistent with the "Black Power" viewpoint. They want better housing, better schools, better jobs, and better personal security within all-Negro areas—and a much stronger Negro voice in controlling all these things. These enrichment-only objectives have apparently eclipsed their desire for greater ability to enter directly into white-dominated portions of the society. This rather dramatic change in values appears to rule out much possibility of Negroes' accepting either dispersal strategy.

In my opinion, the main cause of this shift in objectives is the failure of white society to offer any real hope for large-scale integration. After years of seeking equality under the law, Negro leaders have discovered that even removal of legal barriers is not producing much progress toward a true sharing in the life of white-dominated society. Why should they keep knocking on the door if no one will answer? Why not turn instead to existing all-Negro communities and try to improve conditions there? Indeed, I believe continued white refusal to engage in meaningful, large-scale integration will make it impossible for any self-respecting Negroes to avoid espousing some version of the "Black Power" viewpoint. Understandably, they will not be able to accept the conclusion that most of the millions of Negroes whom whites force to live racially segregated lives must therefore be condemned to inferior educations, housing, culture, or anything else.

Rather, they will reason, there must be some way to make the quality of life in all-Negro portions of a racially segregated society just as good as it is in the all-white portions. And if equality in terms of the indices of desirability accepted by whites cannot be achieved, then some of these "Black Power" advocates will be willing to attain at least nominal equality by denouncing those indicators as specious. They will further claim—with some justification—that life in all-white portions of society cannot be better and may be morally worse because whites suffer from racial blindness.

The reason why this argument is and will be advanced so strongly is certainly understandable. Those who advance it would hardly be human if they were not at least tempted to do so. As long as present white attitudes and behavior persist, adopting any other view amounts to despairing of any chance at equality for most Negroes.

Can the Enrichment-Only Strategy Create "Separate But Equal" Societies?[32]

The "Black Power" viewpoint essentially argues that racially separate societies in America can provide equal opportunities for all their members if Negroes are able to control their own affairs. Yet there is a great deal of evidence that this argument is false.

Certainly concerning employment, equality of opportunity for Negroes cannot possibly be attained in a segregated labor market. Negroes must be provided with full freedom and equality regarding entry into and advancement within the white-dominated enterprises that are overwhelmingly preponderant in our economy. Only in this way can they have any hope of achieving an occupational equality with whites.

In education, the evidence is far more ambiguous. The recent reports of the Office of Education and the Civil Rights Commission contend that both racial and economic integration are essential to the attainment of educational equality for Negroes.[33] Yet critics of these reports point out that many types of enrichment programs were not tested in the studies conducted by the authors. Unfortunately, most alternative approaches have not yet been tried on a scale large enough to determine whether any of them will work. Yet one conclusion does seem reasonable: Any real improvement in the quality of education in low-income, all-Negro areas will cost a great deal more money than is now being spent there, and perhaps more than is being spent per pupil anywhere.

Thus, society may face a choice between three fundamental alternatives: providing Negroes with good-quality education through massive integration in schools (which would require considerably more spending per pupil than now exists), providing Negroes with good-quality education through large-scale and extremely expensive enrichment programs, or continuing to relegate many Negroes to inferior educations that severely limit their lifetime opportunities. The third alternative is what we are now choosing. Whether or not the second choice—improving schools in all-Negro areas—will really work is not yet known. The enrichment alternative is based upon the as-yet-unproven premise that it will work.

Regarding housing, the enrichment-only strategy could undoubtedly greatly improve the quantity, variety, and environment of decent housing units available to the disadvantaged population of central cities. Nevertheless, it could not in itself provide Negroes of *any* economic level with the same freedom and range of choice as whites with equal incomes have. Clearly, in this field "separate but equal" does not mean *really* equal. Undoubtedly, all-white suburban areas provide a far greater range and variety of housing and environmental settings than can possibly be found in central cities or all-Negro suburbs alone.

Moreover, there is an acute scarcity of vacant land in many of our largest central cities. Therefore, greatly expanding the supply of decent housing for low-income families in those cities at a rapid rate requires creating many new units for them in the suburbs too.

Thus, if society adopts one of the many possible versions of the enrichment-only strategy, it may face the prospect of perpetuating two separate societies—one white and one Negro—similar to those that would develop under the present-policies strategy. If the enrichment programs carried out proved highly effective, then the gap between these two societies in income, education, housing, and other qualities of life would be nowhere near so great as under the present-politics strategy. Hence, the possibility of a potentially catastrophic "confrontation" between these two societies sometime in the next twenty years would be greatly reduced.

Nevertheless, I do not believe it will really be possible to create two separate societies that are truly equal. Therefore, even if the enrichment-only strategy proved extraordinarily successful at improving the lot of disadvantaged central-city residents of all races and colors (which is by no means a certainty), it would still leave a significant gap in opportunity and achievement between the separate white and Negro societies which would continue to emerge over the next twenty years. This gap would remain a powerful source of tension that might lead to violence, for experience proves that men seeking equality are not placated by even very great absolute progress when they perceive that a significant gap remains between themselves and others in society who are no more deserving of success than they. And that would be precisely the situation twenty years from now under the enrichment-only strategy—whether linked to "Black Power" concepts or not.

Why Dispersal Should Be Seriously Considered

As pointed out earlier, either of the two dispersal strategies would require radical changes in current trends and policies concerning the location of Negro population growth. Moreover, it is likely that massive dispersal would at present be opposed by *both* suburban whites and central-city Negroes. Many of the former would object to an influx of Negroes, and many of the latter would prefer to live together in a highly urbanized environment. Why should we even consider a strategy that is not only socially disruptive, but likely to please almost nobody?

In my opinion, there are five reasons why we should give enrichment plus dispersal serious consideration. First, future job-creation is going to be primarily in suburban areas, but the unskilled population is going to be more and more concentrated in central-city ghettos unless some dispersion occurs. Such an increasing divergence between where the workers are and where the jobs are will make it ever more difficult to create anything like full employment in decent jobs for ghetto residents. In contrast, if those residents were to move into suburban areas, they would be exposed to more knowledge of job opportunities and would have to make much shorter trips to reach them. Hence they would have a far better chance of getting decent employment.

Second, the recent U.S. Office of Education and U.S. Civil Rights Commission reports on equality of achievement in education reach a *tentative* conclusion that it is necessary to end the clustering of lower-income Negro students together in segregated schools in order to improve their education significantly.[34] As I understand these reports, they imply that the most significant factor in the quality of education of any student is the atmosphere provided by his home and by his fellow students both in and out of the classroom. When this atmosphere is dominated by members of deprived families, the quality of education is inescapably reduced—at least within the ranges of class size and pupil-teacher ratios that have been tried on a large scale. Therefore, if we are to provide effective educational opportunities for the most deprived groups in our society to improve themselves significantly, we must somehow expose them to members of other social classes in their educational experience. But there are not enough members of the Negro middle class "to go around," so to speak. Hence this means some intermingling of children from the deprived groups with those from not-so-deprived white groups, at least in schools. Because of the difficulties of bussing large numbers of students from the hearts of central cities to suburban areas, it makes sense to accomplish this objective through some residential dispersal. This consideration tends to support the integrated-dispersal strategy to some extent, even though these reports have received significant criticism, as noted above.

Third, development of an adequate housing supply for low-income and middle-income families and provision of true freedom of choice in housing for Negroes of all income levels will require out-movement of large numbers of both groups from central cities to suburbs. I do not believe that such an out-movement will occur "spontaneously" merely as a result of increasing prosperity among Negroes in central cities. Even the recently passed national open-occupancy law is unlikely to generate it. Rather, a program of positive incentives and of actual construction of new housing in suburban areas will be necessary.

Fourth, continued concentration of large numbers of Negroes under relatively impoverished conditions in ghettos may lend to unacceptably high levels of crime and violence in central cities. The outbreak of riots and disorders in mostly nonwhite areas in our central cities in the past few years is unprecedented in American history. As the report of the National Advisory Commission on Civil Disorders indicates, continuing to concentrate masses of the nonwhite population in ghettos dominated by poverty and permeated with an atmosphere of deprivation and hopelessness is likely to perpetuate or intensify these disorders. This could lead to the disastrous outcome already discussed in connection with the present-policies strategy.

Fifth, a continuation of ghetto growth will, over the next three or four decades, produce a society more racially segregated than any in our history. We will have older, blighted central cities occupied by millions of Negroes, and newer, more modern suburban areas occupied almost solely by whites. Prospects for moving from that situation to a truly integrated society in which race is not a factor in key human decisions are not encouraging. In fact, by that time we will be faced with a fantastically more massive dispersal problem than the present one if we really want to achieve a society integrated in more than just words.

Thus, only the two enrichment-plus-dispersal strategies explicitly seek to create a single society rather than accepting our present perpetuation of two separate societies: one white and one Negro. Dispersal would involve specific policies and programs at least starting us toward reversal of the profoundly divisive trend now so evident in our metropolitan areas. It may seem extraordinarily difficult to begin such a reversal. But however difficult it may be now, it will be vastly more difficult in twenty years if the number of Negroes segregated in central cities is 8 million larger than it is today.

In doing so, we must keep in mind that a significant increase in dispersal is perfectly compatible with a very large increase in Black Nationalism, or even with strong dominance of the Black Power viewpoint among Negroes. Very few Negroes are now moving into suburban areas, except into segregated portions of certain older suburbs which contain extensions of central-city ghettos. In most metropolitan areas, the number of Negroes moving into suburban areas could rise several hundred per cent without significantly reducing the total size of the central city's racial ghetto. Therefore, even if the desire for geographic racial solidarity associated with the Black Power viewpoint becomes strongly dominant among most central-city Negroes, dispersal could still rise many-fold as long as some Negroes still wanted to achieve higher-quality schools, housing, and other amenities through the traditional route of moving to the suburbs. In my opinion, it is incredible to believe that all the many millions of Negroes living in central cities will adopt a single viewpoint concerning dispersal, any more than they—or whites—do concerning any other subject. Therefore, it is not inconsistent to support *both* Black Nationalism and dispersal simultaneously. In fact, such dual support is implicit in the two dispersal strategies, since each embodies both dispersal and enrichment.

The Difficulty of Gaining Acceptance for Dispersal

I am fully aware that any strategy involving significant dispersal may now seem wholly impractical to responsible politicians and social leaders. The voluntary movement of large numbers of Negroes from ghettos to the suburbs encouraged by federal programs presupposes radical changes in existing attitudes among both suburban whites and central-city Negroes.

In spite of our social mobility, Americans are extremely sensitive to class differentiations. We have deliberately developed class-stratified suburban areas. Residents of each suburb use zoning, tax rates, lot-size requirements, and other devices to exclude persons considered farther down the ladder of social and economic prominence. As each group and each family moves upward in our mobile society, they become more concerned about creating social distance between themselves and those now below them—including those who were once equal to them.

I certainly do not deplore the historic traditions of self-improvement and protection of amenities and privileges that have been won through hard work and perseverance. These traditions should and will continue in some form, because it is proper for successful people to enjoy the fruits of their efforts.

Nevertheless, it is at least possible that the social objective of upgrading the lowest and most deprived groups in our society cannot be accomplished if we simultaneously insist upon excluding those groups from nearly all daily contact with other more fortunate people—as we do now—by maintaining extremely rigid class distinctions by geographic area. Thus, the best dispersal policy might be one that promoted day-to-day inter-class and inter-racial experiences without changing the dominant socio-economic character of the receiving suburban areas. This would allow persons moving out from the inner city to benefit from the existing character of those suburbs. Such a policy implies that the newcomers would comprise a minority in each area into which they went. This means that an integrated-dispersal strategy might ultimately provide the most desirable form of dispersal. It would enable the group that was already there to maintain nearly intact their conception of the proper standards for that community, while sharing the benefits of those standards with others.

Even this change in attitude, however, presupposes a shift in values of profound magnitude among white middle-class Americans. Furthermore, I doubt that most Negroes today want to live in white communities in which they would be relatively isolated from other Negroes. Hence they might prefer a segregated-dispersal strategy, if they were willing to accept dispersal at all. Yet, since most suburban areas are already incorporated into predominantly white communities, where and how could such a strategy be initiated?

Some Tactical Mechanisms for Encouraging Dispersal

Any attempt to achieve dispersal must involve specific answers to two basic questions:

What *mechanisms* can be designed to encourage voluntary out-movement of large numbers of Negroes into the suburbs and their peaceful acceptance and welcome by whites there?

What *incentives* can be developed leading particular interest groups in society to press politically for—or at least support—employment of those mechanisms?

Let us consider the mechanisms first. Americans have always used one basic approach to get people to overcome inertia and make voluntarily some socially desirable change. It consists of providing a significant economic or other reward for persons who behave in the desired manner. That reward might be free land (as for homesteaders and railroads in the nineteenth century), or tax reductions (as for homeowners or investors in equipment in the past few years), or direct payments (as for farmers), or services and income supplements tied to participation in specific programs (as for users of the G.I. Bill in education).

In the case of dispersion, I believe the system of rewards used should probably have the following characteristics:[3][5]

1. Advantages should accrue both to the Negro households moving out from central cities and to the suburban households into whose communities the newcomers move.

2. Whenever possible, these advantages should consist of rewards administered under metropolitan-area-wide organizations specifically set up for such a purpose. These organizations could be quasi-private bodies able to cooperate directly with existing local governments and other geographically limited organizations. Hence they would *not* be metropolitan governments.

3. Advantages to out-moving households might include the following:

The possibility of sending their children to top-quality schools that receive special grants because of participation in programs involving out-moving children.

Home-buying or renting financial aids available only to out-moving families or at least with assigned proportions of their total funding available only to such families.

Top-priority access to special programs concerning employment and on-the-job training in suburban industrial and other firms. In my opinion, such programs might be effectively built around the self-selection principle embodied in the G.I. Bill—that is, eligible persons would be given certificates enabling those firms who hire them to receive special benefits to compensate for their lower productivity or training costs. Such benefits might include tax credits or direct payments. The persons receiving these certificates would then make their own choice of employers among firms participating in such programs. This would preserve maximum individual choice among program participants.

4. Advantages to households already living in the receiving areas might include:

Special aid to schools receiving children of out-moving Negro families. Such aid should consist of funds linked to the students in such families (as Title I funding under the Elementary and Secondary Education Act is now linked to low-income families). But the per-student amount of aid given should greatly exceed the added direct cost of teaching each out-moving student. Hence the school district concerned would have a positive incentive to accept such students because of the financial "bonuses" they would bring with them. Those bonuses could be used to upgrade the entire receiving school or cut locally-borne costs therein.

"Bonus" community financing to participating suburban local governments. Again, the payments involved should significantly exceed the added costs of servicing in-coming families, so that each participating community would be able to improve other services too.

Giving higher priority in other federal programs to communities participating in out-movement programs than to those refusing to participate. These related programs could include sewer and water financing, planning aid, and selection as locations for federal installations.

5. Benefits available for out-moving families and receiving areas could be restricted by geographic area to avoid either paying people discriminately by race or wasting funds paying families who would move out anyway. A precedent for giving residents of certain neighborhoods special benefits already exists in the urban renewal and Model Cities programs. Thus, specific ghetto neighborhoods could be designated "origination" areas and largely white suburban communities designated "receiving" areas. Benefits would accrue only to persons moving from the former to the latter or to residents of the latter participating in reception programs.

6. If these programs were part of an integrated-dispersal strategy, they could be linked to quota systems concerning newcomers to each school or community involved. Thus, the special bonus aids would be available only up to a certain fraction of the total school enrollment or residential population of a given receiving community. This restriction would be aimed at retaining in the schools or communities concerned the dominance of the groups originally residing there. It is to be hoped that the result would be suburban integration, rather than a shift of massive neighborhood transition from central cities to suburbs.

The above suggestions are highly tentative and exploratory. Yet I hope they at least indicate that practical mechanisms can be created that might achieve a substantial amount of peaceful Negro out-movement—*if* they were adopted in a general atmosphere of social encouragement to dispersal.

Some aspects of the basic approach described above may seem terribly unjust. In particular, this approach rewards the advantaged (those already living in suburbs) as well as the disadvantaged (those moving out of deprived areas into suburbs) in order to get the former to accept the latter. Yet that is a key mechanism, one which free-enterprise systems have always employed when they seek to attain high-priority ends through voluntary action. Our society abounds with arrangements that provide special economic advantages to those who are already privileged, presumably in order to evoke socially desired behavior from them. Examples are oil depletion allowances, stock option plans for top executives, profitable contracts for defense firms, lower tax rates on capital gains, and subsidy payments to wealthy farmers. I am defending neither the equity nor the effectiveness of these particular examples. Yet they illustrate that we often adopt public policies that pay the rich to undertake behavior which presumably benefits society as a whole.

A second aspect of the approach to dispersal I have described which might seem harsh is that no benefits apparently accrue to disadvantaged persons who fail to move out to the suburbs. As stated earlier, however, I believe dispersal programs should only be undertaken simultaneously with large-scale ghetto enrichment programs. The latter would provide comparable, or even greater, benefits for those "left behind" in central cities—who will undoubtedly comprise the vast majority of Negroes in our metropolitan areas for many years to come.

Developing Political Support for Dispersal

The concept of dispersal will remain nothing but an empty theory unless a significant number of Americans decide their best interests lie in politically supporting specific dispersal mechanisms. It is conceivable that such support might result from a massive "change of heart" among white suburbanites. They might view dispersal as a way to "purge themselves" of the kind of "white racism" which the National Advisory Commission on Civil Disorders discribed. I do not think this will occur. In fact, I believe recent urban violence has tended to make white suburbanites more hostile than ever to the idea of having Negroes live next door to them.

Yet, on the other hand, several specific groups in society are beginning to realize that dispersal might benefit them immensely. The motivation of persons in these groups varies widely, from pure moral guilt to sheer self-interest. But almost all significant social change in the United States has occurred because a wide variety of different types of people with diverse motives have formed a coalition to accomplish something. In my opinion, only through that kind of process will any of the basic strategies I have described (except the present-policies strategy) ever be achieved.

I believe the groups favorable to dispersal now include, or soon will include, the following:

Suburban industrialists. In many metropolitan areas, they are experiencing acute labor shortages, particularly of unskilled workers. They will soon be willing to provide open and powerful political support for the construction of low-income and moderate-income housing for Negro workers and their families in currently all-white suburbs.

Downtown-oriented retailers, bankers, restaurant operators, hotel operators, and other businessmen in our larger cities. In cities where disorders have penetrated into central business districts (such as Milwaukee and Washington), many former patrons have stopped visiting these areas altogether—especially at night. If disorders in these areas get worse, the impact upon both consumer patronage and future capital investment in big-city downtowns could be catastrophic. Those whose enterprises are "locked in" such areas will soon realize they must vigorously support both stronger law enforcement and positive programs aimed at alleviating Negro discontent. At first, these programs will consist primarily of ghetto enrichment, but these groups will soon begin to support dispersal too.

Home builders. They would benefit from any large-scale programs of housing construction. But the delays and difficulties of carrying out such programs within central cities are much greater than they are on vacant suburban land. Hence they will eventually exert at least low-level support for dispersal if it means large-scale subsidy of privately built homes.

White central-city politicians in large cities. As the populations of their cities shift toward Negro majorities, they will be more and more willing to support some dispersal policies, as well as the enrichment programs they now espouse.

Businessmen in general with plants, offices, or other facilities "locked in" large central cities. An increasing number of such persons will realize that they will emerge losers from any major "confrontation" between black-dominated central cities and white-dominated suburbs, as described earlier.

Persons of all types whose consciences influence them to accept the National Advisory Commission's conclusion that dispersal of some kind is the only way to avoid perpetuating two separate societies, with the Negro one forever denied equality.

Since these groups now constitute a small minority of Americans, a great many other Americans must change their existing values considerably if large-scale dispersal is ever to occur. Yet the alternatives to such a strategy—especially the one we are now pursuing—could conceivably lead us to equally grave changes in values. For example, if there is an extremely significant increase in violence in Negro ghettos which spills over into all-white areas, the white population might react with harshly repressive measures that would significantly restrict individual freedoms, as noted above. This, too, would call for a basic shift in our values. But it is a shift which I regard with much more alarm that the one required by a dispersal strategy. In fact, in this age of rapid technological change, it is naïve to suppose that there will not in the future be significant alterations in attitudes that we presently take for granted.

The Scale of Efforts Required

The foregoing discussion emphasizes that any strategy likely to have a significant impact upon ghettos will require a very much larger effort than we are now devoting to this problem. Even a "pure" ghetto-enrichment strategy, which does not eliminate or even slow down the growth of the racial ghetto, would require a significantly greater allocation of financial and manpower resources to coping with the problems of the urban poor. A dispersal strategy that addresses itself to breaking up or at least slowing down the growth of the racial ghetto would also require even more profound changes in values and attitudes. Only the first strategy—that of continuing our present activities—requires no immediate change in effort or values. But it may eventually result in significant value changes too—and perhaps far less desirable ones than are required by the other two alternatives.

Thus, there is simply no easy way to cope with this problem. In my opinion, past federal programs and many currently suggested approaches have suffered from the desire to find a cheap solution to what is an extremely expensive problem. The program is expensive in terms not only of money, but also of our national talents and our willingness to change our basic values. In one way or another, we must and will accommodate ourselves to this problem. We cannot evade it.

Creating the Programs and Incentives Necessary to Achieve Any Desired Ghetto Future

Each strategy contains two basic parts: a desired outcome and a set of actions designed to achieve that outcome. I have not placed equal emphasis on these two parts in discussing each of the five strategies concerning ghetto futures. For example, the present-policies strategy as I have described it is essentially a set of actions—the continuation of present policies. Hence it does not emphasize a desired outcome. In fact, I have pointed out several reasons why its outcome might be quite undesirable. Conversely, my discussion of the enrichment-only strategy has focused upon its outcome. Hence I have not made many suggestions about how that outcome might be brought about. Similar emphasis upon the outcome rather than the means of attaining it also marks the discussion of the integrated-core strategy. Even my tentative analysis of how dispersal might be carried out hardly represents a complete blueprint for action.

Any strategy is really just wishful thinking until it links the outcome it envisions with some feasible means of attaining that outcome. This is especially true regarding several of the ghetto futures I have described, since they embody such radical changes in society. They are likely to remain largely fantasies, rather than real alternatives, until specific programs for achieving them can be defined. I have made some program suggestions in connection with dispersal strategies in order to prove that dispersal is not totally unrealistic. Unfortunately, the complexity of developing similar suggestions for the other strategies involving social change prevents my attempting to do so in this article.

Nevertheless, there are five basic principles crucial to formulating such programs.

1. No proposed "solution" to ghetto problems that is not eventually supported by the majority of the white middle class can possibly succeed.[36]

2. The actions designed to bring about any desired outcome must be linked to incentives that will appeal both to the self-interest of all groups concerned and to their consciences. In fact, the most difficult part of implementing any strategy (other than the present-policies strategy) will be providing effective incentives for the relatively well-off white majority. This group must be persuaded to expand many resources, and alter its own traditional behavior, in order to produce outcomes that appear to

benefit mainly a small minority of the population. As indicated in the discussion of dispersal, each segment of the white majority (such as business, labor, suburbanites, senior citizens, farmers, and so forth) must be presented with arguments and incentives which appeal specifically to its interests. An example is the argument that business suffers great losses of potential profits and output because of the failure of poor Negroes to engage in high-level consumption and the inability of poorly educated Negro workers to help meet high demands for skilled labor.

3. Any program designed to achieve a given outcome should involve significant action by the private sector. Otherwise, society may relegate ghettos to a position of dependency upon government that is inconsistent with full equality in American life. On the other hand, it is naïve to suppose that the private sector can or will bear the huge expense of coping with ghetto problems unaided. Society as a whole must pay the extra costs of on-the-job training programs, new factories located in ghettos, union training of unskilled Negro apprentices, and other actions aimed at helping the unskilled or otherwise "left out" enter the main stream of our economy. These actions must be carried out by nongovernmental organizations, but financed by the government through direct payments, tax credits, or other means.

4. No program involving ghettos can be effective unless it involves a high degree of meaningful participation by ghetto residents, and significant exercise of power and authority by them. We must realize that ghettos cannot be drawn into the main stream of American life without some redistribution of authority and power, as well as income, for equality in America means exercise of significant self-determination. Admittedly, lack of skill and experience may cause that exercise to be disorderly, inefficient, and even corrupt at first—as it was among the Irish, Italians, Jews, and others in the past. Therefore, turning over more power in ghetto areas to local residents may actually cause a short-run decline in the professional quality of government there—whether in schools, the police, or local government in general. Yet it will greatly alter the attitudes of residents toward those institutions and begin to draw them into the real functioning of our society. So it should and must come.

5. The more benefits that most ghetto residents receive through programs aimed at helping them, the more dissatisfied and vocally discontent certain small parts of the ghetto community are likely to become. This makes the problem of persuading the white

majority to support large-scale aid programs doubly difficult. It also means that socio-economic programs will have to be accompanied by greatly enlarged and improved law-enforcement efforts, particularly those in which ghetto leaders themselves play significant roles. Yet emphasis on improving law enforcement alone, without massively trying to meet the other needs of ghetto residents, will probably prove disastrous. Such one-sided emphasis on "law and order" could easily provoke steadily rising violence shifting in form toward guerrilla warfare. The need to avoid this outcome further emphasizes the importance of relying more and more on ghetto communities to develop their own internal controls of violence, with outside aid, as is consistent with the preceding principle of greater self-determination.

Merely stating these principles emphasizes how far we are from having designed practical programs to achieve most of the outcomes set forth in this article. In my opinion, one of the most important tasks facing us is the formulation and public discussion of the specific ingredients needed for such programs. But even that cannot be done until we have recognized more explicitly the various possible futures of American ghettos and weighed their relative advantages and disadvantages.

At present, most public discussion and thought about racial and ghetto problems in America suffer from a failure to define or even to consider explicit possible long-range outcomes of public policy. This is one reason why such discussion seems so confused, inchoate, and frustrating. I hope that the ideas set forth in this article can serve as a nucleus for more fruitful public discussion of this crucial topic, for the future of American ghettos will determine to a large extent the future of America itself.

Notes

[1] The first draft of this article was written in the early summer of 1967. Subsequently, the author became a consultant to the National Advisory Commission on Civil Disorders. In that capacity, he wrote the rough drafts of several chapters in the Commission's final report. One of these (Chapter 16) contains many of the ideas set forth in this article. Nevertheless, there are sufficient differences between the contents and presentation of Chapter 16 in the Commission's Report and this article to warrant separate publication of

the latter. The contents of this article express the thoughts of its author only and do not necessarily represent the views of either the National Advisory Commission on Civil Disorders or Real Estate Research Corporation.

[2] Data from the Social Security Administration.

[3] *Report of the National Advisory Commission on Civil Disorders* (Washington, D. C., March 1, 1968), p. 127. This document will hereafter be referred to as the *NACCD Report*.

[4] *Ibid.*, pp. 121, 127.

[5] Based upon the Census Bureau's Series D projections of future population—the ones assuming the lowest of the four levels of future fertility used by the Census Bureau. See U. S. Bureau of the Census, *Statistical Abstracts of the United States, 1967* (88th Edition; Washington, D. C., 1967), pp. 8–10.

[6] *NACCD Report*, p. 121.

[7] *Ibid.*

[8] *Ibid.*

[9] Open-occupancy legislation appears to be aimed at shifting the location of some future nonwhite growth to presently all-white areas. Experience in those states which have had open-occupancy ordinances for some time indicates, however, that they have little, if any, impact in altering the distribution of nonwhite population growth.

[10] *NACCD Report*, p. 227.

[11] Surveys conducted annually by Real Estate Research Corporation, results unpublished.

[12] *NACCD Report*, p. 216.

[13] See Raymond J. Murphy and James M. Watson, *The Structure of Discontent*, Mimeographed (Los Angeles: University of California at Los Angeles, June 1, 1967).

[14] *NACCD Report*, pp. 123–31.

[15] Specific recommendations concerning these subjects are set forth in the *NACCD Report*, Chapter 17.

[16] See John F. Kain, "The Distribution and Movement of Jobs and Industry," in *The Metropolitan Enigma*, ed James Q. Wilson (Washington, D.C., 1967)

[17] These include legislative proposals made by Senator Javits, the late Senator Robert Kennedy, and Senator Percy.

[18] William Baumol and William Bowen, *The Performing Arts: The Economic Dilemma* (New York:20th Century Fund).

[19] *NACCD Report*, p. 217.

[20] Insofar as I know, this principle was first formulated by my father, James C. Downs, Jr.

[21] Two well-known urban specialists with such views are Jane Jacobs and Victor Gruen. See Jane Jacobs, *The Life and Death of Great American Cities* (New York, 1961), and Victor Gruen, *The Heart of Our Cities* (New York, 1964).

[22] This phenomenon explains why it is so difficult to halt "massive transition" from white to nonwhite occupancy once it begins. It tends to continue even when whites originally living in the area concerned do not "panic" at all. As long as normal turnover continues to produce vacancies, and only nonwhites fill them, such transition is inescapable. The key persons whose behavior must be affected to stop transition are not the whites living in the area at the outset, but those living scattered elsewhere in the metropolitan area or even other parts of the nation. They are the persons who must move into the areas as vacancies appear in order to maintain racial balance therein. Thus, attempts to organize existing white residents so as to prevent them from

fleeing almost always fail to halt transition. Organizers can rarely identify "the whites who aren't there yet," so they cannot influence the decisions of these potential future occupants, and transition continues relentlessly.

23An equally significant problem is convincing at least some Negro families that it is desirable to live in an area where Negroes are in a minority. If all members of *both* groups demand a racially dominant position in their neighborhoods, then integration will be impossible, and *de facto* segregation will prevail everywhere. This results from the racist assumption involved in any desire for racial dominance: that race or color *in itself* is a significant factor in determing a person's nature or character.

24The U. S. Supreme Court will soon have to face up to the consequences of this "Law." In order to attack *de facto* segregation effectively, it must recognize racial discrimination in the form of school quotas as constitutional. At present, our society cannot achieve integration or end segregation without deliberate and explicit racial discrimination by public authorities. This is true in relation to other public facilities besides schools, including hospitals and housing.

25This term and usage were coined by Charles E. Lindblom. See Lindblom and David Braybrooke, *The Strategy of Decision* (New York: The Free Press, 1963).

26See the *NACCD Report*, Chapter 17.

27See their statements as quoted in the Chicago *Daily News*, August 25, 1967.

28*NACCD Report*, p. 227.

29*Ibid.*, p. 121.

30These figures are based upon the Census Bureau's Series D population projections. If higher fertility projections are used, the suburbs would contain slightly higher proportions of total population in 1985. See the reference cited in footnote 5.

31*NACCD Report*, pp. 216–17.

32This section of the article was written after Chapter 16 of the *NACCD Report* had been completed and closely parallels the contents of certain parts of that chapter.

33See James Coleman *et al.*, *Equality of Educational Opportunity* (Washington, D. C.: U. S. Office of Education, 1966), and the U. S. Civil Rights Commission, *Racial Isolation in the Public Schools* (Washington, D. C., 1967).

34*Ibid.*

35Many of the programs described in this section have been recommended by the National Advisory Commission on Civil Disorders. See the *NACCD Report*, Chapter 17.

36This fact is recognized by most Negro leaders not committed to zealously militant separatism. For example, see Kenneth Clark, *Dark Ghetto* (New York, 1965), p. 222.

3

Racism in America and How to Combat It [1]

Americans Need To Understand Racism

Racism is a dirty word in America—and a hotly controversial one.

Calling somebody a "racist" is—and should be—a grievous insult. It implies that the person concerned is guilty of committing a serious injustice. Black Americans accuse the Nation's ethnic majority of white racism; while many whites accuse some Negroes of black racism.

What is racism anyway? What significance does it really have in American life today? Unfortunately, almost no one who uses this word defines it clearly or at all. And it is used in such widely varying ways that it hardly seems to have any commonly agreed upon meaning—except that nearly everyone believes racism is evil and un-American. The result is widespread confusion, uncertainty, and disagreement concerning the nature of racism. Even worse, practically any use of the word calls forth strongly emotional reactions. Rather than consider the subject reasonably, Americans of all colors usually adopt self-righteous and defensive views about it, even though racism is one of the most complicated and profoundly important issues in the Nation's history.

Because racism is too important in the destiny of America to allow this confusion to continue unchallenged, this paper seeks to clarify its meaning, to measure its true significance in American life, and to indicate some ways to combat it.

Significance of Racism

Millions of Mexican Americans, Puerto Ricans, Negroes, Indians, and other minority groups in our society suffer from severe

Reprinted by permission of the U.S. Civil Rights Commission from Clearinghouse Publication, Urban Series No. 1, January, 1970. The opinions expressed are the author's and do not necessarily represent the views of Commission members or staff.

deprivation and injustice—not only in the past—but now. Many widely varying factors cause this deplorable situation. They include historical development, economic and physical conditions, technical and population trends, long-established institutional structures and practices, political forces, and social and personal customs and attitudes. An additional factor, racism, is not always the most important one. Therefore, any reduction of deprivation and injustice must involve actions aimed at many things other than racism.

The harmful effects of racism upon American society are immense. These effects are especially injurious to members of certain minority groups, often in ways completely unrecognized by most Americans. Racism worsens the impact upon these minority groups of nearly all the other causal factors listed above. Therefore, no attempts to provide equal opportunities in our society, or to improve conditions among deprived groups, are likely to succeed unless we eliminate *or* counteract racism. Such success will not occur until most Americans—especially whites—understand racism well enough to recognize and counteract its pervasive forms in their own behavior and in the institutions around them.

The great significance of racism in American life received dramatic and widely publicized emphasis in the "Report of the National Advisory Commission on Civil Disorders," in March 1968. Among the most controversial findings in this report are:

What White Americans have never fully understood—but what the Negro can never forget—is that white society is deeply implicated in the ghetto. White institutions created it, white institutions maintain it, and white society condones it.

Race prejudice has shaped our history decisively in the past; it now threatens to do so again. White racism is essentially responsible for the explosive mixture which has been accumulating in our cities since the end of World War II.

These statements were controversial when they were first made because most white Americans did not believe that they had racist attitudes or that they exhibited racist behavior. After all, most whites are far removed from direct contact with what the National Advisory Committee on Civil Disorders called "the ghetto." So they do not see themselves as "deeply implicated" in creating, maintaining, or condoning it. Most of all, they cannot understand why they should be held "responsible for the explosive mixture which has been accumulating in our cities since the end of World War II." The overwhelming majority of whites do not understand how they can be blamed for riots and disorders among people with whom they have very little direct contact, and whose affairs have been—and still are—largely unknown to them.

The National Advisory Commission failed to clarify its accusations by explicitly defining "white racism" in its Report. It did not directly link that term with the many examples of racist institutional practices set forth throughout the Report. These omissions strengthened the initial antagonism of many whites to its findings. Moreover, events since the Commission issued its report have further increased this antagonism, and even caused many whites who at first favored the Commission's findings to change their views. Yet these same events have made it even more imperative for most Americans to understand the real nature and significance of racism in our society.

Racism is one of those words that many people use, and feel strongly about, but cannot define very clearly. Those who suffer from racism usually interpret the word one way while others interpret it quite differently. This ambiguity is possible in part because the word refers to ideas that are very complicated and hard to pin down. Yet, before we can fully understand how racism works or how to combat its harmful effects we must first try to define it clearly even though such an attempt may be regarded as wrong by many.

Perhaps the best definition of *racism* is an operational one. This means that it must be based upon the way people actually behave, rather than upon logical consistency or purely scientific ideas. Therefore, racism may be viewed as *any attitude, action, or institutional structure which subordinates a person or group because of his or their color.* Even though "race" and "color" refer to two different kinds of human characteristics, in America it is the visibility of skin color—and of other physical traits associated with particular colors or groups—that marks individuals as "targets" for subordination by members of the white majority. This is true of Negroes, Puerto Ricans, Mexican Americans, Japanese Americans, Chinese Americans, and American Indians. Specifically, white racism subordinates members of all these other groups primarily because they are not white in color, even though some are technically considered to be members of the "white race" and even view themselves as "whites."

As a matter of further explanation, racism is not just a matter of attitudes: actions and institutional structures, especially, can also be forms of racism. An "institutional structure" is any well-established, habitual, or widely accepted pattern of action or organizational arrangement, whether formal or informal. For example, the residential segregation of almost all Negroes in large cities is an "institutional structure." So is the widely used practice of denying employment to applicants with any nontraffic police record because this tends to discriminate unfairly against residents of low-income areas where police normally arrest young men for minor incidents that are routinely overlooked in wealthy suburbs.

Just being aware of someone's color or race, or even taking it into account when making decisions or in other behavior, is not necessarily racist. Racism occurs only when these reactions involve some kind of subordination. Thus, pride in one's black heritage, or Irish ancestry, is not necessarily racist.

Racism can occur even if the people causing it have no intention of subordinating others because of color, or are totally unaware of doing so. Admittedly, this implication is sure to be extremely controversial. Most Americans believe racism is bad. But how can anyone be "guilty" of doing something bad when he does not realize he is doing it? Racism can be a matter of *result* rather than *intention* because many intitutional structures in America that most whites do not recognize as subordinating others because of color actually injure minority group members far more than deliberate racism.

The separation of races is not racism unless it leads to or involves subordination of one group by another (including subordination of whites by Negroes). Therefore, favoring the voluntary separation of races is not necessarily a form of racism. However, it would become racism if members of one group who wanted to cluster together tried to restrict the locational choices of members of some other group in order to achieve such clustering; for example, if whites tried to discourage Mexican Americans from moving into all-white neighborhoods or if a group of black students forced other black students to live in a specific dormitory. Furthermore, separation of groups is one of the oldest and most widespread devices for subordination in all societies. It is particularly effective in modern urbanized societies because it is extremely difficult, if not impossible, to provide different but truly equal opportunities and conditions for separated groups within an economically integrated society.

WAYS WHITE RACISM APPEARS OR WORKS IN AMERICAN SOCIETY

White racism exhibits itself in hundreds of ways in American society, and acts in hundreds of other ways that are not recognized by most citizens. Yet all of these can be usefully grouped into two basic categories: *overt racism*, and *indirect institutional subordination because of color*. (For convenience, the second category will be referred to as just *institutional subordination*.)

Overt racism is the use of color *per se* (or other visible characteristics related to color) as a subordinating factor. *Institutional subordination* is placing or keeping persons in a position or status of inferiority by means of attitudes, actions, or institutional structures which do not use color itself as the subordinating mechanism, but instead use other mechanisms indirectly related to color. Institutional subordination is particularly difficult to define clearly in a few words. The very essence of institutional subordination is its indirect nature, which often makes it hard to recognize. Furthermore, there are so many different forms of institutional subordination that it is difficult to include all of them in a single definition. Therefore, these two categories of racism, and the relations between them, can best be clarified by discussing them rather than by further refining their definitions.

HISTORICAL DOMINANCE OF OVERT RACISM AND ITS RESULTS

For more than 300 years, overt racism was a central part of American life, particularly in the South. During these centuries, thousands of overtly racist laws, social institutions, behavior patterns, living conditions, distributions of political power, figures and forms of speech, cultural viewpoints and habits, and even thought patterns continually forced colored Americans[2] into positions of inferiority and subordination. It took the bloodiest of all American wars to abolish the most terrible form of legal subordination—slavery—just 100 years ago. But many other overtly racist laws and institutions remained in force until well after World War II. These include legally segregated schools, restrictive covenants forbidding nonwhites to live in certain neighborhoods, laws prohibiting interracial marriages, required racial separation of public facilities like bus seats and restaurants, and denial of the right to vote.

In the past two decades, there has been important progress in striking down legal support for most of the forms of overt racism. The actual effects of many such forms of racism have been greatly reduced, too. Moreover, this type of conscious and deliberate subordination by color is now considered wrong by most

Americans. As a result, many whites *believe* that overt racism—which is the only form they recognize—is disappearing from America.

Yet hundreds of forms of overt racism remain throughout most of the Nation. Examples are the deliberate exclusion of Negroes, Mexican Americans, and other colored persons from labor unions, law firms, school districts, all-white residential neighborhoods, college fraternities, and private social clubs.

Furthermore, the effects of more than three centuries of overt racism upon both whites and nonwhites cannot be overcome in just a few years. For many generations, millions of Negroes, Mexican Americans, Indians, and other nonwhites have been treated as inferiors, given inferior jobs and legal rights, compelled to accept inferior schooling, forced to live in inferior housing and neighborhoods, made to use inferior public facilities, and constantly told that they were inferior human beings and had no chance to be otherwise. They have been—and still are—systematically excluded from most residential areas, most schools, most jobs, most social privileges, and most political opportunities—particularly the best of all these things. This treatment has inescapably had tremendous effects upon a whole range of conditions among nonwhites in America. These conditions include where they live, their incomes, their self-images and degree of self-confidence, the nature and stability of their families, their attitudes toward authority, their levels of educational and cultural attainment, and their occupational skills. Of course, not all members of each nonwhite minority group have been equally affected by these conditions. Yet, taken as a whole, Americans of color are still severely handicapped by the residual effects of past overt racism—plus the many forms of overt racism that still exist.

RELATION OF RESIDUAL EFFECTS OF OVERT RACISM
TO INSTITUTIONAL SUBORDINATION

The deeply embedded effects of overt white racism will not instantly disappear if the white majority suddenly reduces or even eliminates the use of color as an explicit factor in making decisions or influencing its actions. Many whites now say: "All right, we recognize the injustice of overt racism. So we will stop using color as a factor in making decisions. Instead we will use other factors which are clearly and reasonably related to the activities and privileges concerned." Examples of these other factors used in making decisions are skill levels in relation to jobs, place of residence in relation to school attendance, ability to score well on entrance examinations in relation to higher education, self-confidence and leadership of whites in relation to job promotions, and savings plus present income in relation to buying homes.

Usually, the use of such factors is free from overt racism. Hence, it constitutes great progrsss in relation to most of American history. Thus, most civil rights organizations have argued for years in favor of "merit employment" based upon skill and ability without regard to race or color. And achievement of true "merit employment" regarding hiring, promotion, wages, and salaries would be a great advance in most firms. Therefore, whites who succeed in this achievement can rightly feel proud of eliminating an important form of overt racism from their behavior.

Nevertheless, even "merit employment" programs can conceal many forms of indirect institutional subordination by color. In fact, we can use the example of such programs to illustrate how present elimination of overtly racist action does *not* destroy or even significantly weaken the continuing racist effects of *past* overtly racist behavior. This can occur because many of those effects are embedded in institutional structures that no longer appear related to race or color.

Consider an employer who needs workers to fill certain jobs that demand advanced carpentry skills. Naturally, he requires that applicants have such skills in order to be hired. But what if the local carpenters' union excludes all Negroes and Mexican Americans as members? Then this very reasonable behavior of the employer has racist effects because of overt racism of another organization upon which he relies to carry out his own activities. Or what if unions accept minority group apprentices specially trained in local high schools, but the only high schools providing such training are in all-white neighborhoods, either too far from minority group neighborhoods for convenient attendance, or far enough to be placed in different school districts because all school district boundaries are based upon the "neighborhood proximity" principle? In this case, no decision-makers are using overtly racist principles. Yet the result clearly continues systematic subordination of minority groups by excluding them from important economic opportunities. Returning to the example, assume that the employer saves money by never advertising available job openings. Instead, he relies solely upon word-of-mouth communications from his present employees to their friends to find applicants—but all his present employees are white. This is an extremely widespread practice, since most workers find their jobs by hearing of openings from friends. Yet it has the effect of excluding nearly all minority group members from consideration for available jobs. Because of past overt racism, most whites have mainly white friends, particularly since they live in all-white neighborhoods.

Again, the employer is taking actions which are not overtly racist in either nature or intent—but which nevertheless have racist effects—that is, they subordinate people because of their color. In this case, these effects occur because the seemingly reasonable and "unbiased" behavior of the employer takes place in an institutional context that still contains profoundly racist elements remaining from three centuries of overt racism. If the employer had carefully examined his recruiting practices to see whether he was giving members of all groups an equal chance to compete for his job, he might have discovered this situation. But he was not engaging in any overtly racist behavior; so it never occurred to him that his customary practices might have indirect racist effects because of institutional subordination.

'INVISIBILITY' OF MUCH INSTITUTIONAL SUBORDINATION

This "invisibility" of institutional subordination is even more striking concerning those forms which result from *geographic exclusion* of minority group members from all-white areas, or *perceptual distortion* in the way people see reality. Overt racism—both past and present—is the main cause of the special separation of where most whites live from where most nonwhite minorities live. The major form of such racism is deliberate discouragement of Negro and other nonwhite families from buying or renting homes in all-white neighborhoods. Such discouragement is systematically practiced by white realtors, renting agents, landlords, and homeowners. This clearly racist behavior has become so well entrenched that many minority group members no longer even try to find homes in all-white areas because they fear they will "get the run-around" or receive hostile treatment from at least some neighbors. So the pattern of exclusion is continued—in spite of recent laws and court decisions to the contrary.

Yet dozens of other forms of institutional subordination are indirectly caused by the absence of nonwhites from white residential areas. For example, most new jobs are being created in suburban shopping centers, industrial parks, new office buildings, and schools or universities. But American suburban areas are overwhelmingly white in population (about 95 percent in 1966). So the suburban sources of new employment are usually far from where nonwhites live. This makes it very difficult for the latter to know when such job openings exist, to get transportation to look for them, and to commute to work once they are found. Even if they do get jobs in the suburbs, they have great difficulty finding housing near their work. This difficulty does not result only from overt racism: it is also caused by zoning laws which deliberately discourage any housing serving relatively lower-income groups, or local actions which prevent use of federal subsidies for such housing. Such laws are usually defended on grounds of "maintaining high community standards" of housing and open space, or protecting the existing residents from tax increases that would be caused by building more schools to serve new low-income residents.

All these conditions discourage minority group members from even trying to get suburban jobs. This perpetuates their exclusion from all-white suburban areas. Yet many of the best quality schools, housing developments, recreational facilities, and general residential environments are found in the suburbs. So most minority group members find themselves cut off not only from the fastest growing sources of new jobs, but also from many of the best amenities in American society. This is clearly racism or "institutional subordination."

Moreover, this exclusion is accomplished by very few acts of overt racism carried out by a small number of people—supplemented by thousands of acts of indirect institutional subordination carried out by millions of white suburbanites. But most of the latter are completely unaware of the subordinating nature of their behavior. In fact, many sincerely avoid any actions they believe are overtly racist. That is why so many whites become righteously indignant at the claim that American society is "racist." They have carefully purged their own actions of overtly racist behavior, and they sincerely believe their own communities "have no race problems" because there are practically no minority group members there. The institutionally subordinating nature of the processes that cause this exclusion remain completely hidden from them.

This invisibility of institutional subordination occurs in part because minority group members themselves are "invisible" in the normal lives of most white Americans—especially white children. Most white children are brought up in neighborhoods where Negroes, Mexican Americans, and other nonwhite persons are totally absent, or constitute an extremely small minority—usually engaged in menial jobs. These children form an unconscious but deeply rooted mental image of "normal" society as consisting only of white people, and of all colored persons as "strange" and "different" from "normal people." This image is further reinforced by the world they see on television. Until very recently, "normal" American society as depicted by television programs contained few Negroes, Indians, Mexican Americans, or other nonwhites in positive or realistic roles. Members of these groups were seen only as villains, or professional athletes, or entertainers, or servants, or on newscasts engaged in crime or violence. Recent introduction of many more Negroes into television commercials and some major roles is certainly an improvement. But television still depicts a largely segregated society, especially in the situation shows and cartoons which children watch—and particularly regarding such minority groups as Puerto Ricans and Indians. Moreover, this perception of whites as the only "normal Americans" was further reinforced for more than 100 years by the elementary and other textbooks used in almost all American schools. The exclusion of minority group members from such texts is one more way in which millions of Americans were—and still are—made both "invisible" and "strange" in the minds of the white majority.

The same distortions in perception that make whites unconsciously feel "normal" and superior in relation to nonwhite persons have exactly the opposite effects upon the latter. Most colored children also group in neighborhoods where they meet few people not in their own ethnic group. However, they learn from adults who must deal with whites that people in their own group have relatively little power and status in society. Television has devastatingly confirmed this impression because the world of "normal Americans" they see on the screen almost totally excludes them, or shows \them mainly in inferior or marginal roles. School textbooks and other educational materials further confirm this view. It is, therefore, not surprising that many members of nonwhite groups unconsciously come to believe that perhaps they really *are* inferior. Otherwise, how can the pictures of reality which society shows them be explained? But once a person begins to believe he is inferior, he starts losing confidence in his ability to overcome any obstacles he may run into. This often causes him to reduce his efforts when confronted by such obstacles—which in turn produces failures that confirm his feelings of inferiority. So his subordination is not only perpetuated, but becomes justified in the eyes of others by his behavior.[3] Thus, geographic exclusion of nonwhites by whites, plus perceptual distortions in white-controlled mass media, combine to produce largely unrecognized psychological and behavioral effects upon both groups. These effects perpetuate the institutional subordination of nonwhites because of their color.

The pervasive nature of institutional subordination, and its continuance over long periods, is illustrated by the Negro quest for good quality education in American public schools. Obtaining quality educations for their children is a central concern of all American parents. But among Negro parents, this desire has been continuously thwarted by a series of white-dominated institutions. Each time Negroes overcome or bypass the obstacles posed by one such institution, another blocks them with some new form of subordination.

As late as the 1940's, Negroes tried to get good quality schooling within the legally segregated separate school systems which then prevailed. But experience proved that the education their children received was definitely inferior in quality to that received by whites. For example, the few Negroes who managed to complete college in this inferior system discovered they could not earn incomes even as high as those of white high school graduates, both because their training was inferior and because of discrimination in hiring.

In response, Negro civil rights organizations launched a long legal battle for racial integration in the public schools so they could share in the good quality education received by whites. The legal struggle was finally won in the Supreme Court's monumental 1954 decision striking down segregation. But then they found themselves confronted by a whole new series of white maneuvers and institutions preventing meaningful integration. In the South, most areas simply ignored the Supreme Court's command to integrate schools. Other areas engaged in token integration of just a few students, or devised "voluntary selection" schemes that nullified integration. As of 1966—*12 years* after the Supreme Court decision—the proportions of Negro elementary and secondary school students in schools with white students were 4.4 percent in Alabama, 8.8 percent in Georgia, 3.4 percent in Louisiana, 2.5 percent in Mississippi, and 5.6 percent in South Carolina. In only four of the 11 southern states was this fraction more than 16 percent. However, it was more than 75 percent in five of the seven border States. So the strikingly low fractions in the deep South unquestionably resulted from deliberate white policy rather than any necessity stemming from high proportions of Negroes in the total population.

Northern white resistance to school integration was also strong, but it employed different forms of institutional subordination. Overtly racist practices in real estate markets strongly discourage Negroes from moving into most all-white neighborhoods in order to gain access to the better schools serving those neighborhoods. So Negro residential expansion necessarily remains focused on areas near the edge of massive all-Negro concentrations. But as soon as Negroes begin moving into all-white areas, white residents cease moving in. Eventually, most whites withdraw, causing the neighborhood to become rapidly almost entirely Negro. This *de facto* residential segregation was linked to school segregation by the neighborhood school principle—that is, the concept of having all children attend schools near their homes.

To cope with this form of *institutional subordination*, Negroes proposed busing students from where they lived to schools in other areas so as to achieve racially mixed student bodies in each school. This idea evoked two hostile responses from many of the white parents whose children were concerned. The first was an even stronger defense of the neighborhood school principle. This principle had originated mainly for convenience reasons, but now formed a useful instrument for continued institutional subordination. The second was opposition to *all* busing of students as inherently undesirable because of delays, child fatigue, added costs, and other ostensibly "technical" reasons. White parents even opposed schemes that did not move their own children, but involved only the busing of Negro children from overcrowded all-Negro schools to underutilized all-white schools. *Such opposition to all busing as undesirable is clearly racist in nature.* This is indicated by the high proportion of white students in rural areas, suburbs, and Catholic big-city school systems who have used buses for years to get to school—and still use them—without arousing any such complaints. Yet white opposition to publicly supported busing schemes aimed at integrating schools has effectively stymied this route to improved educational quality for Negro children. It is one form of the adamant white refusal to integrate that is driving most Negroes to abandon integration as a goal, and instead turn to Black Nationalism.

Still searching for ways to improve the quality of education received by their children, Negro parents and educators have now begun emphasizing the idea of community control over public schools. Recent statistical evidence proves conclusively that present school systems in our largest cities are failing to provide equal or even minimally decent educational opportunity to most Negro students. So Negroes in some cities have urged that local school boards be set up in each neighborhood or group of neighborhoods with real power over the schools in each area vested in such school boards. These school boards would be dominated by members of the minority group living in the area and providing most of the students in its schools. Hopefully, such local minority group members will be far more sensitive to the educational needs of their own children than the professionals in giant citywide school bureaucracies have proved to be. Moreover, having Negro children realize that their schools are controlled by black people might add to their self-respect and sense of control over their own destinies. This could markedly improve their attitude toward learning, thereby raising their achievement levels. Finally, creating closer links between local schools and parents may affect the encouragement toward education which children receive in their homes. The whole concept of local community control is new within large cities. Therefore, whether these hoped-for benefits will actually result cannot be evaluated until this concept has been tried out in practice. However, it does not differ very much from the idea of local control of schools already used throughout most of white suburban America.

But this latest attempt by Negroes to achieve good quality schools is already facing mounting opposition from several white-dominated institutions. Professional educators who control big city school bureaucracies claim such decentralization may result in *lower* quality education because of lack of professional skill and training by those who would then control schools. Teachers' unions seem ready to fight delegation of any authority over their members to local groups more likely to insist on evaluating teacher performance than professional administrators do now. This battle is so bitter that it closed the giant New York City public school system for many weeks. And similar opposition seems likely in other big cities where decentralization is being seriously considered.

This series of moves by Negroes seeking to give their children a decent education, and countermoves by white institutions preventing this desirable outcome, clearly illustrates why so many nonwhite Americans believe our society is permeated with racist institutions. No matter what course Negro parents have pursued, their efforts have been frustrated by white-controlled institutions using a wide variety of arguments and tactics. The result is always a refusal to allow Negroes either equal access to good quality white schools, or control over the schools to which they have been relegated. On the one hand, they are compelled to use predominantly Negro schools by the neighborhood school principle; but on the other hand, they are prevented from applying the same principle to control over those schools so they can try to improve them.

No doubt there is often some truth in the "technical" arguments used by white-dominated institutions to oppose each attempt by nonwhites to improve their children's education. But the same dual denial of either equal access to white facilities or self-control over the inferior facilities relegated to nonwhites exists in many other spheres—such as housing and politics. It is no wonder that nonwhites now look past the "purely technical" arguments advanced by whites to support each set of tactics, and instead see the terribly frustrating underlying pattern of institutional subordination. It is time that all Americans saw it—and attacked it vigorously.

SUMMARY OF HOW INSTITUTIONAL SUBORDINATION WORKS

The above discussion illustrates how institutional subordination constantly produces racist effects from actions which are usually *not* overtly racist in either content or intention. This type of transformation occurs whenever apparently nonracist actions are:

a. Directly linked to other actions that are overtly racist (such as basing employment policies on acceptance of unions that deliberately exclude Negro members).

b. Heavily reliant upon personal qualifications or skills which minority group members have not been permitted to achieve because of past overt racism (such as requiring passage of academically oriented tests for getting a job, or basing early ability groupings of children in public schools on tests administered only in English in areas where many children have been reared in Spanish-speaking homes).

c. Dependent upon institutional arrangements which embody the residual results of past overt racism (such as policies—like the neighborhood school policy—which mainly benefit persons living near facilities in all-white neighborhoods).

d. Likely to perpetuate any of the three causal factors cited above—that is, overt racism, low achievement among minority groups of key skills or traits, or residual institutional arrangements from past overt racism (as distortions of reality in mass media and textbooks do).

These relationships between seemingly nonracist actions and other actions or institutions which involve either present or past overt racism are rarely recognized by most whites. They see only the nonracist actions in themselves, not the institutional context in which they are embedded. Moreover, there are almost always "sound" economic or other reasons why these seemingly nonracist actions—and all the institutional structures surrounding them—have been adopted. But such "soundness" has been calculated from the unconsciously restricted "white only" viewpoint that most Americans have been absorbing since birth. This viewpoint is simply not aware of the impacts of any action upon Mexican Americans, Indians, Negroes, or other colored groups. So it normally does not consider such impacts at all in deciding whether or not any given action is desirable. In recent years, more whites have become conscious of overt racism. Yet they still do not realize how many of their everyday actions continue to indirectly subordinate minority group members in the ways described above.

IS INSTITUTIONAL SUBORDINATION REALLY 'RACIST'?

If institutional subordination is one of two basic types of racism, should people who engage in it be considered "racist," even if they do not realize the effects of their actions? How can someone be guilty of racism when he does not realize that his actions have racist effects? After all, guilt is a matter of intention as much as effect.

There are several reasons why it would be both wrong and harmful to consider persons who support institutional subordination as "racists" in the same sense as those who practice overt racism. For one thing, many actions which involve institutional subordination seem perfectly fair, reasonable, and "unbiased" to most Americans. An example is adoption of "merit employment." Accusing people who follow this policy and others like it of being "racists" contradicts commonsense—as well as the longstanding policy of many civil rights groups. Moreover, such accusations might simply infuriate persons who were sincerely trying to eliminate overt racism from their lives. Their outrage at this seemingly unjustified insult might blind them to any understanding of institutional subordination at all. The proper ways of offsetting institutional subordination may not require changes in the policies of some of the people who cause it. For example, the way to get rid of the subordinating impacts of "merit employment" is certainly not to have all employers put unqualified workers in every job. Rather it is to eliminate unfair union practices or have society as a whole pay for extra training for certain workers, etc. So what good would it do to make supporters of "merit employment" feel guilty about a policy that was actually producing many benefits, merely because it also produced costs which they could not remove themselves anyway? Finally, almost every white American supports some form of institutional subordination. Therefore, we might remove nearly all significant meaning from the term—or cause many people to reject our whole analysis—for they *know* they are not "racists" in the overt sense.

On the other hand, most white Americans *are* causing impacts upon Negroes, Mexican Americans, Puerto Ricans, Indians, and other colored Americans that unfairly subordinate the latter. To this extent, they are all "unintentional racists," even though they are certainly not guilty of the same kind of deliberate injustice as those who practice overt racism.

How Racism Provides Benefits to Whites

American racism probably originated in slavery, the most extreme form of subordination by color. That type of racism, and all other later types, came into being mainly because subordination of colored people provides definite benefits to those who do the subordinating. In fact, overt racism persists mainly because it still yields significant psychological, economic, and political advantages to millions of white Americans—and even to a few nonwhites.

Successful efforts to combat racism will necessarily reduce or eliminate these benefits, thereby imposing a significant cost upon people who now enjoy them. That is why attempts to combat racism have been so strongly resisted. Moreover, such resistance is far more widespread than most people realize because so many whites receive significant but only dimly realized benefits from the subordination of nonwhites. Even many whites who sincerely abhor racism in principle, and openly combat overt racism, sometimes find themselves resisting clearly antiracist actions for "intuitive" reasons they do not fully understand. This usually means such antiracist actions threaten to reduce certain almost subconsciously perceived psychological benefits these whites have been gaining from living in a society where they are considered members of a "superior" group.

A necessary step in weakening this widespread but unexpressed support for racism is clearly identifying the benefits which whites receive from continued subordination of colored people. True, some whites will still resist losing these benefits even after they realize that such benefits result from unjust subordination. But, hopefully, many whites who are opposed to overt racism in principle will begin to see how they have been profiting unawares from either overt racism or institutional subordination or both—and will therefore begin supporting the antiracist strategies set forth later in this analysis.

ECONOMIC BENEFITS DERIVED FROM RACISM

Overt racism and institutional subordination provide the following economic benefits to a significant number of whites:

1. Reduction of competition by excluding members of certain groups from access to benefits, privileges, jobs, or other opportunities or markets. The ability to easily identify members of the subordinated group by sight is a key factor linking such reduction of competition to color. An example is the refusal of many hospital medical staffs to accept Negro or Mexican American doctors as staff members.

2. Exploitation of members of the subordinated groups through lower wages, higher prices, higher rents, less desirable credit terms, or poorer working or living conditions than those received by whites. Where racial or color discrimination *per se* is illegal, such exploitation probably cannot be effectively carried out unless the subordinated groups are spatially segregated from the white majority. Then differentials in wages, prices, credit terms, and other policies actually based upon color can be more easily concealed and even rationalized as based upon geographic differences.

3. Avoidance of certain undesirable or "dead-end" jobs (like garbage collection) by creating economically depressed racial or ethnic groups which will be compelled by necessity to carry out

those jobs, even though their potential skill levels are equal to those of other groups.

POLITICAL BENEFITS DERIVED FROM RACISM

All the political benefits of racism involve receipt by whites of a disproportionate share of the advantages which arise from political control over government. Their share is disproportionate because they prevent nonwhites from receiving what the latter would get if true political equality prevailed. The benefits of political control over government include ability to control government actions and policies as well as jobs. Therefore, political racism is an extremely important device for maintaining other forms of racism.

The main ways political racism occur are as follows:

1. Manipulation of potential nonwhite voters in order to maintain exclusive white control over an entire governmental structure (such as a county government in the South), or some portion of such a structure (such as a ward in a northern city), which would be controlled by nonwhites if all citizens enjoyed equal voting rights, since nonwhites are a majority of the potential electorate in that area.

2. Manipulation of political district boundaries or governmental structures by whites so as to minimize the ability of nonwhite voters to elect representatives sensitive to their needs. This includes "gerrymandering" congressional districts, creating "at-large" electoral systems in big cities with significant nonwhite minorities, and shifting to metropolitanwide government when nonwhites appear likely to constitute a majority of voters in a central city.

3. Exclusion of nonwhites from a proportionate share—or any share—of government jobs, contracts, and other disbursements through the decisions of white administrative officials.

4. Maintenance of the support of nonwhite voters by either white or nonwhite politicians who fail to provide reciprocal government policy benefits and other advantages to the same degree as for white groups in the electorate. This can occur when nonwhites as a group feel themselves too subordinated in general to demand such benefits, when competitive parties are somehow excluded from effective operation in all-nonwhite areas, or when voters are so poor they can be influenced by small monetary rewards and favors.

5. Voter refusal to support a politician who is clearly superior to his opponent merely because he is not a member of the same racial or color group as the voters themselves and his opponent is. This kind of racism can also occur among nonwhite voters in relation to a white politician. Even though basing votes on group solidarity is a long established American tradition, it must be considered racist if it subordinates any candidate solely because of his race, color, or ethnic background.

PSYCHOLOGICAL BENEFITS DERIVED FROM RACISM

Both overt racism and institutional subordination provide the following psychological benefits to many whites in America:

1. Creation of feelings of superiority in comparison to nonwhites. These feelings are extremely widespread among whites, though not always openly expressed or even consciously recognized. Hence it is important to examine their true implications. All whites who gain ego support from feeling superior to nonwhites basically believe that nonwhites are somehow inherently or biologically inferior because of their color. This is the "purest" form of racism. It is so blatantly "un-American" that few whites will admit they believe it—or even consciously accept it. Yet all whites who feel the least bit superior to nonwhites as persons—in contrast to believing they live in *environmental surroundings* superior to those of nonwhites—basically adopt such a "pure" racist viewpoint. This is true because the obviously inferior economic, political, and social *status* of nonwhites can result from only two factors. Either nonwhites *are* inferior as persons, or white racism has prevented their natural equality with whites from asserting itself in actual attainments during their more than 300 years in America. Therefore, whites who deny that overt racism and institutional subordination are essentially responsible for the currently lower status of nonwhite groups are basically implying that those groups are biologically or otherwise inherently inferior.

2. Suppression in oneself or one's group of certain normal traits which are regarded as undesirable. This is accomplished by projecting an exaggerated image of those traits and "legitimizing" attacks upon them. For example, many American whites unjustly accuse Negroes of laziness, sexual promiscuity, and general irresponsibility. These are exaggerated versions of normal human impulses. But they happen to be the very impulses which the

Puritan ethic, long dominant in America, seeks to suppress in favor of extreme industry, sexual purity, and individual self-reliance.

3. Promotion of solidarity and reduced tension among white nationality and social class groups. Racism enables them to focus the inevitable hostilities and antagonisms which arise in modern life upon the subordinated colored groups, and to identify themselves together in contrast to those groups.

4. Avoiding the necessity of adopting difficult or costly policies to solve key social problems by falsely blaming those problems upon "immoral behavior" by members of the subordinated groups. For example, many whites erroneously blame unemployment and high welfare costs upon laziness and sexual promiscuity among Negroes. In reality, more than three-fourths of all unemployed persons are white, most persons on welfare are white, and more than 90 percent of all persons on welfare are incapable of supporting themselves because they are either too old, disabled, children, or mothers who must care for children. By falsely converting these problems into "the results of sin," such scapegoating provides a moral excuse for relatively affluent whites to reduce their economic support for the unemployed and the dependent poor without feeling guilty about doing so.

5. Diverting one's own energies from maximum self-improvement efforts by claiming that white racism makes any significant self-help attempts by colored people ineffective and useless. Such "reverse scapegoating" occurs—often unconsciously—among many minority group members. It is possible only because white racism *does* seriously inhibit—though not entirely nullify—nonwhite self-improvement efforts. This phenomenon can lead to two opposite results: excessive apathy or suicidal violence. Thus, by helping to create such "reverse scapegoating," white racism encourages some nonwhites to exhibit two of the very characteristics—"laziness" and tendencies toward violence—that it often falsely attributes to all nonwhites.

REINFORCEMENT OF RACISM BECAUSE OF HEIGHTENED ANXIETIES IN MODERN SOCIETY

Recent events have emphasized the rising level of tensions, anxieties, and other psychologically threatening factors in modern American life. These things result from a combination of rapid technological change; high economic productivity; instant and universal communication of problems; dissent and prevailing affluence through television; and the inertia and rigidities of legal and social institutions. The ways in which these basic causes interact are too complex to explore fully here. But their net effect is to heighten the needs of many whites for precisely the kinds of psychological benefits that racism provides.

For example, television has focused great attention recently upon the new life-style espoused by "hippies." This style features drugs, hostility toward authority, sexual freedom, unorthodox styles of dress, rejection of work as a central value, and willingness to engage in violent protests and demonstrations. These traits pose powerful psychological threats to many Americans. They are a direct threat because they imply that the values upon which most middle class families have built their lives are really worthless. Moreover, "hippie" values also threaten to "seduce" middle class children, causing profound cleavages between them and their parents. These values are also an indirect threat because they appeal to the suppressed desire of every normal person to engage in such activities to some degree. Thus, they may weaken the adherence of middle class citizens to their existing values.

Such psychological threats are bound to produce anxieties—both conscious and unconscious—among many of the middle class Americans who form the vast majority of our population. One way to cope with such heightened anxiety is to lean more heavily upon the psychological benefits which can be derived from racism. This can take the form of more vociferously blaming social problems upon minority groups, or projecting traits one wants to suppress in oneself upon members of such groups, or gaining feelings of solidarity with other whites by uniting in greater antagonism against nonwhites, or emphasizing the inferiority of others so as to reassure oneself about one's own worth. Consequently, powerful recent trends in American life may be significantly increasing the dependence of many whites upon the psychological benefits they derive from racism, whether consciously or unconsciously. Unless the anxieties caused by these trends can be alleviated in other ways, it may be increasingly difficult to get these whites to give up such benefits. This suggests that antiracism strategies must include, or be linked to, policies that will help reduce the threatening nature of these recent trends to the white middle class.

The fact that overt racism and institutional subordination produce benefits for many whites does not mean that these benefits outweigh the costs of racism. In the first place, such benefits are wholly illegitimate, since they spring from an unjust subordination of others. Second, creation of these benefits imposes immense costs upon millions of nonwhite Americans. Finally, by preventing nonwhites from developing their maximum productive potential, racism also inhibits them from creating much greater economic, social, and cultural wealth than they do now. This makes all of society poorer than it would be without racism—including the very people who benefit from racist behavior and institutions.

Basic Strategies for Combating Racism

Racism in America is extremely complex and deep-rooted. Consequently, only an equally complex and profound set of actions can possibly eliminate or counteract it effectively. Summarized under eight basic headings, each of the kinds of actions involved describes a basic strategy which aims at one or both of two essential objectives: *changing the behavior of whites* so they will no longer consciously or unconsciously support racism; and *increasing the capabilities of nonwhite groups* so they can overcome the handicaps racism imposes.

The nine basic strategies can be briefly summarized as follows:

1. *Make all Americans—especially whites—far more conscious of the widespread existence of racism in all its forms, and the immense costs it imposes on the entire Nation.* Most whites are completely unaware of the many kinds of institutional subordination they themselves support. A crucial task facing those who wish to combat racism is converting this "blindness" into acute consciousness of the many unrecognized ways in which white attitudes, behavior, and institutional structures continue to subordinate minority groups.

Economic costs, including the loss of national output due to holding minority group members below their maximum productive potential, the loss of markets because the incomes of these groups are kept low by institutional subordination, and large social costs of policies aimed at remedying conditions partly caused by subordination, such as poverty, crime, poor housing, and poor health.

Political costs resulting from tensions in national life caused by unjust subordination of minority groups. These include civil disorders, restrictions of individual freedoms and rights, tendencies toward a weakening of the two-party system, possible rising difficulty in gathering sufficient congressional support for *any* cohesive set of national policies, and decreasing respect for the United States abroad.

Social and human costs caused by the loss of human potential due to institutional subordination, and by the distortion of values in the white majority necessary to sustain such subordination. The first kind of costs includes loss of personal self-respect, weakened family stability, widespread frustration and apathy, frequent resort to narcotics and criminal behavior, and a declining respect for authority among minority groups. The second kind includes excessive narrowness of viewpoint; defensiveness and hostility feelings; resistance to constructive change; lack of human sensitivity; and overly technological (rather than humane) orientation of social policies and activities.

It is impossible to quantify these costs in this analysis. But some future attempts should be made to measure at least the economic costs so as to show what giant losses are involved. For example, in 1965, if Negro families had received the same average income as whites, incomes received by all U.S. families would have been $15.7 billion higher.

The process of education necessary to change white perceptions will never work if it consists mainly of some people "lecturing" others. Rather, it must involve intense participation by two types of people. First, various groups of whites must thoroughly examine their own behavior in order to uncover all the subtle and unconscious forms of racism embedded in it. This should be done by teachers concerning schools, by property managers and realtors concerning real estate practices, by personnel directors concerning employment practices, etc.

Second, whites must overcome their habitual exclusion of Negroes and other minority group members in this process of self-examination. Whites, themselves, are not likely to discover all the forms of subordination they impose on others without the help of the latter. This may require planned confrontation of whites by Negroes or others who deliberately take an accusing posture, or simply insightful advice from well informed members of minority groups. But, in any case, unless white self-examination incorporates significant contributions from nonwhites, it will embody a form of racism in itself.

2. *Build up the capabilities of minority group members, and greatly strengthen their opportunities and power to exercise those capabilities, especially regarding public and private activities that directly affect them.* This strategy embodies one of the ultimate objectives of all the others: enabling presently subordinated groups both to achieve and to exercise their maximum potential. The capabilities and opportunities concerned therefore include all types: economic, political, social, aesthetic, and cultural. It is especially crucial to provide Negroes and other minority group members with direct experience and power in designing, running, and evaluating both public and private programs and activities in their own neighborhoods. This will not only enhance the capabilities of many deprived minority group members, but also permit many others who already have such capabilities to demonstrate their skills and competence both to themselves and to the Nation as a whole.

Four key observations are relevant to this strategy:

a. *An essential ingredient is expressing strong political support for key national policies concerning housing, education, civil rights, employment, welfare programs, tax reforms, and other measures with antiracist effects.* Many problems associated with racism cannot be effectively solved, or even attacked, by local or State governments. They are inhibited by lack of financial resources within their boundaries, or competitive pressures from other cities or States which force them to keep taxes down. Older central cities containing large Negro, Puerto Rican, or Mexican American minorities are especially incapable of supporting effective antiracism policies by themselves. The concentration within their boundaries of low-income groups requiring expensive services, and the shift of most new growth to suburbs, cause them to sustain rapidly rising costs while their real property tax bases stagnate or decline. Only the use of nationwide taxing powers can effectively shift resources from wealthier areas to where the problems associated with racism are now most concentrated.

Yet Congress has been reluctant to launch many of the programs suggested by the National Advisory Committee on Civil Disorders. So far, its members have perceived very little support for such programs among their white constituents. *Until such white political support is both created and forcefully expressed to Congressional representatives, no effective nationwide attack on racism is possible.* Because the white middle class constitutes a large majority of the American electorate, no significant federal programs can possibly be adopted unless they are supported by a great many Congressional representatives of that group. Therefore, however tiresome and unexciting it may seem, keeping informed about national legislation and writing one's local Congressman to support appropriate measures comprise an essential strategy for combating racism. Equally significant is persuading other citizens—especially whites in areas where few nonwhites live—to do likewise.

b. *In primarily Negro areas, this strategy is closely related to the concepts of "Black Power" and "Black Nationalism," but it need not involve support of geographic separatism.* Undoubtedly, one effective way to build up capabilities quickly among the most deprived members of the black population, and to enhance the self-respect of the already capable members, is for Negroes to dominate most public and private activities in predominantly Negro neighborhoods. This includes the design as well as the execution of such programs. It also might involve voluntary transfer of many white-owned stores and firms in all-Negro areas to black ownership through some type of purchase plans, or creation of new black-owned facilities there.

These and other Negro economic resources can be generated fastest if most Negroes deliberately direct their consumer trade and other business to Negro-operated stores, banks, service firms, professional firms, restaurants, etc. Clearly, such behavior involves taking race and color into account in making decisions; hence some might consider it "black racism." But it can be more accurately viewed as a form of "black pride" analogous to the nationality-conscious behavior of many Irish, Italian, Polish, German, Czech, Jewish, and other citizens in earlier periods—which still persists in some cities. This kind of selective patronage is really a nonsubordinating exercise of free choice by Negroes in an essentially white-dominated society. Therefore, even though it certainly involves discrimination by color, it is not truly a "reverse" version of the white racism that institutionally subordinates so many nonwhites.

c. *One important device for developing Negro and other minority group business capabilities is the "third-party contract" for providing both public and private services.* For instance, if expanded government services concerning neighborhood maintenance were to be carried out, the local government could contract that function in mainly Negro areas to a Negro-owned and operated firm organized for that purpose, rather than enlarging the government itself. An example is PRIDE, Inc., in Washington, D.C. Similarly, white-owned firms procuring or providing services in mainly Negro areas should make every effort to use Negro-owned and operated firms, or Negro franchise operators, as intermediaries between them and their final customers. In some cases, it will take major efforts by the white firms concerned to help minority group members organize new firms and manage them successfully. These efforts are a key input which whites can contribute to the success of this basic strategy.

d. *One of the objectives of this basic strategy is to equip Negroes and other minority group leaders with much greater bargaining power in dealing with whites.* This would enable such leaders to more successfully persuade whites to carry out some of the institutional and behavioral changes necessary to eliminate racism. For example, a Negro mayor of a large city who can form a coalition with Negro councilmen to control local property tax rates is in a strong position to influence white-dominated employers there to alter discriminatory hiring practices. Similarly, a Mexican American-dominated union of hospital workers might be able to persuade all hospitals to adopt nondiscriminatory policies toward Mexican Americans and other doctors and patients. Thus, *the more successful this strategy is in building Negro and other minority group capabilities, the more likely it is that conflicts will arise between these minorities and some or all of the white majority.* Consequently this strategy embodies significant risks of at least temporarily "back-firing" and generating antiminority sentiments. Whites who support this strategy should be well aware of these risks, and prepared to counteract such sentiment in themselves as well as others. Yet no efforts to combat racism in America can succeed without greatly building up the capabilities of presently subordinated minorities and actually transferring significant power to them, since prevention of such outcomes is the essence of racism.

3. *Develop legislative and other programs which simultaneously provide benefits for significant parts of the white majority and for deprived or other members of nonwhite minority groups, so it will be in the immediate self-interest of the former to support programs which aid the latter.* Publicly supported programs which benefit the most deprived persons in society, regardless of color, often have difficulty obtaining vital white middle class

support. An example is the federal antipoverty program. Such programs provide benefits for a minority of the population by imposing taxes or inflation on the remaining majority. In reality, there are significant long-run benefits to the majority in thus aiding the minority. But these more distant benefits are not always obvious; whereas the immediate costs are clear. The same thing is true of programs which primarily benefit Negroes or other ethnic minorities, such as housing programs concentrated in ghetto areas.

(Actually, almost all public programs—including public housing and welfare—mainly benefit whites, but many whites do not realize this.) Consequently, major programs benefiting *any* group which is a minority of the population—whether ethnically or economically or in any other way—would have a much better chance of gaining the necessary political support if they also provided benefits for many members of the large white middle class majority. For instance, it might be easier to get Congress to aid poor female-headed households with children by passing a family allowance that assisted *all* families with children than by expanding welfare payments that assisted only the poorest such families.

This strategy seems especially significant now because of the apparent discontent of the "silent majority" comprised of lower-middle-income and middle-income whites. Recent political developments indicate that millions of these white Americans believe public programs in the past few years have unduly focused upon the problems of ethnic minority groups and the poor. Regardless of whether or not this belief is accurate, it constitutes a significant political force. Moreover, it is extremely relevant to whether or not Congress can be persuaded to adopt legislation with significant antiracist impacts. Chances for such legislation appear critically related to the ability of its sponsors to develop "program packages" that will appeal to the immediate self-interest of large portions of the white middle class, while simultaneously providing key benefits to minority groups who are deprived or discriminated against.

There are two important qualifications to this strategy. First, such programs will not improve the *relative* position of the minority groups concerned unless they provide larger benefits to those groups than to members of the middle class majority they also aid. From the viewpoint of persons seeking to reduce or eliminate the effects of racism, this "gap-closing" aspect is vital. For example, high-level national prosperity tends to raise everyone's income to some degree. But if all incomes go up to the same degree, then the subordinating effects of racism are not counteracted. The incomes of subordinated persons are still artificially suppressed below the incomes of others. Certainly absolute improvements are important—especially to poor people. But the subordination inherent in racism is essentially a relative condition. Therefore, it is also important not to sacrifice all possibility of gaining relative improvements for deprived or subordinated minority groups in order to form an effective coalition with parts of the white middle class majority.

This leads to the second qualification: it is virtually impossible to create programs which provide *net* benefits both to most severely deprived people and to most of the middle class white majority. Any program which redistributes income to poor people must cause a net loss to some other group. The only group with enough total income to support a meaningful redistribution of this kind is the middle-income majority. So no program can cause *net* redistribution favoring all of the lowest-income group and all of the middle-income group simultaneously. However, programs can be devised which provide net benefits to most of the lowest-income group and to large segments of the middle-income group. The net expenses they create could fall on the remainder of the middle-income group and on most of the upper-income group. For example, certain federal-aid-to-education programs might help all families with children in both income groups at the net expense of all households without children in the middle class group. Moreover, such "program packages" can be designed or promoted in ways that soften their negative impact upon those who bear it. For instance, they could be financed out of the "automatic" increase in federal income tax receipts which occurs because of economic growth without any increase in tax rates. Or they can provide net benefits to only part of the lowest-income group, along with part of the middle-income majority, so their net burden is not extremely large. Congressional supporters of minority-favoring legislation benefiting the wealthy have been successfully designing such "packages" for decades, as the urban renewal program illustrates.

4. *Insure that minority group members are in a position to contribute to the design, execution, and evaluation of all major social policies and programs. This will improve the quality of such policies and programs by introducing a certain sensitivity to human values which is too often lacking in the overly technology-oriented*

behavior of the white majority. Persons who are outside "the established system" which dominates economic, political, and cultural life in America have an important contribution to make in improving the output and operation of that system. Without question, the American economic and political system has been an unprecedented success. It has created the highest material standard of living in world history in an atmosphere of great individual freedom and opportunity. Yet the very orientation toward efficiency and high productivity responsible for this success often overlooks, suppresses, or distorts important human value. *Racism itself is a stunning example.* Others include the dehumanizing routines required on high speed assembly lines, the shattering impacts on family life of migration caused by farm mechanization, and the demeaning procedures incorporated in welfare programs. People who receive significant net benefits from "the system" which commits these dehumanizing acts tend to overlook them entirely, or simply to regard them as a price society must pay for high output. In contrast, people who are essentially "outside the system" are far more acutely conscious of these effects. They suffer from such effects more often, and they are not given a strong incentive to accept them by receipt of other net benefits from the system. Such "outside" groups include not only the minorities subordinated by racist institutions, but also many university students, intellectuals, artistically oriented citizens, and even "hippie dropouts." Partly because they do not receive many material or other rewards directly from the dominant system, these "outsiders" tend to develop life styles centered on values that emphasize personal characteristics rather than technological efficiency or material success. These values include great sensitivity and openness to the personal expression, individuality, and needs of others—far greater than is typical of the behavior of many middle class Americans incorporated within the system. Such heightened sensitivity is a potentially uplifting contribution to American society in general—indeed, to the operation of the very system in reaction to which it developed. But that contribution can only become effective if such persons can exert significant influence on the design, execution, and evaluation of most major social policies.

An example may help clarify this reasoning. For two decades, many urban highways were constructed through low-income neighborhoods, thus forcing thousands of poor families to move. No compensation was paid to those uprooted unless they owned their own homes, and even then it was grossly inadequate. No relocation services were provided; no alternative housing was built to make up for the destruction of thousands of units in the midst of a shortage of housing for poor people; and little thought was given to the losses caused by destroying local schools, stores, parks, and even whole neighborhoods. This striking insensitivity to the problems of poor people—most of whom were "outside the system"—resulted from the almost completely technological orientation of the highway engineers responsible for building roads. They were concerned solely with moving traffic from point to point in the technically most efficient manner.

Moreover, the middle class majority which used the resulting roads did not want them to behave otherwise. Recently, however, there have been mounting protests from those threatened with displacement—most of whom are Negroes. And local politicians have become far more sensitive to Negro demands, because of recent disorders. So in 1968, federal policies regarding highway construction were changed to include much more adequate compensation to displaced owners *and* renters, and the provision of relocation assistance and perhaps even new housing. This is a clear example of heightened sensitivity to human needs partly counteracting an overly technological-oriented social policy. Similarly increased sensitivity, particularly to the negative impacts of institutional subordination, should be introduced into other social policies of all kinds—including economic and political—and at all levels—including federal, state, local, and private. In this way, the dominant part of American society could benefit from the humanizing influence of those whom it has heretofore excluded from any significant power in relation to most major policies. The result should be a society that is different from, and superior to, both the presently dominant system itself and the alternative life style developed by those whom the system has made "outsiders." This is what Martin Luther King, Jr. meant when he insisted that Negroes and other minorities did not simply want to become part of the white middle-class America as it is now. Rather, they want to help build a new society far more sensitive to certain human values than white middle class America has proved to be in the past. Hopefully, it will combine the best of both worlds. But this ideal outcome will be possible only if minority group members are able to influence policy design, execution, and evaluation at all levels in all major social institutions. These include predominantly white institutions which have significant impacts upon both nonwhite and white Americans. Examples are federal government agencies, large insurance companies, state governments, local school systems, and nationwide retail firms.

Therefore, placing minority group members in real positions of power and influence within such organizations is not simply a matter of making more and better jobs available to them. It is also a key means of implementing this vital antiracist strategy in society as a whole.

5. *Influence local, state, and national policies and programs—both public and private—so they have certain characteristics which will reduce their possible racist effects.* Two such characteristics have already been discussed: heightened sensitivity to human values, and "gap-closing" improvement of the most deprived or subordinate groups relative to others benefited by the same policies. Others include:

a. *Avoidance of any action or arrangement that unnecessarily produces, sustains, or emphasizes derogatory or stigmatizing forms of differentiation.* These could involve differentiation by race or color, or by social and economic class. For example, current public housing regulations require that all the families living in a public housing project have very low incomes. This tends to stigmatize such projects as undesirable, especially if they become dominated by unstable multiproblem households. Conceivably, public housing projects could contain a majority of stable moderate-income families who paid higher rents. Then such projects would not be stigmatized as for low-status households only. Similarly, locating all the public housing projects in a city (except those for the elderly) so that nearly all occupants are Negroes has racist effects. This practice causes most whites to identify the need for public housing with race, even though over half of all low-income persons in U.S. central cities are white. Thus, simultaneous differentiation of any programs by *both* poverty and color causes several very undesirable results. First, political support for such programs often declines because racism leads many whites to oppose funding anything they believe mainly aids Negroes. Second, this dual differentiation reinforces the erroneous belief among some whites that most Negroes are dependent, and therefore inferior. Third, participants in such programs are exposed mainly to other deprived people; so their own sense of differentiation and inferiority is reinforced.

b. *Emphasis upon participation by, and within, the private sector rather than direct dependency upon government at any level.* In attacking problems of poverty, poor housing, unemployment, poor health, and other undesirable conditions in large urban centers, the natural tendency will probably be to rely on direct government action as the primary weapon. This is likely because the people suffering from these maladies usually cannot pay enough to support private remedial action. That is why they are not getting any now.

However, it is vital that society avoid creating low-income minority group neighborhoods that are almost totally dependent upon direct public expenditures aimed at self-maintenance, rather than at producing services consumed by society as a whole. Such a position of primarily nonproductive dependency discourages initiative among residents, reinforces their feelings of inadequacy and inferiority, results in a very low standard of living because of legislative economizing, and tends to confirm existing stereotypes that the residents are lazy and incompetent. It could even lead to a permanent publicly maintained "underclass" in slum areas differentiated by dependency, location, and color. Experience with American Indians conclusively demonstrates the failure of such "public reservations."

This means that as much direct participation by the private sector as possible should be encouraged in remedial programs for these areas. Such programs include education, job creation, training, housing, and even welfare administration. Moreover, as many persons as possible now dependent upon direct public support should be transferred to positions in the private sector. These positions could be in either the kinds of remedial programs mentioned above or truly self-supporting private activities.

However, two vital qualifications must be made. First, this emphasis on the private sector does not imply that positions in government are not productive or desirable. Instead it is simply a balancing counterforce to the natural tendency to use direct government action as the main way to attack these problems. Second, public subsidies will play an essential role in this entire process, even if private firms carry out many of the programs concerned. Training unskilled workers, teaching low-achieving students, or building housing and pricing it so that poor families can afford it all require public subsidies. They cost more than those who are benefited can either pay themselves or provide through their participation. These extra costs are the real costs of eliminating accumulated deprivation, poverty, ignorance, and racism. It is unreasonable and naïve to expect private firms to bear these costs themselves, any more than they bear the costs of achieving other public objectives, such as building highways or putting a man on the moon. The purpose of encouraging private participation is therefore not primarily to reduce costs. Rather it is to tap the many talents in the private sector, to get more of its members personally "involved" in combating racism and poverty, and to reduce the ultimate dependency of those being aided.

c. *Use of a metropolitan areawide geographic focus whenever possible.* Carrying out housing, employment, health and other programs on a metropolitanwide basis will both discourage the development of geographic separatism, and encourage a realistic view of each metropolitan area as an economically interrelated whole.

At present, racial cleavages on a geographic basis within metropolitan areas are indeed striking. Taken together, the central cities within all 224 U.S. metropolitan areas were 21 percent Negro in 1966. But over 100 percent of their population growth from 1960 to 1966 was Negro (they lost white population). In contrast, the portions of metropolitan areas outside central cities were 95 percent white in 1966 and their population growth from 1960 to 1966 was 98 percent white. In most of the largest metropolitan areas, if these trends continue, central cities will contain Negro majorities within two decades; whereas the surrounding suburbs will remain almost entirely white. This could lead to a political conflict between large central cities and their surrounding suburbs along racial lines. Such a conflict could in turn cause fiscal bankruptcy in the large cities, and could even lead to racial violence and suppression.[4] Conducting programs aimed at reducing racism on a metropolitanwide level will at least maintain communications between these two racially diverging areas, and may help to counteract emerging racial separatism.

However racially divergent central cities and suburbs become, they are still critically dependent upon each other economically and physically. Central cities contain a majority of the jobs in metropolitan areas, to which millions of suburban commuters travel daily. They are also the nerve centers of many vital networks, including telephone systems, utility systems, water systems, sewage disposal systems, railroads, and highways. Most of the largest corporations in the Nation, and many small firms, have their headquarters and many major plants in central cities. The Nation's key financial institutions are located primarily in large downtown areas, and most cultural and entertainment activities take place in large cities. Most of the leading universities in the country have huge physical plants tying them to central cities. On the other hand, the suburbs supply many of the workers that operate these central city facilities, and contain most of the vital air transportation links in the Nation.

In spite of these intimate interconnections, many white suburbanites are not aware of their dependence upon central cities. They rarely go into such cities, since the suburbs in larger metropolitan areas contain a broad spectrum of shopping facilities, hospitals, banks, entertainment facilities, and even jobs. So some white suburbanites may be led by their spatial isolation to think they can disregard the fiscal and other problems of central cities, especially as the latter become more and more occupied by minority groups. The development of antiracist policies and programs on a metropolitan areawide basis would help to counteract such erroneous views, particularly if it included educating suburbanites concerning their dependence upon central cities.

This conclusion does not contradict the earlier observation that adoption of metropolitan government could be a form of institutional subordination. It would be if it were aimed at preventing nonwhites from dominating a central city government. But many antiracist policies other than local government itself can be carried out on a metropolitan areawide basis without creating such subordination at all. Examples are job training, housing development, educational enrichment, job placement, and transportation programs.

6. *Create recognition among all Americans that overcoming the burdens of racism will cost a great deal of money, time, effort, and institutional change; but that this cost is a worthwhile investment in the future which both society as a whole and individual taxpayers can bear without undue strain.* There is no precise way to estimate the costs of significantly reducing the impacts of racism in the United States. However, the recommendations set forth by the National Advisory Commission on Civil Disorders (NACCD) embody a program that would probably accomplish a major part of that job and would greatly reduce poverty and deprivation among whites, too. Rough cost estimates of this program indicate that its many components would add from $15 to $40 billion per year to the federal budget, depending upon exactly at what levels certain programs (such as building new housing and raising support payments for poor, dependent families) were carried out. These costs are roughly

equivalent to from 1.8 to 4.7 percent of our gross national product of about $850 billion in 1968.

To some extent, such costs could be financed through future increases in federal tax receipts that will occur without any rise in tax rates. Because the federal tax structure is progressive (that is, it contains higher percentage rates for higher dollar incomes), federal tax receipts rise automatically as American families earn higher incomes. Moreover, these receipts go up *faster* than national income as a whole. This "national dividend" has been estimated to be about $14 billion per year, or more than $150 billion in the next decade. However, a significant portion of it will be spent on programs which have already been adopted with built-in future cost increases. Therefore, some increase in federal taxes might be needed to launch a major program against racism and deprivation along the lines suggested by the NACCD. A survey recently completed by the NACCD indicated that more than half of all white adult respondents would be willing to pay 10 percent more in income taxes to carry out the kind of program set forth in the NACCD report. That would have yielded an added $12.9 billion in 1969 (including higher corporation taxes). Thus, although the money costs of combating racism and deprivation are very large, it would be possible to pay those costs without placing any overwhelming strain upon either the economy as a whole or most individual taxpayers.

But the costs of effectively combating racism are not limited to money alone. Most Americans would have to reexamine and change their own behavior patterns and many of the structures and practices of the institutions which serve them and in which they participate. This might impose significant psychological costs upon some people—especially those who now benefit either consciously or unconsciously from racism. Yet those costs would surely be tiny compared to the gain of eliminating all the *existing* costs imposed upon the Nation by racism, as discussed earlier. More important, all the costs necessary to combat racism and deprivation are essentially investments in a greater future output. These investments would gradually increase the economic and other capabilities of millions of persons whose potentials are now inhibited by racism and poverty. Since there are more than 22 million Negro Americans, and millions of other Americans in smaller minority groups, a significant increase in their economic, social, cultural, and political productivity would add immensely to future benefits shared by the entire Nation.

7. *Search out and develop alliances of nonwhites and whites organized to obtain common practical goals, particularly in combating racism.* At present, white and Negro or other minority group communities in most American cities act almost completely independently of each other. This is true in nearly all social, economic, and other nongovernmental activities, though somewhat less so in relation to government. Even efforts to combat racism tend to be conducted separately by both communities. As a result, those efforts are frequently far less effective than they would be if members of each community shared the insights, experience, capabilities, and contacts of the other. Moreover, such nearly complete separation of whites and nonwhites breeds mistrust, fear, and hostility between these groups, and generates both rumors and stereotypes based upon ignorance. Leaders in both communities should therefore take the initiative in organizing and carrying out well defined joint projects (perhaps of existing organizations) to reduce racism.

One effective type of project would link influential whites with members of low-income Negro communities. They could jointly support continuous surveillance and evaluation of the quality of various local and national programs in those communities. The programs involved could include everything from garbage collection to on-the-job training. The whites could bring their influence to bear upon local and national government and private officials, using information and insights furnished by Negro observers living in the affected areas. This would in turn greatly enhance the effective power of Negro residents and their influence upon the design of future programs.

8. *Create many more positively oriented contacts between whites and Negroes and other minority group members—including personal contacts, intergroup contacts, and those occurring through mass media.* It is an unfortunate fact that most whites have few, if any, personal friends or even acquaintances who are Negro or Mexican American or members of other minorities—and vice versa. The resulting dearth of "normal" contacts between people of different races and colors but of like interests and capabilities is one of the main reasons why erroneous prejudices and rumors continue to flourish in each community about the other. Moreover, many interracial contacts which do occur (such as those between white police and Negro citizens, or white television viewers and Negro rioters shown in newscasts) are negatively rather than positively oriented. Therefore, persistent efforts in increasing positively oriented contacts between races should be made by

private individuals, private groups, and the mass media (which have markedly increased such contacts in the past 2 years).

9. *Open up many more opportunities for minority group members in now predominantly white organizations (such as businesses), areas (such as suburban neighborhoods), or institutions (such as public schools)*, and encourage other arrangements where members of different groups work, live, or act together. This *strategy of integration* is implicit in many of the eight others. Discussing integration fully would require another long essay. However, I believe *integration* implies much more positive action than desegregation. The latter consists of removing discriminatory barriers so that all have equal access to opportunities in proportion to their existing abilities to compete "within the system." Hence, desegregation is a vital first step toward integration. But such removal of unfair barriers makes no allowance for the fact that the existing competitive abilities of many minority group members suffer the effects of prolonged repression. Until those effects have been overcome, true social justice in many situations will require positive supplementation of the impaired abilities of many minority group members. I believe the term *integration* should imply such a policy.

Any situation regarding two groups can therefore be considered *integrated* if all the following conditions exist:

Enough members of both groups are *actually present* so that everyone in the situation constantly perceives both groups in day-to-day experience.

Enough members of the minority group in that situation (who might be white) are present so that as individuals they do not feel isolated or lost within the majority group.

The minority group in that situation exercises power and influence at least proportional to its numbers there. In some cases, the average capabilities of the minority-group members will be lower than those of the majority-group members. Then minority-group power and influence proportional to their number will be more than proportional to their overall competitive abilities. That is where the majority might deliberately supplement the competitive abilities of the minority group, or the influence that group would wield based on such abilities alone. An example is providing special training for some black workers in mainly white firms.

Integration aims at achieving equality of access to the opportunities and benefits of society both immediately and in the long run. It also seeks to promote more daily intergroup experience so members of each group will learn to accept others fully as individuals. Such experience will not result from just *potential* equality of access by minority group members to facilities or areas now predominantly occupied by majority group members. Instead, it requires *actual mixing* of these groups on a daily basis. That is one reason why integration implies positive programs rather than just the removal of discriminatory barriers.

Effective integration of many kinds, including jobs and schools, is often inhibited because such a high proportion of Negroes and other minority groups live in segregated areas. Thus, achieving significant integration implies much greater Negro movement into now predominantly white residential areas as the National Advisory Commission on Civil Disorders stated. At present, this seems out of favor with many minority group leaders seeking group solidarity and stronger political power through group concentration. Yet, as the NACCD concluded, significant integration is essential for true equality of opportunity in America—especially economic opportunity—because separate societies cannot be made equal.

The nine strategies described above are not mutually exclusive; nor do they exhaust all the possible ways to combat racism. Yet they encompass the key approaches that must be carried out over the next few years—and decades—if racism is to be reduced to an insignificant factor in America.

Conclusion

Americans seeking to combat racism should understand three additional points. First, racism in this country is the product of more than 300 years of systematic subordination of Indians and Negroes by the white majority, plus later subordination of still other groups. The racist attitudes, behavior patterns, institutional structures, and cultural heritage built up over these three centuries are profoundly embedded in our society. They cannot be eradicated overnight, or in just a few years. Therefore, effectively combating racism will require continuous and prolonged persistence by both whites and Negroes. They must be deeply committed—indeed, dedicated—to this goal.

However, there are signs that many white Americans are already tired of hearing about "the race question." Because most whites conceive of racism only in the overt forms, they believe it is rapidly disappearing or has already diminished to an insignificant level. For example, in 1966, 70 percent of the national sample of whites interviewed by the Louis Harris organization thought that Negroes were moving too fast toward integration.

This leads to the second point: the principal task of those white Americans combating racism lies within the white community, rather than within nonwhite communities. As pointed out earlier, no policies or programs aimed at improving conditions in black America or among Mexican Americans or other minorities can possibly succeed unless they are politically supported by a majority of whites. Such support is essential to obtain the money and institutional changes required to alter those conditions. Yet that support will not be forthcoming unless most whites significantly revise their present views concerning racism. Many whites, especially those living in suburbs, are almost completely isolated from any direct contacts with life in Negro ghettos or Puerto Rican neighborhoods or other minority group areas. Hence, they fail to perceive the compelling need for further remedial actions there. Moreover, they do not understand how institutional subordination works. Therefore, these whites think the plight of ghetto dwellers is largely their own fault, rather than largely the product of racism expressed by institutions controlled by whites.

Only two forces can change this dominant view. The first consists of the dedicated efforts of well informed white leaders within white communities who understand all forms of racism, and why much more must be done to eradicate them. The second is development of greater capabilities and power within the Negro community and other nonwhite communities. By its very nature, this development must occur primarily through the efforts of nonwhite Americans themselves. Once such development begins, it will better demonstrate the true potentialities and abilities of those Americans, and give their leaders a stronger bargaining position from which to influence public and private policies. These changes may in turn persuade the white majority to devote more resources to the task of still further developing nonwhite capabilities, both in nonwhite communities and throughout society.

Thus the process of overcoming racism involves a continuous feedback between changing the views of the white majority and expanding the capabilities and power of nonwhite communities. It is clear that the most critical role in this process for whites fighting racism is influencing the opinions of other whites. Similarly, the most critical role for nonwhites is developing their own communities.

This conclusion certainly does not imply that no whites should work in nonwhite areas, or vice versa. In fact, such joint action is one of the nine basic strategies for combating racism. But the predominant efforts of whites in this combat should nevertheless involve those strategies focused upon the white community itself. For no one else can carry out those strategies—yet without them, the entire struggle is doomed.

Opposing racism is indeed a worthy objective for all Americans. It is the highest tradition of democracy to promote equality of opportunity and freedom of choice for all citizens in fact as well as in theory. But such equality and freedom cannot exist as long as racism continues to operate through long-established and pervasive institutional structures and behavior patterns. No other single issue in domestic affairs has more profound implications regarding America's success in achieving its own ideals, or the kinds of social changes that must be carried out to attain them. That is why a clear understanding of racism and how to combat all its many unrecognized forms, plus a strong dedication to doing so, are essential for every true American.

Notes

[1] I am profoundly indebted to John McKnight of Northwestern University for his key contributions to this essay, including many of its central ideas.

[2] The terms colored and nonwhite in the remainder of this paper refer to Negroes, Puerto Ricans, Mexican Americans, Japanese Americans, Chinese Americans, and American Indians because this is how most whites really view and identify them.

[3] The key idea of "Black Nationalism" is precisely to reverse this process by generating pride in being Black, instead of feelings of inferiority. Such pride is designed to lead to greater self-respect and self-confidence—and, therefore, to more success in overcoming obstacles. This in turn is supposed to reinforce self-confidence and reaffirm initial pride in being Black. "Black Nationalism" and "Black Power" seek to create a positive counter-identity to offset the negative "loss of identity" felt by Negroes as a result of the forces described above.

[4] Discussed in chapter 16 of the "Report of the National Advisory Commission on Civil Disorders."

4

Moving Toward Realistic Housing Goals

The Housing Act of 1949 set forth a national housing goal: "Realization as soon as feasible . . . of a decent home and a suitable living environment for every American family." Yet almost two decades later, the National Advisory Commission on Civil Disorders discovered that inadequate housing was one of the major complaints among residents of every area where civil disorders had occurred.

Consequently, the Housing and Urban Development Act of 1968 starts by declaring that "Congress finds that this (1949) goal has not been fully realized for many of the Nation's lower-income families; that this is a matter of grave national concern; and that there exist in the public and private sectors of the economy the resources and capabilities necessary to the full realization of this goal." The 1968 act further states that "Congress reaffirms this national housing goal and determines that it can be substantially achieved within the next decade by the construction or rehabilitation of twenty-six million housing units, six million of these for low and moderate income families."

This paper seeks to determine (1) whether these quantitative housing targets adopted by Congress represent a reasonable estimate of the nation's needs; (2) what actions would have to be undertaken by the public and private sectors to achieve those targets in the period 1970 through 1980; (3) whether these actions are likely to be carried out; and (4) what public policy recommendations can be derived from the above considerations.

What Is "The Housing Problem"?

According to the official national goal, every American household which does not enjoy "a decent home and a suitable environment"

Reprinted from *Agenda for the Nation*, edited by Kermit Gordon (Washington, D.C.: The Brookings Institution, 1968), pp. 141–78, by permission of the publisher. Footnotes have been renumbered. Copyright 1968 by The Brookings Institution.

is part of the housing problem. Unfortunately, this statement utterly fails to convey the appalling living conditions which give the housing problem such overriding urgency to millions of poor Americans. In fact, most Americans have no conception of the filth, degradation, squalor, overcrowding, and personal danger and insecurity which millions of inadequate housing units are causing in both our cities and rural areas. Thousands of infants are attacked by rats each year; hundreds die or become mentally retarded from eating lead paint that falls off cracked walls; thousands more are ill because of unsanitary conditions resulting from jamming large families into a single room, continuing failure of landlords to repair plumbing or provide proper heat, and pitifully inadequate storage space. Until you have actually stumbled through the ill-lit and decaying rooms of a slum dwelling, smelled the stench of sewage and garbage and dead rats behind the walls, seen the roaches and crumbling plaster and incredibly filthy bathrooms, and recoiled from exposed wiring and rotting floorboards and staircases, you have no real idea of what bad housing is like. These miserable conditions are not true of all inadequate housing units, but enough Americans are trapped in the hopeless desolation of such surroundings to constitute both a scandal and a serious economic and social drag in our affluent society.

I am deliberately emphasizing this point at the outset of my analysis, because the remainder is necessarily dispassionate in tone and focuses primarily upon statistics rather than graphic descriptions of what life in substandard housing is really like. Yet behind the dry data lurk the faces of thousands of suffering human beings, whose basic need for decent shelter is not being met. Sadly, this failure is often caused by public policies that benefit wealthier Americans. I have tried not to let the moral urgency of meeting this need, and of righting the injustices underlying some of it, blur my vision concerning what remedies are actually possible in our society. But neither should the objective tone of the analysis obscure the raw human realities encompassed in "the housing problem."

HOW MANY UNITS ARE NEEDED?

Most experts measure inadequate housing by using the data for "substandard housing units" published by the U.S. Bureau of the Census. These include all units that are physically dilapidated and all that do not have hot water and full plumbing within the unit, regardless of physical condition. The number of such units has been declining in recent years, but is still very large, as Table 1 indicates.[1]

Table 1.   Comparison of Standard to Substandard Housing
Units in the United States

Year	All housing units (millions)	Substandard units (millions)	Percent substandard
1950	46.1	17.0	36.9
1960	58.5	11.4	19.5
1970 (estimated)	69.5	6.9	9.9

In the two decades from 1950 to 1970, the nation will have built 30 million new units, eliminated 10.1 million substandard units, and expanded the net supply of standard units by 80.7 percent (as compared with a 35 percent rise in population), but there will still be almost 7 million substandard units. Moreover, counting only substandard units as inadequate seriously understates the true severity of the problem. If we also consider all overcrowded housing inadequate (that is, all units with more than 1.0 occupant per room), then an additional 3.9 million units would be part of the housing problem by 1970.

Even more important, measuring inadequate housing only by the number of substandard housing units focuses solely upon the housing unit itself. *But housing broadly defined includes three basic ingredients: a physical dwelling unit, its inhabitants and their behavior toward the unit, and the surrounding environment.* Thus, improvements in physical dwelling units cannot be considered in isolation: they must be linked to changes in occupant behavior and to overall environmental upgrading if the housing problem is to be truly solved.

Another complicating factor is that many low-income households live in good quality units with decent surroundings, but must pay a large proportion of their incomes for rent or ownership costs. For example, in 1959, 77 percent of all households with incomes under $2,000 paid 35 percent or more of their incomes for housing. It may be desirable to provide some assistance to the many housholds that can afford to live in adequate housing only by spending more than some reasonable proportion of their incomes on housing. Careful budgetary studies have shown that this proportion should be about 25 percent, varying somewhat with income level and household size. Using this definition, at least 12 million households—and perhaps many more—were part of the housing problem in 1966 (including those in substandard units). [2]

Finally, American standards of what constitutes "a decent home" and "a suitable environment" are constantly rising, so measuring housing needs by these definitions involves elements of both subjectivity and relativity that make precise accuracy impossible. Nevertheless, my rough estimate is that from 10 to 12 million households will be considered inadequately housed in 1970—or about one out of every six or seven U.S. households. To be conservative, I will use the estimate of 10 million.

To solve the housing problem, the nation must not only replace all this inadequate housing, but must also provide enough new or rehabilitated units to accommodate future population growth and to replace units that will be demolished. From 1970 through 1979, about 12.3 million net new households will be formed in the United States. In addition, about 5.4 million new housing units will be needed to replace the net losses from existing inventory caused by demolition, mergers, conversions, and other shifts. Therefore, the nation would have to produce about 17.7 million new or rehabilitated units in the 1970s just to keep even, and at least 27.7 million units to include elimination of all inadequate units.[3] And it would also have to create all the facilities and services necessary to generate "a suitable environment" for those units.

These calculations indicate that the official production target of 26 million units for the next decade—including 6 million for low-income and moderate-income families—represents a reasonably accurate estimate of the output needed to solve the housing problem in that period.

WHERE WILL NEW HOUSING BE BUILT?

Where would these housing units, facilities, and services be located? A recent study indicates that about 90 percent of all population growth from 1960 to 1985 will occur in metropolitan areas—10 percent in central cities and 80 percent in suburban rings.[4] I assume that future housing needs arising from population growth will be spatially distributed in the same way. Housing units likely to be destroyed or demolished in the next decade will probably be heavily concentrated within central cities. But replacement housing for these units will not be similarly concentrated, because the cleared sites will be occupied by new highways and nonresidential structures. Hence I have made an arbitrary spatial distribution of such replacement housing.

Information concerning substandard units, though inadequate, provides the best way to discover where housing deficiencies are located. In 1960, 64 percent of all substandard units in the United States were outside metropolitan areas, 21 percent were in central cities, and 15 percent were in suburban rings. However, the new housing units replacing these deficiencies will not be distributed in the same way. For one thing, continued population migration to metropolitan areas means that replacements outside those areas should be much lower than the proportion of substandard units there. Second, relocation problems will make it almost impossible to replace all the inadequate housing in central cities with new units located inside those cities. These problems are discussed in detail in a later section. Third, the replacement of all inadequate central-city housing units by new units within those cities cannot be achieved by 1980 because of the prolonged time required for clearance operations. Urban renewal projects now take an average of six to nine years from initial concept to final occupancy.[5] In 1967, the annual rate of construction of public housing, urban renewal housing, and interest-subsidy housing combined was less than 100,000 new units. At this rate, it would take over thirty years to replace all the housing units in central cities that were inadequate as of 1960, even if *all* public efforts were focused solely upon those cities. Certainly this snail's pace could be speeded up if housing were awarded a higher priority on the nation's agenda. But it is unrealistic to believe that even a major policy shift would accelerate clearance enough to permit complete replacement of inadequate central-city housing by 1980 without use of vacant land, most of which is in the suburbs.

A fourth factor in redistributing housing, which also emphasizes this need to build on vacant land, is the desire among city planners to reduce residential densities in central cities. Most plans for upgrading cities call for massive expansion of nonresidential land uses, such as parks, schools, and universities. Moreover, much central-city slum housing is inadequate precisely because of its sardine-can density, such as the 67,000 persons per square mile in Harlem.

These considerations all point to the inescapability of replacing many inadequate central-city housing units with new units built on vacant land in surrounding suburbs. But most suburban residents are not very eager to accept thousands of low-income households—many Negro—moving out of central cities. Their reluctance will have a critical influence upon the speed with which society tackles the job of replacing inadequate housing, and where future construction is likely to occur. Therefore, I have made a rather arbitrary distribution concerning the future location of replacement housing. The results are summed up in Table 2.

Table 2.   Housing Units Needed, 1970-80
(In millions)

Type of need	Total needed	Central cities	Suburban rings	Outside metropolitan areas
For population growth	12.3	1.2	9.8	1.3
For replacement of units eliminated (net of other additions)	5.4	2.1	2.3	1.0
For replacement of inadequate units	10.0	1.0	5.8	3.2
Total	27.7	4.3	17.9	5.5

Sources: Patricia Leavy Hodge and Philip M. Hauser, *The Challenge of America's Metropolitan Population Outlook—1960 to 1985*, Research Report No. 3, National Commission on Urban Problems (Washington, D.C., 1968); distribution estimated by author.

HOW WILL THE TYPE OF HOUSING BE DETERMINED?

Until now, the analysis has been solely in terms of undifferentiated housing units. This fails to provide guidance concerning the number of units of each building type, each kind of ownership or tenure, each size, and each type of financing. Many of these choices are best left up to private market forces. But others—especially those concerning type of financing—require public policy decisions. Hence the *quality* of future housing needs should be analyzed, as well as the *quantity*.

The best way to analyze quality is to focus upon those households which will require public assistance to achieve an adequate standard of housing. These consist of three main groups: those now living in inadequate housing because they cannot afford adequate quarters; those now living in adequate quarters but spending an inordinate fraction of their income to pay for those quarters; and households that will form in the future and enter one of the two preceding categories. The second group needs, not new or improved housing, but income supplementation. Consequently, my analysis will focus upon the first and third groups.

In 1960, considering housing in metropolitan areas only:

> Most substandard units were occupied by low-income households—55 percent by those with annual incomes under $3,000, and 24 percent by those with annual incomes from $3,000 to $4,999.
>
> A clear majority of even the lowest-income households lived in adequate housing, even so. For example, only 26 percent of all households with annual incomes under $2,000 lived in substandard dwellings (though many more lived in overcrowded or otherwise inadequate "standard" units).
>
> Negroes occupied disproportionate fractions of all substandard housing in relation to either their total numbers or their incomes. Nonwhites comprised 10 percent of all metropolitan area households, but occupied 31 percent of all substandard housing units in those areas. And for "poverty-level" groups (annual incomes under $3,000), the proportion in substandard units was much higher among Negroes than among whites, even though their incomes were similar (44 percent compared with 25 percent for renter households, and 34 percent compared with 12 percent for owner households).
>
> A very high proportion of large families (six or more persons) lived in inadequate housing.

Outside metropolitan areas, the same general conditions prevail, but substandard housing tends to be even more concentrated among the poorest groups and among Negroes.

Future population growth will undoubtedly create more households which cannot achieve adequate housing standards without public assistance. This will occur because housing of adequate quality, whether new or used, costs more than many low-income households can afford to pay. Moreover, the income which any household must attain to rent or buy adequate quality housing without spending too high a proportion of its total income on housing is significantly higher than the official "poverty level" as defined by the Social Security Administration, which is based on costs of an adequate diet rather than on costs of adequate housing. There are millions more "housing poor" households in the United States than "food poor" households.

Will future population growth increase the number of households that are "housing poor" and therefore need public assistance to procure adequate housing? Incomes will probably rise even faster than population in the next decade. Hence the number of new entrants into any given lower-income bracket will be more than offset by the number whose rising incomes take them out of that bracket. But these future income gains may be at least partially offset by an escalation in the "housing poverty level" resulting from rising costs and prices. The likely outcome of the race between consumer incomes on the one hand, and population growth plus housing costs on the other, is not clear. Nevertheless, I do not believe there will be any really significant increase in the number of households below the housing poverty level, even though the income figure representing that level will rise.

WHAT OTHER URBAN SERVICES WILL BE NEEDED?

Production of 27.7 million new or rehabilitated dwellings during the 1970s would not in itself achieve the nation's housing goal. For creating "a suitable living environment" for every American family also requires providing the many ancillary facilities and services related to housing. The facilities include sewer and water systems, streets, highways, schools, parks, shopping centers, public transit lines and equipment, public buildings, and other private buildings like churches, motels, small stores, and so on. The services include police and fire protection, garbage collection, street cleaning, operation of schools and recreational facilities, and operation of all the private facilities mentioned above.

Clearly, in a paper of this length, it is impossible to analyze all the problems and policies associated with creating this immense spectrum of facilities and activities. Even so, it is appropriate to make a few observations concerning this task. It consists of two essentially different parts: upgrading all the facilities and public services in existing neighborhoods, especially poorer parts of central cities; and creating the new facilities and services necessary to accommodate future population growth, largely in suburbs.

The Model Cities Program has already begun the extraordinarily complex, expensive, and frustrating job of trying to improve the overall environment in a sample of existing low-income neighborhoods. This program provides federal monetary incentives for each of a selected group of local governments to plan and carry out an intensive and highly coordinated upgrading drive in a relatively small part of its area. Each such drive involves activities by all city departments, the local school board, private social agencies, relevant state agencies (such as welfare departments), and key federal agencies. By trying to get all these "actors" to focus their efforts jointly in a well-coordinated attack on the problems in a single slum neighborhood in each city, the Model Cities Program seeks to overcome the excessive fragmentation and diffusion that have weakened the impact of past upgrading efforts. Therefore, a key national task is to carry out this program effectively and expand it. Greater emphasis should be placed on trying out really radical technical and institutional experiments, because we know so little about how to solve many key upgrading problems. For example, we have yet to discover an effective way to improve the educational achievements of children from the most deprived homes. Finally, there must be closer cooperation among the many federal agencies responsible for programs that affect Model City neighborhoods.

Providing adequate nonresidential facilities and services to accommodate future population growth seems strikingly different from upgrading existing deprived areas. Ironically, the same concern that causes reformers to advocate splitting large cities into small neighborhood-oriented jurisdictions simultaneously causes them to press for the merger of small suburbs into larger jurisdictions. This paradox occurs because, in both areas, the existing government is not responsive to the needs of the most deprived people in society. In big cities, this lack of responsiveness masquerades as the impersonal bureaucracy found in many large organizations. So the cure seems to be shifting the locus of decision making to small areas, in the hope that the obvious predominance of the deprived in those areas will compel the government to respond to their needs. However, it is not possible to deal with all the complexities of participation and representation issues here.

In contrast, in growing suburban areas political jurisdictions are already small enough to provide high responsiveness to their residents. But those relatively affluent residents deliberately seek to exclude most of the poor. In this case, the cure seems to be *reducing* local responsiveness by shifting certain policy responsibilities to a larger jurisdiction. Since that jurisdiction will incorporate the people now deliberately excluded, it will supposedly be far more responsive to their needs. Unfortunately, it is not really clear why this larger entity will be any more responsive to the deprived than larger central-city governments are now. But there does not appear to be any other even potentially effective way to sensitize suburbs to a broader viewpoint. Therefore, "escalating" key powers to larger jurisdictional areas should certainly be tried in many metropolitan areas, and perhaps adopted generally.

In both central cities and suburbs, two other ingredients will be vital in creating proper facilities and services ancillary to housing. The first is more effective administration of existing institutions. This requires a greatly increased quality of state and local government personnel. The second consists of large infusions of financial aid from outside the local governments, for creation of adequate environments for new housing will be extremely expensive. A crude estimate of the cost of constructing the necessary ancillary capital facilities (such as streets, schools, water systems, and so forth) is that it will be at least two-thirds as much as the cost of the housing itself. This would amount to about $436 billion from 1970 through 1980. Studies indicate that about $196 billion would consist of private investment and $240 billion of public investment. This is an average public investment of $21.8 billion per year in new construction of facilities related to housing. This compares with $13 billion, my rough estimate of the amount spent on similar construction by all state and local governments in 1966. And these figures include no allowance for the immense expense of operating the new facilities. Thus, the public sector will have to expand its spending greatly to meet the nonhousing parts of the federal government's housing goals by 1980. Much of that expansion will require federal financing.

This conclusion should not be obscured by statements about the potentially increased role of the private sector in solving the urban crisis. No matter how much of the job of creating better urban environments is *performed* by the private sector, a major part of the *costs* of that performance must be borne by the public. And this is perfectly proper. The actions involved benefit society as a whole, and therefore should be paid for by society as a whole.

Meeting National Housing Targets

Creating 27.7 million new or rehabilitated housing units and the ancillary facilities and services they require by 1980 is a heroic target. If the United States actually reached this target, it would have virtually solved its remaining housing problem in slightly more than a single decade. According to the Housing and Urban Development Act of 1968, this is precisely what Congress wants the nation to do. And according to the official statements, exhortations, and policies of the Department of Housing and Urban Development, its leaders believe we can do it.

Yet the obstacles blocking attainment of this target by 1980 are formidable. From 1950 through 1959, an average of 1.5 million new housing units were built each year. From 1960 through 1967, the annual average was 1.4 million, and from 1966 through 1968 it will be about 1.3 million. In only three postwar years have over 1.6 million units been built; 1950 (the all-time high of almost 2 million), 1955, and 1963 (both under 1.7 million).[6] Moreover, annual production of subsidized units for middle-income and and low-income households has averaged less than 60,000 in the past decade. Therefore, meeting the targets in the 1968 act will require an annual rate of total production double that attained in the recent past, and 42 percent higher than the greatest ever achieved. It will also require producing ten times as many housing units for moderate-income and low-income households per year as in the past.

Theoretically, these enormous accelerations in housing production could be achieved only if, throughout *all* of the 1970s, the nation would simultaneously:

> Attract vastly more private capital into residential investment. This would be virtually impossible unless we ended the war in Vietnam immediately, avoided any costly new foreign involvements, placed top national emergency priority on housing, and adopted monetary and fiscal policies that encouraged low interest rates and relatively little inflation.
>
> Greatly expand the available supply of construction workers. This would involve major changes in existing union practices in the building trades.
>
> Pace housing programs to avoid great dislocations between supply and demand.

Subsidize millions of households so that they could pay for adequate housing. This would demand annual congressional housing appropriations much larger than any ever passed before.

Overcome existing bitter resistance to relocation among low-income households so that millions of persons could be peaceably displaced through massive clearance programs.

Achieve a major change of attitude among middle-class Americans—both white and black—concerning their willingness to accept large numbers of low-income households into their communities, and similarly alter the unwillingness of present all-white areas to welcome Negro newcomers. Open up many "exclusive" suburban areas to provide vacant sites for housing lower-income households through fundamental changes in existing zoning laws and practices.

Remove the obstacles to the development of mass production techniques for building housing (such as myriad building codes), attract large-scale operators into the housing industry, and create better institutions in that industry to carry out federal programs.[7]

Slash administrative red tape and delays at all levels of government. This could be done only through basic changes in the incentive systems now built into all public institutions.

Expand local government revenues sufficiently to pay for all the ancillary facilities needed to support the new housing, and for their subsequent operation. This would require major shifts in the fiscal relations among federal, state, and local government institutions.

Merely stating these requirements indicates how unrealistic it is to believe they will all come to pass soon enough for the nation to reach its official housing targets by 1980. This conclusion is certain to be labeled as gloomy and pessimistic by many sincere and well-informed proponents of housing. They contend that the nation could reach these targets by 1980 "if only we would make the effort." Perhaps they are right. But I believe most Americans will conclude that the costs of making that effort are not worth the reward of eliminating nearly all inadequate housing by 1980.

After all, the vast majority of Americans at all income levels live in reasonably adequate housing now. Therefore, they would not benefit directly or immediately from wiping out inadequate housing, though they would receive many indirect benefits. Yet many of the profound institutional and other changes required to eliminate inadequate housing by 1980 would impose large costs upon this well-housed majority and drastically alter institutions they now cherish. Moreover, awarding the housing problem the top national priority—indeed, emergency status—necessary to reach the official targets by 1980 would necessarily downgrade efforts to attack other problems that many citizens believe are even more serious—such as poverty, the need for better quality education, and minority-group unemployment. In fact, focusing national efforts on housing might even raise unemployment generally, as pointed out later.

For these reasons, I do not believe the nation will reach the official housing targets by 1980. This conclusion seems to me an inescapable result of any thorough and realistic assessment of the true probabilities that all the key actors will behave in the ways necessary to carry out the actions set forth above. In the subsequent sections, I will try to support this conclusion by examining in detail each of the nine activities described above. In each case, I will first set forth the actions necessary to reach the housing targets in the 1968 act. Then I will indicate why, in my opinion, some of those actions will not occur in the near future. The purpose of these detailed examinations is not to dispute the desirability of attaining the official housing targets, or to attack those who espouse them. Rather, it is to develop effective policy recommendations which the nation might adopt concerning housing. For discovering what actions would be required to reach these targets by 1980 will also provide crucial insights concerning the actions necessary to solve the housing problem within a longer time-frame. In most cases, the basic policies and institutional changes required will be roughly the same regardless of what the ultimate target date may be—only the pacing and the annual magnitudes will be different.

Admittedly, I cannot determine the proper future pacing. I believe the nation's worst housing conditions are terribly bad, and improving them deserves very high national priority. Nevertheless, solving the housing problem is only one of the many pressing tasks facing the nation. Each of these tasks seems compellingly urgent to those who specialize in it; consequently, they often claim that it should be given top national priority. But, in my opinion, such specialists should not set national priorities—that is the task of our political leaders. Therefore, I will simply indicate what must eventually be done to solve the housing problem and what specific first steps could effectively be adopted within the next few years.

The principal challenges to the federal government regarding housing will not necessarily involve major new legislation. True, Congress must pass much bigger appropriations for many of the programs it has already authorized, and this implies a very different attitude of members of congressional appropriations committees toward the housing problem from the one prevailing in the past. But the really tough challenges will be effectively administering existing and new programs, and persuading key nonfederal actors to carry out their roles in attaining federal housing goals. These nonfederal actors are the local governments in major metropolitan areas, state governments, the three basic segments of the private building industry (lenders, labor, and builders), and the public at large. Thus, administration and leadership—rather than housing legislation—will be the crucial tasks which the President and his administration must undertake with unprecedented effectiveness.

FINANCING EXPANDED OUTPUT

Procuring the capital to invest in 27.7 million housing units involves four basic issues. First, is the required investment in residential construction compatible with the basic structure of the economy? Detailed analysis of the likely cost of creating that number of new housing units from 1970 through 1980 indicates that the total investment in housing required (in current dollars) will be about $654 billion. Assuming gradually increasing output the annual investment rate will rise from about $37 billion in 1970 to about $85 billion in 1980. These requirements will amount to roughly 3.9 percent of gross national product (GNP) in 1970, and 5.1 percent in 1980. In recent years, the share of GNP devoted to residential construction has been from 3.0 to 3.3 percent, but it reached 5.5 percent in 1950. Similar analyses concerning gross private domestic investment and personal income indicate that high, but not impossible, fractions would have to go into housing. These could be attained only if current flows of capital into defense spending were significantly curtailed. Thus, if peace returns and defense spending drops off, it will be structurally possible to hit the 1980 target in terms of capital funds.

Second, will the financial institutions which have traditionally provided mortgage capital be able and willing to pour the required funds into housing in the 1970s? Prospects are not good for attracting such large flows of funds into housing through these channels. They include savings and loan associations, commercial banks, mutual savings banks, and insurance companies. A preliminary analysis of the levels of funds which each of these institutions (and others) would have to put into housing to finance 27.7 million units in the 1970s indicates: savings and loan associations would have to attract as high a share of savers' funds as they did before bank rates became competitive with association rates; American consumers would have to save about 7 percent of their personal disposable incomes throughout the decade—though they have saved a fraction of this size only twice since 1959; pension funds would have to overcome their past aversion to real estate and plunge heavily into mortgage investments; insurance companies, banks, and mutual savings banks would have to alter drastically their antipathy toward residential mortgages (especially for single family homes) during periods of high interest rates when other investments with lower processing costs and comparable returns become available.

Under current institutional conditions, these events are likely to occur simultaneously—if at all—only if there is a sharp slackening of business in all sectors of the economy relative to housing. But it is extremely unlikely that such a slackening would persist throughout the decade.

This raises the third basic question: what kinds of monetary and fiscal policies are needed to encourage large-scale investment in housing? During the postwar period, housing starts have risen whenever interest rates declined, and vice versa. Thus, the economic climate most conducive to massive investment in housing would be one with relatively low or declining interest rates. But interest rates normally fall during periods of receding general prosperity and rise when the economy is booming. This suggests that it is difficult to maintain both high-level prosperity and large-scale investment in housing at the same time—at least over a long period. How could it be done throughout the 1970s?

Some observers believe that huge amounts of money could be channeled into housing even during prosperity if interest rates on mortgage loans rose very high—to, say, 10 percent or more. Traditional lenders would then be willing to make mortgage loans even in prosperous periods, and consumer households would be encouraged to save more. But it is extremely unlikely that high enough mortgage rates can be either achieved or sustained. They are now illegal in most states, though existing usury laws are being changed. More significantly, these rates would probably tremendously reduce the demand for housing, thereby defeating this strategy. Finally, such rates would place severe strains on the huge savings and loan industry. Its large portfolio of past loans made at lower rates means it cannot sharply raise the rates it pays to savers without incurring financial losses. If mortgages could be made at 10 percent, there would be an immense pressure on banks and other savings institutions to raise their savings rates. But savings and loan associations hold over $100 billion in home mortgages; society cannot afford to let them collapse. For all these reasons, this strategy for sustaining a continuous high-level flow of funds into housing will not work.

An alternative might be to use fiscal policy to restrain general demand in the economy and to divert funds into housing. The government could utilize increased income taxes instead of high interest rates to "cool off" the economy. It could also invest all the proceeds of those taxes directly in housing. But when the economy in general cools off, housing demand drops, thereby weakening the desire of builders to create 21.7 million new unsubsidized units.

These considerations raise a fourth major financing issue: Can and will the public sector provide the necessary incentives or supplementary funds to make up for private capital deficiencies? In my opinion, the amounts of capital necessary to hit the target of 27.7 million units by 1980 are so vast (averaging almost $60 billion per year) that it is unlikely that Congress will appropriate any very large fraction of the total. Only a national commitment to this housing goal similar in determination to production commitments during the Second World War would move the federal government to shape the nation's fiscal policy as described above. Because of the current political climate of the nation and strong competitive spending demands for education and other social needs, such an all-out emphasis upon housing seems extremely improbable.

This analysis suggests that the investment capital needed to build 27.7 million new units in the 1970s probably cannot be channeled into housing unless the new administration and its successors elect to slow down economic prosperity significantly. That would injure the very households which many government housing policies are designed to aid. Moreover, it is unlikely that such a slowdown would last throughout the decade. Nevertheless, there are several milder public policies which the administration could adopt to encourage a larger flow of private capital into housing. They are set forth in a later section.

INCREASING MANPOWER

In 1967 there were 3.2 million U.S. workers engaged in all contract construction, but no separate data exist for workers in residential construction. Even this statistic is misleading. Thousands of manufactured components and raw materials go into construction, but the workers producing them are not included in this statistical category. Second, seasonal fluctuations mean that the number of construction workers each August is 20 to 45 percent higher than the number in February. Hence many more workers extract *some* earnings from construction than are considered fully employed therein.

This lack of accurate data makes it difficult to determine whether productivity in homebuilding is rising. Considering aggregate data only, it appears that the real value of each worker's hourly output has not increased significantly in nearly two decades. But recent detailed studies assert that this conclusion ignores significant improvements in product quality and that hourly productivity in construction has actually gone up more than 2 percent per year in the postwar period. If so, doubling the annual average output of housing in the next few years will require somewhat less than doubling the number of workers employed in residential construction.

Even this requirement means increasing residential construction manpower by at least 1 million man-years by 1975, and by even more in the late 1970s, if 27.7 million new housing units are to be built by 1980. But many of the skills required to build a house under present methods take a long time to learn, and there is a chronic shortage of apprentices in building trades unions (though most homebuilding is done by nonunion labor). This situation is likely to create a serious production bottleneck if government programs plus population growth suddenly expand the demand for residential building. Contractors and subcontractors will bid desperately for skilled workers, and wages will rise rapidly. Shortages of workers in key trades have already appeared in those few metropolitan areas where homebuilding has recently boomed. From 1960 through 1966 hourly rates in contract construction rose 25.7 percent, compared with 19.9 percent in all manufacturing. Total weekly pay also went up faster in construction, but by a smaller margin: 28.7 percent compared with 24.7 percent in manufacturing. However, the wages of on-site labor play a relatively small role in determining the ultimate cost of housing to its occupants. They comprise only one-fifth the cost of constructing a single family house, and one-tenth the total cost of occupying it (which includes property taxes, utilities, maintenance, and interest). True, many other costs of housing, such as property taxes, are proportional to construction costs; so on-site labor expenses have a "multiplier effect" on total cost. Nevertheless, if construction wages rose an average of 8 percent per year over the next decade instead of 4.3 percent as from 1960 to 1966, this would raise the cost of building a house by no more than 3 percent per year and the cost of living in it by about 2 percent per year.

These calculations imply that future shortages of construction workers are likely to have more important effects in slowing down the rate of housing production than in raising costs. The bottlenecks arising from such shortages will be aggravated by the unusually high rate of retirement which will prevail in this work force, because its members are relatively old. Consequently, the manpower required to build 27.7 million housing units by 1980 would not be forthcoming in time unless extensive public efforts were directed to increasing the flow of new workers into this field. Even if the ultimate target date for eliminating all inadequate housing is moved well past 1980, such efforts would have beneficial effects in increasing the output capacity of the housing industry.

PREVENTING DEMAND-SUPPLY DISLOCATIONS

To reach its stated housing targets by 1980, the federal government must increase the housing purchasing power of 6 million low-income and moderate-income households who could not afford adequate housing without subsidies. Hence they would form a *net addition* to the demand for adequate housing likely to arise out of future growth and other factors. The result would be an unprecedented level of demand for adequate housing. On the supply side, the federal government would simultaneously be stimulating the production of housing and expanding the total capacity of the housing industry. In theory, this two-sided approach should result in a close matching of rising demand on the one hand and rising supply on the other. But in reality some periods of significant dislocation would arise, with undesirable effects.

Some experts have contended that such dislocations cannot occur because all the programs of the Department of Housing and Urban Development (HUD) embody direct links between supply and demand. For example, rent supplements are not paid to households, but to developers who build or rehabilitate units. Therefore, a rapid expansion of the rent supplement program would automatically create an added unit for every low-income household thus newly put into the market. Nearly all other HUD subsidies similarly are attached to housing units. This linkage was expressly designed to prevent the kind of dislocation between subsidized demand and added supply described.

Nevertheless, major dislocations can still occur because HUD's programs must compete with all other nonsubsidized users of housing for labor, land, capital, and materials. If the production of subsidized units suddenly rose from its current annual average of 60,000 units to the proposed average of 600,000, then 540,000 "one-unit batches" of housing resources would be diverted from building housing for other people. Unless the total capacity of the industry expanded equally fast, this would result in rising prices of all major housing inputs.

Moreover, to reach HUD's 1980 targets, its programs must successfully "capture" large amounts of housing production resources while those resources are still limited in supply. Insofar as this occurred, many nonsubsidized seekers of new housing units would be compelled to continue living in existing adequate units. This would intensify competiton for the present inventory of adequate housing, and the prices and rents of existing good quality housing would rise. This dislocation would injure many of the very households which HUD's programs are designed to assist—especially low-income renters. They would be less able than ever to bid competitively for existing or new adequate housing if rents and prices rose sharply. HUD cannot possibly subsidize all 6 million households at once. Thus in the first few years the number it benefited would be much smaller than the number which would suffer from the impact of its activities upon the existing inventory. Even at the end of the decade, all the poor households paying inordinate fractions of their incomes to rent adequate units would be permanently injured by the higher rents commanded by such units.

But what if HUD's programs have no initial surge? Their proponents argue that HUD will build up its activities gradually to keep pace with expansion of the housing industry's overall production capacity. Such gradualism would necessarily lead to one of two outcomes. The first is failure to build 6 million subsidized units by 1980. The second is a requirement for gigantic annual outputs of subsidized units toward the end of the 1970s in order to reach the target in that decade. For example, if HUD actually stimulated construction (or rehabilitation) of 200,000 units in the first year of its accelerated program and gradually built up to 600,000 units by the fifth year, it would have to generate 900,000 units in the tenth year to reach a ten-year total of 6 million. What would happen in the eleventh year? Would HUD suddenly cut further subsidies down to the ten-year average of 60,000 units? If so, there would be a huge dislocation in the housing industry. Assuming HUD actually built up its subsidized programs to a very high level in the tenth year, some subsequent wrench of this kind could be avoided only if the nation made a permanent commitment to huge annual outputs of subsidized housing.

Thus, however HUD schedules its planned 6 million subsidized units, any attempt to build all of them within a single decade while still serving all other housing demands is likely to result in major imbalances between demand and supply in the housing market.

Other types of more localized imbalances between supply and demand are likely to arise wherever HUD's programs create a large number of adequate units in a very short period. However, these dislocations are inherent results of *any* attempt to attack the housing problem on a large scale. For example, if a large number of new adequate units are built on previously vacant land in some city, the demand for nearby inadequate units will fall sharply. This will lower the rents and prices of these surrounding units, thereby benefiting many poor renters not covered by HUD's subsidies (and injuring poor owners). In contrast, if the new subsidized units are built on land previously occupied by substandard housing, exactly opposite effects are likely. The number of households displaced by such clearance usually exceeds the number of new units built on the cleared site. The "excess" households displaced will increase competition for existing units nearby, thereby raising their rents and prices. Displacement connected with HUD's urban renewal programs has been causing precisely such injurious effects upon nearby renters for many years.

Policy implications drawn from these considerations are given later.

PROVIDING HOUSING SUBSIDIES

Whatever the number of households now living in inadequate housing, a large proportion have very low incomes. Consequently, any program aimed at providing adequate housing for all households must contain a large amount of "deep" subsidies that cover a large share of a household's total housing costs. But why should the government pay housing subsidies at all? Why not just raise people's incomes above the poverty level through various income maintenance and employment programs? Couldn't they then enter the market and obtain adequate housing without any special housing assistance?

They could not, for two reasons. First, the level of income maintenance adequate to remove people from poverty as defined by the Social Security Administration is too low. It does not allow a household to pay for adequate housing without spending an inordinate share of income on shelter, as pointed out earlier. Yet the cost of raising all Americans even to the "food poverty" threshold is huge, so large that society is certainly unlikely to adopt in the near future income maintenance schemes supporting even higher levels. Second, the supply of housing available to many low-income households in deteriorating central-city neighborhoods—especially Negro households—is highly restricted. There are many "frictional" factors inhibiting the market from increasing that supply in response to higher purchasing power, and these factors will not yield easily to public policy remedies. Therefore, suddenly raising the incomes of these people would simply cause their rents to go up sharply, as has already occurred whenever welfare rent allowances have increased. That is why housing programs per se must remain crucial ingredients in providing poor people with "a decent home and a suitable environment."

However, almost all the programs in the Housing and Urban Development Act of 1968 and in HUD's existing arsenal use "shallow" subsidies that do not cover most of a poor household's housing costs. Hence these programs will not reach really poor households directly. But HUD does have two "deep" subsidy programs available: public housing and leased public housing. In order to serve the majority of persons now living in inadequate units, HUD would have to expand these programs tremendously and alter them drastically to make this expansion acceptable in most communities. Specific recommendations to accomplish this are set forth in the final section of this chapter.

The average subsidy for all households receiving HUD assistance would be based upon both "deep" and "shallow" components. My crude guess is that about $800 per household per year would be required for all the households assisted by HUD's programs over the next decade. If 600,000 more households received such subsidies each year (HUD's target), the annual *added* subsidy cost would average $480 million. By the end of the decade, the *annual* cost would be $4.8 billion. This assumes that the federal government would pay only the marginal difference between the return demanded by lenders and the amounts which households in inadequate units could afford to pay. Moreover, this annual cost would continue into the future until all loans needed to build the new units were repaid, or until almost all families had sufficient incomes to take over full debt payments themselves. If consumer incomes rose rapidly, some of the initial subsidy receivers might be paying their own full costs by the end of the decade, so that the annual cost would decline somewhat. Disregarding this possibility, the *total* subsidy cost of a gradual buildup to the target of 6 million subsidized units by 1980 would be about $26 billion for the entire decade. This is 4.5 times all federal costs of urban renewal in the eighteen years from 1949 through 1966.

In reality, these subsidies to relatively low-income households would not be much larger than the housing subsidies which will be received by middle-income and upper-income households during the same period. All homeowners who pay federal income taxes already benefit from three hidden housing subsidies: they can deduct interest and property taxes from their federally taxable income, and the real benefits they get from occupying their homes are not counted as income. It has been estimated that in 1962 these subsidies amounted to about $2 billion per year for just the 20 percent of U.S. households with the highest income. Since the subsidy to wealthier families *rises* as their incomes increase and tax deductions become more valuable, their total annual subsidy may well equal $4.8 billion by 1980. Thus, extending these subsidies to lower-income households would rectify to some degree the present favoritism toward wealthier people.

OVERCOMING RELOCATION PROBLEMS

Earlier calculations indicated that constructing 27.7 million new housing units by 1980 would involve building about 4.3 million units in central cities. In most older central cities nearly all new housing construction requires prior clearance of existing units, because little usable vacant land is left. The present occupants of those existing units must be relocated first. Even large-scale rehabilitation requires relocation. But most of these occupants have very low incomes, and there is an acute shortage of low rent and low priced housing in these cities. One of the key causes of this shortage is the massive earlier demolition of low-income housing to make way for public improvements like highways and urban renewal projects. These improvements have in effect benefited their middle-income and upper-income users by imposing overcrowding and higher rents upon the lowest-income households—a stunning injustice typical of past public policies regarding housing.

Moreover, a high proportion of the households that would be displaced are Negro. They could find relocation housing only in predominantly white neighborhoods. Thus, massive relocation would speed up the already rapid white exodus from these cities by expanding the areas of Negro occupancy even faster than at present. Such displacement is vehemently resisted both by the Negroes to be displaced and by white residents and politicians. Even middle-class Negroes protest when poor Negroes are moved into nearby public housing projects. Consequently, the massive relocation necessary to build 4.3 million units in central cities before 1980 is now politically impossible in almost all metropolitan areas.

Two kinds of policies are needed to remove this crucial obstacle. The first aims at persuading the occupants of substandard housing to move willingly. They refuse to do so now because (1) present compensation practices fall far short of covering all the true costs of dislocation, (2) there is not enough available housing nearby for them to move into without paying much more or experiencing worse overcrowding, and (3) they resent being herded around without being consulted. One key remedial policy would be awarding both owners and renters "displacement grants" large enough to cover all of their dislocation costs. The Highway Act of 1968 authorizes such payments for road displacement, but they should be expanded and extended to all public programs. A second necessary remedy is engaging in politically sensitive negotiations with both neighborhood groups and individual residents, which will be much easier if generous cash compensation is available.

The third required ingredient is prior creation of adequate housing nearby for displaced families. Some observers have suggested a "roll-over" strategy, using mobile housing units near the housing to be replaced. Residents of the latter could move into the mobile units temporarily. Then they could return to new units on the same site after their original homes were rehabilitated or replaced. The mobile homes would then be moved near the next clearance site. But even this strategy requires more vacant land usable for temporary structures than is available in most large cities. Moreover, demolition and rebuilding now take too long for such a "roll-over" process to work on a large enough scale to allow construction of 4.3 million central-city units by 1980. Another strategy has been suggested: the creation of large "temporary way-station" housing projects on vacant suburban land. These would be occupied by displaced central-city households until new units were created on the sites from which they initially moved. After they moved back to those sites, a new group would move into the "way-station" projects until new units were built for them, and so on. But this policy implies that low-income households can be displaced en masse from one spot to another and back again. Years of relocation experience prove this is impossible. A majority of displaced households would refuse to accept such direction, particularly because it would mean leaving "the action" of the city slum and moving into a foreign suburban environment.

Therefore, the best feasible way to offset the impact of massive displacement upon the existing housing inventory is first to build new units for low-income households on vacant suburban land without trying to shift displaced households into those units directly. If these suburban units are made attractive enough, they will be filled with low-income households who will in turn vacate existing units somewhere. This will ease the market pressure caused by displacement of the households from clearance sites, particularly if the whole process is linked to an intensive housing information campaign in low-income neighborhoods.

If we optimistically assume that half of the 4.3 million new or rehabilitated units to be built in central cities by 1980 can be located on vacant sites therein, about 196,000 units per year must be created on land now occupied by existing housing. I estimate that all publicly supported housing programs have recently caused displacement of about 65,000 units per year in central cities. Therefore, reaching the planned housing targets will require at least tripling the amount of displacement recently generated each year by all housing programs. In large cities, this inescapably involves first building large numbers of new units for low-income households on vacant suburban land.

These considerations bring up the second set of policies needed to overcome relocation problems: those aimed at persuading middle-class American, both white and black, willingly to accept significant numbers of low-income households in their communities. These policies will be discussed in the next section.

OPENING UP THE SUBURBS

The hidden assumption in all programs aimed at rapidly improving central-city housing is that large numbers of new housing units for low-income people can be built on vacant suburban land. But up to now almost all suburbs (and many central-city neighborhoods) have vehemently resisted all publicly assisted housing—especially public housing, which is the major "deep" subsidy program now available. Three motives underlie this resistance. First, any influx of low-income households with children tends to add a net burden to local property taxes. Second, Americans who have "made it" into the middle class have traditionally sought to demonstrate their success by segregating themselves from those less affluent. This desire for relative economic and social homogeneity has important functions. It is much easier to pass on cherished values to one's children if they are reared in schools and neighborhoods where only children from families with similar values are found. And personal security is much greater when one lives in an area where nearly all others accept the same standards of public deportment. So each socioeconomic stratum tries to gain control of some local suburban government. It then sets zoning, taxation, education, and other standards which it regards as appropriate to "its own kind." The third exclusionary motive is anti-Negro sentiment, which is still strong among many whites. It is reinforced by their falsely imputing lower-class traits to all Negroes and by their fears that Negro newcomers will depress property values.

No attempts to open up suburban vacant land to low-income central-city households on a large scale are likely to succeed unless they effectively cope with all three motives for exclusion. The first—fiscal self-defense against higher property taxes—can be counteracted only by institutional changes that remove the economic penalties of accepting low-income residents. The following strategies are possible:

> Creating grant-in-aid programs which attach bonuses to the incoming low-income households. These bonuses would go to the suburban governments and school boards concerned, thereby making it "profitable" for them to accept poor newcomers.
>
> "Escalating" key taxation and land-use control powers away from individual suburban governments to larger entities, such as counties and metropolitan areas. If all households were within a single jurisdiction, no one would suffer a fiscal loss when low-income households moved from one portion to another. And each small part could not exclude any of the problem-creating uses which must go *somewhere*, but which most suburbanites do not want near them.
>
> Shifting much of the burden for paying for certain expensive services—particularly education and welfare—from local governments to the federal government. This is also desirable because these services should partly reflect national rather than local policies, since they have nationwide effects. Then the fiscal penalties of accepting low-income households in any given suburb would be much smaller and overall property taxes lower.

The last strategy seems far more politically acceptable than the other two. Even so, it requires profound changes in present federal-state-local fiscal and institutional relationships. I do not believe society will adopt such changes fast enough to allow achievement of the "official" housing targets for the 1970s.

Even these profound fiscal changes would not in themselves open up the suburbs sufficiently. At least some escalation of land-use controls to higher levels of government would have to occur too. Yet this is sure to be bitterly resisted unless it is tied in with some kind of financing benefits like those mentioned above—and perhaps will be resisted even then. Again, prospects are bleak for accomplishing this change soon enough to help achieve federal housing targets in the 1970s. Nevertheless, the nation should place high priority on thus formulating and carrying out proposals for modernization of our obsolete local and state government institutions.

Counteracting the other two exclusionary motives in the suburbs will be almost as difficult. Desires to protect local socioeconomic status will probably remain dominant until land-use controls are escalated to bodies with bigger jurisdictions or the federal government is given the power to override them under certain conditions. Moreover, some degree of residential homogeneity along economic (not racial) lines at the neighborhood level is surely desirable. Racial discrimination in housing is already under assault by federal and many state and local ordinances. Fears about property values associated with Negro move-ins might even be mitigated by some form of federal or even private loss-limiting guarantees for nearby property owners over a specified time period.

Many observers believe that the best way to accommodate future growth is to create "new cities" outside existing metropolitan areas. Up to now, most developments labeled "new cities" are really large scale, multiple-land-use subdivisions within or dependent upon present metropolitan areas. Successful development of true new cities is beyond the capability of private enterprise acting alone. It requires special government powers to assemble land, bear some of the "front money" cost of the long development period, provide special incentives to attract industry, subsidize new housing for low-income residents, and establish viable relations with existing county and state governments. Moreover, new cities are a far more expensive form of growth than peripheral sprawl. The latter allows new subdivisions to use existing employment concentrations, utility plants, older housing for poorer households, and transport networks; all these things must first be built from scratch in new cities. It might be worthwhile to subsidize one or two experimental new cities to test the possibilities of large-scale, comprehensively planned construction using innovative technology, and to discover how much they might reduce environmental pollution. But it is doubtful whether any significant fraction of future growth will be accommodated in this way, though large scale subdivisions near existing settled areas will probably multiply. Politicians deciding whether to spend billions on new cities or on existing metropolitan areas cannot help noticing that the latter already contain millions of voters, whereas there are none in as yet nonexistent new cities.

CHANGING OPERATIONS IN THE BUILDING INDUSTRY

At present, homebuilding in the United States is largely a localized industry dominated by thousands of small operators. This is true partly because there are over 8,300 separate jurisdictions with different building codes. Many of these also have differing subdivision regulations, zoning ordinances, and officials with whom builders must carry out specific negotiations. In addition, housing markets across the nation exhibit wide variations in climate, consumer tastes, topography, and soil conditions. A third reason is that land ownership is so fragmented that private assembly of relatively large parcels is time-consuming, expensive, and often impossible in the absence of any way to compel owners to sell or merge their holdings. The resulting fragmentation of the building industry has serious effects which keep costs higher than they might otherwise be and discourage comprehensive land-use planning. Nearly all builders have businesses so small that they cannot afford to experiment or do research that might cut costs. Also, they cannot sustain national advertising campaigns likely to persuade consumers to accept a standardized product. Even big builders have difficulty undertaking large-scale housing production.

Comprehensive community planning requires development of very large parcels under a single plan. Then the various types of land uses necessary for a balanced community can be laid out with full consideration of their interrelationships. This should result in a spatial pattern that provides nearly optimal efficiency for the area as a whole and maximum economies of scale in construction. A minimum size of at least 1,500 acres is probably necessary for such a development. But now almost every landowner controls a parcel that is tiny compared to this minimum. The result is a helter-skelter development pattern marked by ugliness, inefficient placement of related land uses, skipping over parcels in otherwise developed areas, and failure to take maximum advantage of land-use interrelations or possible economies of large-scale production. In theory, existing zoning arrangements take all such "external" relationships into account. But in practice, zoning laws are altered almost at will by powerful developers. Moreover, there is no effective way to coordinate the zoning in all the many small communities in each metropolitan area.

Several types of remedies are necessary to counteract these deficiencies. First, much greater uniformity of local building codes and other regulations should be required by each state. Second, a national agency—perhaps quasi-private—should be created to set standards for building materials and techniques so that each locality does not have to test every new idea. Third, the federal government should sponsor extensive research in new technology, as it has done so successfully in agriculture. Finally, development on a large scale in at least some areas should be encouraged or even compelled. Clearly, it would be both impossible and highly undesirable to create a single detailed "master plan" controlling every development in an entire metropolitan area. But it might be practical to require developers in at least some parts of each metropolitan area to operate at a minimum scale—say, 1,500 acres—and to help assemble such parcels. The regulations governing such development could then call for the kind of comprehensive planning described above, as "planned-unit-development" zoning now does. The problems springing from such a requirement are no more severe than the objections originally raised against land-use zoning.

Another constraint blocking technological improvement in housing is insistence by building trades unions on retaining obsolete jurisdictional lines and work practices that render many promising technical ideas economically impractical. Entry into the industry of large manufacturing firms—which have industrial, rather than craft, unions—could conceivably introduce a new element of competition to offset these practices, if local union dominance of building codes and other regulations were ended by adoption of statewide standards. Such large firms would also be more likely to engage in research and development of new products and employ systems analysis and mass production techniques. It is true that the reductions in housing costs which large firms might make are often exaggerated. Many components that go into homes are already manufactured and marketed on a nationwide basis. Moreover, even large firms cannot overcome some of the basic cost-raising aspects of building houses. Yet surely *some* significant economies of scale and technical innovations would result from the entry of large firms into this industry.

The Department of Housing and Urban Development is promoting the entry of large firms into homebuilding also because they may be better adapted to its subsidized programs. Most small builders are oriented toward relatively rapid turnover of land and capital (whereas HUD's programs take years), close tailoring of their product to local markets (whereas HUD imposes many nationally standardized requirements), and small-scale, nonbureaucratic operations (whereas dealing with HUD requires expert paper-shufflers). Therefore, it is unlikely that most existing builders will ever be strongly motivated to participate in HUD's programs, particularly since the direct profits of doing so are limited. Nevertheless, small builders still have a huge role to play in meeting the nation's housing targets. Over three-fourths of the 27.7 million units needed in the 1970s will *not* be directly subsidized, so small builders are well suited to construct most of them. Furthermore, large manufacturing firms may prove to be not much more attracted to HUD's programs than small builders. Most big firms demand higher profit rates than HUD is willing to allow on subsidized projects. The 1968 act allows investors to gain sizeable tax-sheltered cash flows, but these may not be tempting to large corporations seeking earnings to raise their stock values. However, individual investors in high brackets can indeed benefit from tax-sheltered cash flows. HUD should encourage such individuals and syndicates to participate in its programs by providing maximum technical assistance to limited profit as well as nonprofit housing sponsors (as in the 1968 act).

INCREASING ADMINISTRATIVE EFFECTIVENESS

If all HUD's new programs become burdened with the same administrative red tape snarling existing programs, the nation will not come close to producing 6 million subsidized housing units by 1980. In spite of recent attempts to cut processing time, "administrative overkill" is still the basic condition. Ironically, any potential savings to the federal government are more than canceled by the resulting delays. Moreover, these tactics cause most builders—even big ones—to shun government projects.

Whenever confronted by these facts, HUD blames Congress, with much justification. Congress must face the fact that higher risks of failure, mishandling of funds, and other errors are the inescapable price of moving fast to meet ambitious production goals—in housing or any other program. Reduction of administrative complexity is especially crucial in programs dealing with unsophisticated low-income households, and in attempting to encourage participation by private developers while restricting their profits.

This shift in viewpoint would not be just a trivial concession. It requires an entirely new method of rewarding program administrators at every level. Now, no matter how many new housing units an official expedites, he receives the same reward. But one visible error costs him serious penalties. In contrast, administrators should be given strong positive incentives—including spot promotions, financial bonuses, and special recognition—for their net productivity (total output minus mistakes) rather than for avoidance of gross errors. This may require a revolution in Civil Service regulations, but it is long overdue at all levels of government. In fact, *the most crucial innovations which any federal agency can make in the immediate future concern better ways to administer existing programs rather than new program designs.*

USING FISCAL REFORM TO SPUR INSTITUTIONAL CHANGE

Solving the housing problem will require both state and local governments to alter existing institutions radically and to receive large funds from the federal government. Therefore, it makes sense for the federal government to use the promise of large-scale assistance as a means of encouraging institutional change. Moreover, it would be irresponsible for the federal government to provide massive funds for state and local governments without demanding major institutional changes. Some programs have already attempted to do this. Generally, the more radical the changes they call for, the less successful they have been. However, the financial carrots offered have been quite small. Two kinds of fiscal incentives would be more effective. The first would be federal assumption of a major share of *all* costs of education and welfare. The institutional changes to be sought in return are described in the policies section. The second fiscal carrot would be federal revenue-sharing of a certain fraction of the income taxes collected from a state (modified by appropriate redistribution formulas among states) in return for basic state constitutional changes, such as those described in the discussion of opening up the suburbs.

The same political power which has prevented Congress from supporting programs to aid large cities or the poor on a massive scale might be arrayed against these institutional changes. After all, the people who live in deprived urban neighborhoods or occupy inadequate housing units form a minority of the total population—no more than 20 percent. Aiding them imposes an immediate cost upon the more affluent majority without providing any instantly perceptible benefits in return. Given these facts, how can sufficient political support be mustered for any of the programs or institutional changes suggested herein?

The only answer is through effective political leadership. It first must find those of the affluent majority who would directly gain from each specific change needed and persuade them to lend intensive support to that action. For example, many suburban industrialists would probably support middle-income and lower-income housing on suburban vacant land because they need more workers. Second, leadership must present to the public as a whole the most persuasive case possible for the entire set of institutional changes and programs needed to achieve its goals. Third, it must develop means of "packaging" key changes so that they become linked to other actions that provide clearly evident benefits to the majority described above.

Summary of Policy Recommendations

These are some of the policies that could move the nation toward its housing goals, even if those goals cannot realistically be achieved by 1980.

ANCILLARY FACILITIES

1. Forcefully carry out and expand the Model Cities Program, emphasizing more radical experiments and technical innovations and enlarging inventives for participation.

2. Prepare national public opinion for the large costs of both upgrading existing deprived neighborhoods and building adequate new environments for future housing.

3. Greatly improve coordination among federal agencies controlling components of the Model Cities Program.

4. Provide substantial federal aid for expanded administrative staffs of state and local governments and for improved training of such staffs.

5. Seek larger federal appropriations for facilities that will aid in both upgrading deprived neighborhoods and serving new population growth.

6. Sponsor comprehensive surveys and studies to measure accurately our real needs for housing and evironmental improvements.

7. Have the Internal Revenue Service disallow all depreciation allowances, property tax deductions, and interest deductions on properties in designated "high deterioration" zones within large cities unless the owners' tax returns are accompanied by certificates of full code compliance issued by local authorities. Also, federal examiners of banks and savings and loan associations should not count mortgages on properties in such areas as valid assets unless they are similarly documented.

8. Obtain new legislation to support subsidized home and neighborhood maintenance services in designated "high deterioration" neighborhoods. These services would be operated through contracts with newly formed firms run by local residents.

FINANCIAL POLICIES

1. Attract large manufacturing corporations into the housing construction and ownership business by developing attractive tax credits and other incentives and removing obstacles to large-scale housing production (as recommended elsewhere in this paper). Such corporations could tap sources of funds not now used for housing, conduct national advertising campaigns to win acceptance for standardized housing, carry out large-scale production, engage in greater research and development activities, utilize industrial unions with less restrictive work rules, and bargain more effectively with building trades unions because of their size. The 1968 act aims at this objective by offering depreciation advantages to corporations and other investors, but more incentives will probably be needed.

2. Continue liberalization of state usury laws which now prevent rates on mortgage loans from rising to levels competitive with other investments in times of "tight money."

3. Use income taxation and other fiscal devices to "cool off" the economy as inflationary pressures mount rather than rely upon higher interest rates.

4. Develop a form of mortgage with variable interest rates tied to movements in the prime bank rate or some other index. To keep monthly payments constant, varying interest rates could take the form of changeable loan length.

MANPOWER PROGRAMS

1. Expand the supply of construction workers tremendously by overhauling existing apprenticeship practices in the building trades unions. Union agreements to allow low-skilled nonunion labor to work on local projects at wages which are less than union scale need to be made on a much broader basis.

2. Pay monetary fees to unions which participate in on-the-job training.

3. Set up special training programs to teach currently unemployed residents of central-city low-income neighborhoods the skills necessary for constructing housing.

4. Contract and subcontract as many portions of central-city housing tasks as possible to firms run by residents of low-income areas, especially Negroes.

SUPPLY AND DEMAND POLICIES

1. Apply major federal efforts to expand the production capacity of the housing industry, starting immediately.

2. Keep the buildup of subsidized demand generated by federally supported housing programs gradual enough to avoid major dislocations that might cause rising prices for all basic housing inputs.

3. Reconsider the stated national policy of trying to "lump" so much housing production in a single decade, and instead strive for targets which are both more realistic and less likely, if attained, to generate major dislocations in the housing industry.

HOUSING SUBSIDIES

1. Alter and greatly expand public housing and public leasing programs as follows: (a) Emphasize small-scale projects on scattered

sites utilizing low-rise apartment, townhouses, and detached duplex or single family units. These characteristics should be promoted regarding both newly constructed and leased units. The key objective is not to overwhelm the local neighborhood or dominate the local public school with residents of public housing, but rather to have those residents form a relatively small part of both overall and school populations. This would help make public housing acceptable in many areas that now reject it. (b) Sell units within existing projects to tenants whose incomes have risen above existing eligibility, as allowed in the 1968 act. (c) Drastically reduce supervisory and administrative review requirements for "turn-key" construction of public housing. (d) Develop new public housing units in "mixed" projects with other publicly assisted units serving higher-income families. The public housing units should be physically integrated with other units as closely as possible and kept to a minority of each mixed project. Their tenants should be screened to minimize overloading with families in the most difficult circumstances. (e) Eliminate existing unit-cost restrictions on public housing and build many more amenities and better design into new units, thereby making them easier to convert to ownership and more acceptable in better areas. (f) Intensify social services in large projects inhabited mainly by "multi-problem" families; pay residents to run the services. (g) Improve project administrative procedures; encourage greater tenant participation, with monetary incentives for better maintenance.

2. Set up and carry out the many subsidy programs newly created in the 1968 act.

3. Seek much larger appropriations for existing and newly passed programs.

4. Set up locally run educational services to teach participants in new housing programs proper methods of housekeeping, financial responsibility, and management.

RELOCATION AND COMPENSATION PRACTICES

1. Speed up the entire site selection, acquisition, relocation, and demolition process.

2. Pay much higher compensation to most displaced households and business, whether owners or renters.

3. Link demolition of housing units in specific projects to "compensating" construction or rehabilitation of similar units

nearby, or on vacant land in nearby suburbs if that is the only feasible location. An extreme version of this policy would be that no public agency—federal, state, or local—could tear down any housing unit without first putting up another one somewhere in the same metropolitan area available to the same income and ethnic group, and offered to the displaced household. Some such policy (though not necessarily on a one-for-one basis) would halt the current practice of constantly making the poorest big-city households worse off by reducing the total supply of low-priced housing.

4. Provide many more options for displaced low-income families to relocate in subsidized housing (assuming that more such housing is built).

5. Explicitly face the impact of relocation upon the ethnic change of big cities, and take account of it in planning, rather than ignoring it as at present.

POLICIES TO OPEN UP THE SUBURBS

1. Abolish the present "Workable Program" requirement that compels all cities to meet certain prerequisites to receive any federally subsidized housing programs within their boundaries (including explicit local legislative approval of such programs). If this cannot be done, make all forms of federal urban construction, planning, or other assistance (including sewer and water grants and highways funds) contingent upon adoption by local legislatures of Workable Programs. At present, many suburbs deliberately refuse to adopt them so as to exclude all federally subsidized housing.

2. Seek legislative changes to enable public housing authorities in large cities to lease units outside the boundaries of those cities.

3. Persuade county or state public housing authorities to build new relatively small projects on unincorporated land outside central cities.

4. Provide planning grants to metropolitan housing agencies privately formed to build housing in suburban areas, and help those agencies get project funding under the new programs in the 1968 act.

5. Require that the new ownership assistance program in the 1968 act (which aids low-income households in home purchases via

interest subsidies) insure that at least 30 percent of the units it subsidizes in any metropolitan area are located outside the central city in that area.

6. Offer grants to state planning agencies for studies of the socioeconomic impact of existing zoning ordinances and for developing "model" zoning codes or reformed zoning legislation.

7. Expand existing programs which set up housing information services in low-income central-city areas. These local offices should provide data on suburban housing available to minorities from both private parties and public agencies.

8. Put pressure on all firms receiving federal manufacturing contracts to help insure that workers of all races and creeds can freely obtain housing in the immediate vicinity of their plants.

9. Experimentally develop one or two "new cities" outside of major metropolitan areas, using the entire spectrum of HUD and other federal programs.

POLICIES TO IMPROVE THE BUILDING INDUSTRY

1. Provide funds for states to develop standardized building codes to apply to all communities in each state, with some elements uniform in all states.

2. Set up a single code-certification and testing agency (run by a combination of private and public members) to develop building and housing code standards, certify and test new products and processes (or approve such tests conducted by other bona fide agencies), review and certify existing codes insofar as they meet national standards, and act as a clearinghouse for other aspects of code improvement and standardization.

3. Expand HUD's existing research program (which is now under $20 million per year, as compared with over $7 billion in defense research, $600 million in agricultural research, and over $4 billion in space research).

4. Try to persuade building trades unions to break down some of their jurisdictional rigidities as part of overall market expansion and of new training programs.

5. Encourage states to formulate and adopt new land development regulations that would generate more large-scale, comprehensively planned projects.

6. Provide technical assistance and counseling to limited-profit corporations willing to participate in HUD's programs.

ADMINISTRATIVE REFORMS

1. Radically alter existing HUD procedures for application approval and project review. Initial cost calculations should be delegated to the long-term lender and merely reviewed by HUD. Much of this review process should be computerized. Later reviews of progress should be done on a randomized, sample basis like that used by the Internal Revenue Service.

2. Eliminate present congressional requirements to reduce HUD's staff.

3. Completely reverse the incentive structure of program administrators, as explained earlier.

FISCAL REFORMS TO ENCOURAGE INSTITUTIONAL CHANGE

1. Shift almost all welfare costs and a large fraction of basic educational costs from local governments to the federal government (perhaps via states) in return for adoption of reduced property taxes, more uniform property tax rates, broadening of educational district boundaries to link central cities and suburbs, shifts in educational fund allocation to favor the most deprived groups, reform of welfare regulations, standardization of welfare benefits, and shifts in powers to control land use to jurisdictions covering larger geographic areas.

2. Offer major revenue sharing of federal tax receipts to states for a five-year period in return for certain basic constitutional reforms, including escalation of land-use controls.

Conclusion: Rhetoric Versus Reality

The preceding analysis indicates that there are overwhelming obstacles to the construction of 27.7 million new or rehabilitated housing units—or even 26 million—by 1980. The same obstacles make it extremely unlikely that the United States will create 6 million such units for lower and moderate income groups by that date. In fact, adoption of the national priorities and policies necessary to reach these official targets might cause adverse effects that would injure more low-income households than the housing would benefit. What, then, should we think of the housing targets set forth in the Housing and Urban Development Act of 1968, and endorsed by HUD?

In my opinion, a fair appraisal must take into account the dilemma faced by responsible politicians in our democracy. In order to overcome widespread congressional and public resistance to new expenditures, the administration is tempted to exaggerate the potential effectiveness of anything it proposes. It therefore makes rhetorical promises that each new program will provide a "total solution" to the problems concerned. The antipoverty program will "end" poverty; the Model Cities Program will "completely renovate" slum areas; and HUD's housing programs will "wipe out" substandard housing—all in the very near future.

These rhetorical claims appear patently false to anyone who knows much about the problems concerned. Moreover, they have a devastating long-run impact upon the citizenry's confidence in government programs—and even authority in general. For such claims at first tend to generate great expectations among the relatively poorly informed persons suffering from the ills concerned. But repeated disillusionment eventually induces a deep cynicism toward all government programs. Even though most federal programs actually produce many benefits, they inevitably fall far short of carrying out the promises made in order to get them passed.

In setting a goal of 26 million new or rehabilitated units in the 1970s, including 6 million publicly assisted units, Congress and HUD have once more engaged in this dubious strategy. They have substituted rhetoric for reality, thereby almost guaranteeing the "failure" of their own programs to reach the overoptimistic goals they have set. I sympathize with their desire to spur the nation to higher housing production by setting idealized targets beyond our present capacity. Moreover, a great many of the policies that society would have to adopt to reach those targets are probably worth doing sooner or later. The sooner we adopt many of them, the more quickly we can achieve the national housing goal of "a decent home and a suitable living environment for every American family."

Nevertheless, I believe our housing targets should be both more realistic and more flexible. The nation cannot simply measure the housing needs that have accumulated throughout its history and decide to satisfy all those needs within a single decade, regardless of what happens in any other aspect of national life.

Housing is both too important and not important enough for this approach to work. Its major importance in our economy means that how much housing we produce is inescapably bound up with other key aspects of national performance, such as the levels of employment, defense production, and spending on other social needs. But housing is not so crucial that we must shape our entire economic and institutional behavior solely to solve the housing problem in one decade.

Therefore, even though the targets in the 1968 act are an accurate measure of our current housing needs, I do not believe we should commit ourselves to reach them by any precise date. We should use them to identify the major directions of change needed to solve the problem, and start moving in those directions as fast as possible—as the rest of the 1968 act does. We should set precisely quantified targets only for the short run.

This approach is perfectly suited to the requirement in the 1968 act that the President report to Congress each year what his annual housing goal is and what progress the nation has made toward the previous year's goal.   Even more important, this approach recognizes that government programs should reinforce the credibility of public authorities by producing results consistent with their official promises. Only in this way can housing officials build national confidence in their capabilities rather than contribute to growing public doubt that any government program can accomplish its objectives.

Furthermore, fostering such confidence is vital in moving the nation toward its basic housing goal of "a decent home and a suitable environment for every American family." The preceding analysis has shown the enormous complexity and depth of the changes in public policies and institutions at all levels necessary to reach that goal. Only outstanding leadership supported by strong public confidence will enable us to make those many changes as swiftly as the urgency of our housing needs warrants. Armed with such leadership, with the tools in the 1968 act and earlier legislation, and with a comprehensive understanding of what must be done on many action fronts involved, the nation can and should press toward solving the housing problem as fast as possible. We may not arrive at a solution within one decade, but we certainly can move much faster than in the past. The crucial role of housing in the lives of millions of Americans—especially those now suffering from miserably inadequate shelter—demands such a high priority effort.

Notes

[1] These and other data concerning total and substandard housing units are from a report by Frank S. Kristof, "Urban Needs and Economic Factors in Housing Policy," prepared for the National Commission on Urban Problems, completed in May 1968.

[2] Based upon a study conducted by SYSTEMETRICS for the U.S. Department of Housing and Urban Development, completed in July 1968.

[3] Estimates of future household formation and needs to counteract net losses in the inventory are taken from the Kristof Report.

[4] Projections from Patricia Leavy Hodge and Philip M. Hauser, *The Challenge of America's Metropolitan Population Outlook—1960 to 1985*, Research Report No. 3, National Commission on Urban Problems (Washington, D.C., 1968).

[5] Based upon a study by members of the staff of the National Commission on Urban Problems.

[6] All these data do *not* include mobile homes as housing units. If they are counted, then annual average production from 1966 through 1968 was 1.61 million units, rather than 1.36 million.

[7] Another major activity which could be added to this list is expanding the capacity of the building materials industry. However, limitations of both space and my knowledge prevent discussion of this possibility here.

5

Home Ownership and American Free Enterprise

Owning one's home plays an important role in maintaining our economy's orientation toward free enterprise. For many Americans, home ownership represents their major experience as property owners of any kind. Nearly 64 percent of all American households were owner-occupants in 1968. So about 128 million Americans had some stake in the privileges of private property, and some experience with its joys and responsibilities. This represents a sharp contrast with many European nations, where a majority of households live in rented accommodations.

In general, renters are far more likely to favor extensive government regulation of property ownership than owner-occupants. They are also less sensitive to rising local government costs because they do not pay property taxes directly. For example, New York City and several other cities in New York still have rent control. I believe this is mainly because a majority of their residents are tenants, who therefore receive short-run benefits from holding rents below free-market levels. Similarly, European electorates have traditionally favored stronger government intervention in their economies than the American public. This outcome is certainly not caused solely by differences in home ownership, but that factor is significant.

The qualities of home ownership that create favorable attitudes toward private property in general are not necessarily those honored by folklore and tradition. The typical American family moves every five years, and an estimated one-third of all renter-occupants move each year. This implies that the average home-owning household moves every eight years. Clearly, most Americans do not sink deep roots—physical or psychological—in their own homes by remaining there for a lifetime, or even for many years.

However, this turnover itself plays a crucial role in creating a stake in free enterprise. With few exceptions, land and housing prices have risen steadily in the United States ever since World War

This is an original work that has not previously been published.

II. In the immediate postwar period, and especially the early 1950's, it was possible for lower-middle-income households to buy small suburban homes with tiny down payments and low monthly payments. Whenever they moved, they sold such houses at a significant profit. This process, often repeated several times, resulted in the buildup of a sizable cash equity for millions of households. Most reinvested that equity in another house. Nevertheless, it was—and remains—by far their biggest chunk of private property.

Thus, home ownership, plus rising land and housing prices, created a positive stake in the privileges of private property for nearly two-thirds of all Americans. A 1963 survey by the Federal Reserve Board showed that households typically had more dollars invested in their own homes than in any other type of tangible assets—including stocks and securities combined—for all income groups up to $15,000 or more per year. Only among the very wealthiest households (which comprised fewer than 7 percent of all households in 1968) did any one other form of assets surpass home ownership in value. In 1968, there were about 24 million different shareholders of stock in the United States, over half of whom were women. If this represents about 18 million different households, then 30 percent of all households own stocks—or less than half the number that own their own homes. It is true that 83 percent of all households owned some life insurance in both 1960 and 1965, but the average asset-value of their holdings was lower than their average equity in home ownership. The same is true of accounts in banks and savings and loan associations.

Past and Future Trends in Home Ownership

Home ownership remained fairly constant at around 43 to 48 percent of all United States households from the beginning of this century until the end of World War II. Then it began a steady climb towards its present high level, reaching 55 percent by 1950, 62 percent by 1960, and 63.8 percent by 1968. This increase resulted partly from the high proportion of single-family homes built during the early postwar period. But lately there has been a shift towards higher fractions of multiple family units in total starts, as shown in Table 1.

Table 1.   Types of Nonfarm Housing Starts*
As Percentage of Total

Year	Single Family	Three or More Units
1950	83.0	14.0
1955	90.0	8.0
1960	77.4	18.6
1965	63.9	32.2
1968	58.2	38.3
1969	54.1	42.0

*Figures do not include mobile home construction.

Thus, in the past few years, the proportion of single-family homes in total housing starts has been *below* the proportion of home ownership in total occupied units. Therefore; it might appear that new housing production is actually reducing the overall proportion of home-owning households in the United States. But official housing start figures (at least up through 1969) have never included mobile homes, even though over 400,000 were produced in 1969. The rising importance of mobile homes in total housing starts is illustrated in Table 2.

Table 2.   New Units Started (millions)

Year	Conventional Housing, Farm and Nonfarm	Mobile Homes	Total Housing	Mobile Homes as Percentage of Total Starts
1959	1.554	.121	1.675	7.2%
1960	1.296	.104	1.400	7.4%
1961	1.365	.090	1.455	6.2%
1962	1.482	.118	1.600	7.4%
1963	1.642	.151	1.793	8.4%
1964	1.562	.191	1.753	10.9%
1965	1.510	.216	1.726	12.5%
1966	1.196	.217	1.413	15.4%
1967	1.322	.240	1.562	15.4%
1968	1.548	.318	1.866	17.1%
1969	1.500	.405	1.905	21.3%

Clearly, since mobile homes constituted more than one out of every five new dwelling units in 1969, they ought to be included in housing starts. But all mobile homes are single-family units. (Some stacked, modular housing is used for apartments, but these units are not yet numerous and are not counted as mobile homes.) If mobile-home production is added to conventional housing start figures, the proportion of single-family homes in total housing production (Table 3) is significantly higher.

Table 3.   Single-Family Nonfarm
Housing Starts As Percentage
of Total

Year	Including Mobile Homes	Excluding Mobile Homes
1960	77.4%	79.5%
1965	63.9%	68.5%
1968	58.2%	65.3%
1969	54.1%	63.9%

Mobile homes are counted in data concerning the percentage of all housing that is owner-occupied. Therefore, the proportion of single-family units being produced (counting mobile homes) is still higher than the proportion of all units that are owner-occupied. Presumably, almost all new single-family units are owner-occupied. Therefore, the rising fraction of apartments in total *conventional* housing starts is just barely high enough to start reversing the long-term trend towards greater owner-occupancy in the nation as a whole.

This conclusion, however, does not apply within every metropolitan area. In some of the largest such areas (Los Angeles, Chicago, and New York, for examples) the proportion of renter-occupied units in all housing starts (including mobile homes used in those areas) is now well above the existing fraction of all housing units that are owner-occupied. This tends to reduce the overall percentage of all units that are owner-occupied. Nevertheless, the existing housing stock in these areas is very much larger than annual additions to it, so it will take many years of adding high-renter-occupied increments to the existing stock to reduce significantly the total proportion of owner-occupied units.

Therefore, high levels of owner-occupancy are likely to persist in the United States for quite some time, especially when mobile homes are taken into account. True, mobile homes have much shorter economic lives than conventional units, and are financed over shorter time periods. They also cost much less, and are usually located on rented sites. For these reasons, mobile-home occupants may have a somewhat less proprietary attitude towards their homes than owner-occupants of conventional units. Nevertheless, it appears that home ownership is likely to remain a solid pillar of support for an economy based upon private property for some time to come.

The Biggest Home-owner of Them All

Most American real property owners do not realize that they have a silent partner as co-owner: their local government. After all, every local government (and often the state government too) collects a significant share of the gross income from each real property in its jurisdiction in the form of real estate taxes. For example, apartment owners generally pay from 15 to 20 percent of their gross rent receipts in property taxes—and that is usually larger than their net income from the property. True, local governments furnish important services in return for such taxes. But the cost of the services property owners receive as a direct benefit to their property is generally less than the taxes collected from that property, though the exact difference is hard to measure. The local government then, essentially shares in the net income earned by the property, which means it is part owner.

This is also true of owner-occupied units. The existence of their net income is hidden because owner-occupants do not go through the motions of paying rent (as occupants) to themselves (as owners). Keeping the income-earning power of owner-occupied homes hidden in this way also provides a very large tax benefit to owner-occupants. They do not have to pay income taxes on the implicit "profits" they earn by renting their homes to themselves. But home-owners do have to pay a share of those profits to the local government in the form of real estate taxes. Therefore, in every community, the local government is every home-owner's silent partner. So it is really the biggest home-owner of all.

This fact has critical implications regarding any "tax reforms" that would directly affect real estate investment. Insofar as any change in tax laws reduces the attractiveness of real estate as an investment, it will tend to reduce property values. It is a penalty imposed on whoever owns the property affected at the moment the market takes account of the tax change. The biggest such owner is local government, since it is everyone's real estate partner. Consequently, tax reforms aimed at creating more revenue for the federal government, or more equity among federal taxpayers, may seriously injure local governments. Individual owners who suffer capital losses will probably ask for, and get, lower assessed values. Consequently, the local government's tax income will fall. It will have to either raise real estate tax rates to compensate or find other revenue sources, or both. But higher tax rates without improved services will be bitterly resisted by voters. So local officials will have to take all the "political heat" of somehow raising tax rates without improving services, and of assuming implicit ownership of larger fractions of total property values.

For this reason, local government officials ought to be among the leading opponents of tax changes that are likely to reduce property values. However, most of them do not realize that they are co-owners of all the real estate they tax. They abhor the very thought that we have allowed a "socialistic" thing like government ownership of property to creep in through the back door of free enterprise. This tends to blind them to the impacts of many tax "reforms."

Property Ownership and Housing the Poor

Home ownership, like every legal right, carries definite responsibilities. One is maintenance of the property in good condition so that (1) it provides a safe and comfortable home for its occupants, and (2) it has a positive, rather than a negative, impact upon the surrounding neighborhood. But proper maintenance requires money, especially when the home is relatively old. Older homes are often occupied by low-income households, who cannot afford to pay for adequate maintenance and still pay for food, transportation to work, and mortgage debt service.

This situation creates a dilemma for the owners of many homes occupied by low-income households—including owner-occupants. The occupants cannot afford to pay enough to cover debt service, taxes, operating expenses, and sufficient maintenance to keep the building up to code standards (and in the case of tenants, a reasonable return on the owners' investment). As a result, one or more of the following *must* occur: the unit is illegally overcrowded in order to generate more rent; maintenance is neglected and the unit deteriorates below legal standards (often an additional result of overcrowding); the occupants are compelled to spend an inordinately high fraction of their incomes on housing; the owners receive an uneconomically low rate of return on their investment; or property taxes are not fully paid. If the unit is owner-occupied, then the owner can accept a lower-than-normal profit easily (since his "profit" was noncash return anyway), and he can do much of the maintenance himself. But if it is renter-occupied, then the owner is more likely to crowd more people in and allow the building to deteriorate.

Throughout this country's history, urban governments have coped with this dilemma by allowing owners to violate the laws concerning crowding and property maintenance on a massive scale. Rigid enforcement of the law would have meant (and would still mean) that hundreds of thousands of poor families would have no place to live. They would have to dwell in the streets, as in Calcutta, or build shacks in suburban outskirts, as in Brasilia, Caracas, Lagos, and countless other cities. Yet both these alternatives are also illegal under United States statutes. *For the plain fact is that many hundreds of thousands of United States households cannot afford to pay the cost of living in minimum-quality dwelling units, as defined by existing housing and building codes.* Their poverty conflicts with the legal standards defined by those codes, because the latter are based on what is desirable for everyone, rather than what is attainable for everyone. Yet authorities keep telling such poor households that they *ought* to live in decent housing even though they cannot afford it. So, more and more of these residents are demanding that their landlords rehabilitate their housing up to code standards, and some refuse to pay their rent until this occurs.

How can society respond? The only possible alternatives are:

1. Increase the ability of the poor to pay for housing by providing massive housing or income subsidies.

2. Reduce the housing and maintenance standards required by law, so that what is now considered poor and illegal would no longer be illegal.

3. Enforce the present laws regarding quality of *existing* housing, but allow poor people to build new, now-illegally-low-standard units (as they do now in most of the world).

4. Enforce the present laws regarding quality of *new* housing, but allow massive violations to persist concerning older existing housing.

At present, the United States has rejected any reduction in housing quality standards concerning either the laws themselves, or enforcement of them regarding *new* units. Instead we provide a small amount of subsidy (relative to total need), and rely mainly on massive violations of the law concerning older existing units to cope with this situation.

This creates a cruel choice for owners of many homes occupied by poor households, including many owner-occupants. They are compelled either to act illegally or sustain economic disaster. Many so-called "slum landlords" have ruthlessly exploited poor tenants for decades, but this fact must not blind us to the basically uneconomic position into which society forces many homeowners. It unjustly tries to make *them* resolve the conflict between poverty and the high housing standards written into our laws. The problems of these homeowners are often worsened by the high rate of vandalism in many poor urban neighborhoods.

Under these circumstances, enforcing the law makes home ownership an unsustainable liability, rather than a source of wealth. Compelling owners to make their buildings legal forces them to spend much more than can be economically justified by the resulting ability to collect higher rents. Consequently, more and more owners in big cities are simply abandoning their rights of ownership, thereby turning the property over to their silent partner: the local government. But the local government has no money to resolve the conflict between poverty and high housing standards either. So the more local governments attempt to enforce housing laws upon private owners, the more they place themselves in the position of becoming the owners themselves—and equally in violation of their own codes. When that happens, many tenants will refuse to pay rent to their government landlords, who will be very reluctant to evict them for obvious political reasons. We could conceivably wind up with thousands of poor households living rent-free in government-owned urban slums.

This unwholesome situation indicates that *unsubsidized ownership of property occupied by many of the poorest people in our society is not economically feasible.* It is not feasible for owner-occupants, since they cannot keep up their own properties without some kind of subsidy. It is not feasible for landlords, since they cannot keep their properties in legal compliance and still make a profit—or even avoid a drastic loss. It is not even feasible for the government, but the government cannot avoid ownership if everyone else eschews it.

Until we are willing either to lower housing standards, or to help the poor pay the cost of meeting those standards, we will continue compelling hundreds of thousands of home owners—including governments—to violate housing laws and seemingly shirk the responsibilities of ownership. Openly flaunting violations of the law is hardly a way to encourage respect for law and order, or to generate zeal for the rights of private property or free enterprise. Yet it is just as real an aspect of home ownership as the pride of new suburbanites in their first home—and perhaps just as powerful in its long-run impact upon America.

6

Housing the Urban Poor:
The Economics of Various Strategies

Helping to provide decent housing for low-income households is a
worldwide challenge to national governments, especially in
countries where most citizens are adequately fed. However, it
would be euphemistic to use the term strategies to denote public
policies concerning the housing situation in most countries,
particularly those dominated by free markets. Their governments
simply do not have well reasoned, realistic, long-range policies for
coping with housing needs. Nevertheless, for purposes of analysis,
it is useful to view the public efforts to improve the housing of
low-income households in each nation as resulting from at least an
implicit strategy.

Key Background Factors and Relationships

The analysis requires understanding of the following key
background factors and relationships:

QUALITY STANDARDS FOR NEW CONSTRUCTION

I will arbitrarily define three different quality standards actually
used by various nations to control new housing construction (as
distinct from those verbally professed). High standards are
equivalent to the housing consumed by upper-middle-class families
in terms of unit size, land per unit, quality of construction, and
utilities. In the United States, all new urban housing construction
(except mobile homes) must meet high standards. Moderate
standards embody far more modest quality levels, but still qualify
as decent housing. They govern new construction in most

Reprinted from the *American Economic Review*, Vol. 56, No. 4 (Sept.
1969), pp. 646–51, by permission of the American Economic Association.
Footnote added by author.

European nations. Zero standards mean that any type of new housing construction is allowed, including crude shacks built by squatters. Zero standards prevail in most of the world.

RELATIONSHIPS AMONG HOUSING STANDARDS, HOUSING COSTS, AND PUBLIC SUBSIDIES

The public subsidy necessary to enable the average low-income household to live in a newly built decent home is much larger if high quality standards are required than if moderate quality standards are required. (If zero standards are required, the housing units concerned are not decent in quality.) Therefore, requiring high standards means that (1) a higher proportion of households in the economy cannot buy new housing without subsidies; (2) fewer badly-housed poor households can be provided with "decent" new housing per million dollars of public subsidy; (3) the total cost of providing all presently ill-housed poor households with "decent" housing is vastly greater; and (4) among middle class voters, political opposition to large scale housing subsidies is greater, since many appear to be paying taxes to put poor people in housing better than their own. Also, the higher the standards required for new housing, the more citizens of all incomes must resort to debt financing in buying homes. Therefore, the higher the fraction of total cost they pay that goes to interest instead of direct construction. In contrast, zero standard housing can be paid for entirely out of current income without debt financing, especially because the land is often expropriated.

EFFECTS OF RISING INCOMES AND RISING OCCUPANCY COSTS

If real incomes rise faster than housing occupancy costs (which include land, interest, and construction costs), then most households upgrade their housing. They do so either by moving into higher quality units, or improving the units they now occupy. Improvement without movement is most likely where: social class mixture and racial mixture in any given neighborhood are common and socially accepted; zero standard construction is common, so residents can gradually upgrade initially skimpy housing by adding improvements wholly financed out of current income; there is an acute overall shortage of housing; or housing is rationed by public authorities who control the supply, or at least control all new units. Where opposite conditions prevail, upgrading is usually accomplished by moving to a better neighborhood, as in the United States. If occupancy costs rise faster than real incomes, then little upgrading occurs, and the amount of subsidy required per household to put ill-housed families into decent housing rises.

THE IMPACT OF POPULATION GROWTH AND MIGRATION UPON LOCAL HOUSING CONDITIONS

In any given metropolitan area or neighborhood, the number of households can normally fluctuate much more rapidly, both up and down, than the total supply of "decent" quality housing units. Thus, rapid natural increase in population plus heavy inmigration can lead to an acute local housing shortage. This situation absolutely compels one or more of the following indecent housing conditions to result at least temporarily: overcrowding of existing "decent" units, division of such units into smaller substandard units, construction of many new substandard units (or even zero standard units), or households living in the streets or in the open without housing. Public authorities may attempt to prevent such outcomes by prohibiting migration into a given metropolitan area. However, experience throughout the world, even in totalitarian nations, shows that such prohibitions are ineffective if strong pressures are driving people out of rural areas. Hence a critical factor influencing housing conditions in any locality is the pressure of population growth on the local housing supply. Where such growth occurs mainly among poor households, the only way to prevent the above indecent results from lasting a long time is through huge public housing subsidies, since the new households cannot afford to purchase new housing on the free market.

THE IMPORTANCE OF PUBLIC POLICIES IN STIMULATING TOTAL HOUSING PRODUCTION

In any locality, the relationship between the total supply of decent housing units and the total number of households determines to what extent the indecent housing conditions described above will occur. Any rapid increase in total supply relative to total needs, even consisting solely of more new luxury units, tends to loosen the entire housing market, thereby eventually improving conditions for all households, even the poorest. Unless demolition offsets new building, the prices of all units decline relative to incomes, and more options are available to all households, though frictions may weaken this effect in poor areas. Thus, any public policies which stimulate total housing production tend to improve housing conditions among the poor to at least some extent, other things being equal. Clearly, the bigger the total direct public subsidy put into housing, the more new units will be built. In addition, because so much new housing employs debt financing, national monetary and fiscal policies that reduce interest rates can greatly increase the amount of new housing produced in free markets.

THE EFFECT OF VARYING PUBLIC HOUSING SUBSIDY DISTRIBUTIONS

Public housing subsidies have two effects which improve housing conditions among poor households: they always increase total housing output, thereby tending to loosen the entire housing market; and they may provide direct access to new housing for poor households if they focus upon aiding such households. But, the lower the household's income, the greater the per-household subsidy needed to close the gap between ability to pay and the cost of a new decent unit. Therefore, any given sized public housing subsidy can generate more new production of decent units if concentrated upon middle-income and upper-income groups than if concentrated upon the poorest groups. True, the frictions of the housing market mean that the immediate impact of such larger outputs upon the poorest households will be far less than a lower total output directly distributed to them. Yet focusing housing subsidies upon middle income groups (as in the United States) enables the government to assist more households per million dollars of subsidy, and therefore may be considered politically more efficient than direct housing aid to the poor.

APPROACHES TO SECOND BEST SOLUTIONS

In all nations and all historic periods, providing decent housing for every household has been far too expensive for society to achieve without sacrificing other objectives which it considers more desirable. Hence, a variety of second best solutions have been tried. Where the poorest groups are politically powerful, there is usually a combination of (1) allowing urban squatters to expropriate housing sites without payment, especially on publicly owned land;

(2) allowing large amounts of zero standard housing to be built privately by poor urban squatters; and (3) building some publicly subsidized decent units for poor households in large cities. Where middle-income groups are politically dominant, there is more pressure to prevent squatting and zero standard new construction, and to shift subsidies to directly benefiting middle-income or high-income households.

THE LOCATION OF LOW-INCOME HOUSEHOLDS IN URBAN AREAS

Throughout the world, most new urban construction occurs on vacant land at the edges of existing built-up areas. It is almost always much cheaper and faster to build on vacant sites than to acquire existing properties, relocate their occupants, demolish them, and then build on their sites. Also, where acute housing shortages prevail, it is politically difficult to destroy existing units because it is so hard to relocate their occupants.

The edge of most urban areas lies on the outskirts relatively distant from the central business district. However, in some cities, more close-in areas have remained vacant because of undesirable features that caused earlier developers to bypass them. For example, in Caracas, close-in hillsides were skipped by early urban developers because of the high costs of building on steep slopes.

In societies which cope with rapid increases in low-income population by housing poor households in new units, the poorest people tend to live at these edges of the developed area, mostly on the periphery, but sometimes also on initially bypassed hillsides, public parks, or swamps. Since it is too expensive to provide decent new units for most such households, the majority usually live in zero standard shacks clustered around these outskirts.

In contrast, societies which prohibit zero standard new construction generally cannot afford to house all or even most low-income population growth in new units. Instead, poor households must concentrate in the lowest price existing units. These tend to be the most dilapidated and obsolete houses, which are usually the oldest in the area. Almost all cities were historically built up in concentric rings outward from their points of origin. Hence the oldest units are close to central commercial areas. Thus, prohibiting poor households from building new zero standard or low standard housing on vacant land radically shifts the spatial concentration of the poor from the outer periphery of a metropolitan area to the inner core, as in the United States. Conversely, in these societies, only relatively affluent families or those receiving public subsidies can afford to occupy the decent new units built on vacant land at the edge of the urban area. True, a few very wealthy households live close to the center in older units they rehabilitate, or new units created through clearance. But these are exceptions to the general rule that whoever lives in older units dominates the near-core area.

Basic Strategies for Providing Housing for Low-Income Urban Households

Using the background factors and relationships described above, we can systematically analyze the basic strategies employed in various nations to provide housing for low-income urban households. Each such strategy occurs in a setting influenced by three key exogenous factors: the rate of population growth and population migration patterns; the rate of change of average real income per household; and the rate of change of occupancy costs per household for newly built decent housing units. Variations in these factors influence both the selection of particular housing strategies by public authorities, and the outcomes of whatever strategy is selected. Clearly, a myriad of other exogenous factors can influence these things too, but these three are especially critical.

For purposes of analysis, I will arbitrarily view each basic housing strategy as containing four main elements: the quality standards actually enforced regarding new housing construction, the degree of overall public stimulation of total new housing production, the total amount of public subsidy for housing, and the way this public subsidy is allocated among income groups. A huge number of possible combinations and variations of these elements can be conceived of. But I believe it is useful to narrow down these possibilities to the following three major types of strategies:

Filtering strategies involve strict enforcement of high or moderate quality standards for all new construction, and either (a) no public housing subsidies at all or (b) public subsidies focused mainly on middle-income or high-income households. Thus, nearly all new housing units are occupied by non-poor households. Poor households receive decent units through filtering down of older units from higher income households.

Low-income subsidy strategies also involve strict enforcement of high or moderate quality standards (usually the latter) for all new construction, but include large scale public housing subsidies allocated directly to low-income households. High standard versions require either larger total public subsidies or reach fewer poor households than moderate standard versions. The latter are better able to use the economies of mass produced or industrialized housing.

Minimal standard strategies involve only partial enforcement of any housing quality standards in urban areas, primarily in existing good quality neighborhoods. A great deal of the new construction under such strategies consists of zero standard units built by their occupants. Any housing subsidies employed can be either concentrated on the poor or spread over all income groups.

Additional variations of these strategies can result from differences in the magnitude of both total stimulation of housing production and total public housing subsidies.

The Likely Results and Effectiveness of These Strategies

The key results and effectiveness of these strategies can be assessed in terms of their locational outcomes and how well they cope with large scale migration of poor households to urban areas.

THEIR LOCATIONAL OUTCOMES

Filtering strategies cause a concentration of low-income households in or near the central cores of urban areas. Moreover, poor households can gain more housing units only by taking over those formerly occupied by wealthier households. Therefore, if the low-income population in an urban area expands rapidly, it must progressively displace more and more somewhat wealthier households through gradual outward expansion of the areas it occupies. This displacement or transition process causes systematic instability in residential occupancy patterns. It also tends to generate antagonism between the poor newcomers and those groups pressured to leave their existing neighborhoods. If older parts of the urbanized area are under a political jurisdiction different from newer peripheral parts (as in the United States), the concentration of poor households in the older parts can cause major political and fiscal disparities between the core and periphery in the urbanized area.

In contrast, since the other two strategies provide new housing for poor households, those households become concentrated on the outskirts of the urbanized area. Under a minimal quality strategy, nearly all poor households are located in shacks at least partially encircling older built-up areas. But under a low-income subsidy strategy, total subsidies are almost never large enough to house all badly housed poor urban households in new decent housing built on vacant land. Hence at least some poor households, often a large fraction of all those newly entering the urban area, must still concentrate in older existing units near the central core, as in a filtering strategy.

These locational variations have important social class impacts. Where all housing for low-income groups is provided through filtering (as in the United States), the poor are almost completely spatially separated from middle-income and upper-income groups. The central core becomes dominated by the former, and outlying growth areas by the latter. An opposite pattern of spatial segregation occurs in minimal quality strategies, with the poor living outboard of middle- and upper-class groups. However, many households who start out in shacks may gradually improve them as their incomes rise, thereby remaining in a primarily poor neighborhood. But in low-income subsidy strategies (as in Sweden and the Soviet Union), the new units occupied by low income groups are likely to be spatially close to or intermixed with those occupied by higher income groups.

Consequently, any attempt to introduce strong elements of low-income subsidy into what has long been a nearly "pure" filtering strategy (as the Department of Housing and Urban Development is proposing) requires moving from strong social class segregation (and in the United States, racial segregation) to much greater spatial mixture of social classes in peripheral areas. The political acceptability of this aspect of the strategy shift may be more important in determining its success than either the physical availability of sites or the cost of required subsidies.

COPING WITH LARGE-SCALE URBAN IN-MIGRATION

Large scale movement of low-income households from rural areas into urban centers has been a worldwide phenomenon in the past few decades. How well can these strategies cope with such movement, and what are the differences in their effectiveness?

During periods of really rapid inflow of poor people into a given urban area, none of the strategies can provide decent housing for all the newcomers, even in the wealthiest nations. Hence there is an inescapable surplus housing need which must somehow be met. If public authorities still prohibit construction of new zero standard or sub-standard units, this need is met through over-crowding or cutting up existing units. Sometimes public authorities themselves build new lower standard units on a temporary basis (such as the Veterans Housing at United States universities right after World War II). Where a minimal quality strategy is official policy (usually because the nation cannot afford any other), whole cities of new shacks spring up on the edge of existing urban areas.

No one really knows whether it is more desirable to overcrowd or cut up existing units than to build new substandard ones. Therefore, it is hard to compare the effectiveness of these different approaches. However, low-income subsidy strategies are clearly far more effective than filtering strategies at remedying these conditions among low-income households per million dollars of total public and private investment in housing. This is true because the former provide new decent units directly to poor households. On the other hand, the resulting interference with free markets tends to spread the impact of the housing shortage to middle-income and upper-income groups too, and to distort normal allocations of resources in the economy.

SOME TENTATIVE POLICY IMPLICATIONS

Space limitations prohibit any extensive analysis of the strategies summarized above, or their many policy implications. However, two related policy suggestions can be tentatively derived from them. Both spring from the undesirable results of a society's trying to require poor urban households to meet housing quality standards which are in reality beyond their capacity, or the society's, to achieve.

For example, in the United States filtering strategy, rigid prohibition of any new construction at less-than-high quality standards forces many poor urban households to live in over-crowded slum conditions. Thus, unrealistic insistence upon high quality in fact produces more low quality than is necessary. The low-income households concerned would be much better off if the United States allowed construction of new moderate standard units.[1] Then the limited subsidies voted by Congress for direct housing aid to poor households would generate far more units. Also, Congress might be willing to increase these subsidies because it would not seem to be putting poor people into better units than those occupied by the taxpayers providing the subsidies. The widespread insistence of poor households themselves upon very high standards for public housing thus requires them to endure miserable housing conditions longer than would acceptance of moderate quality standards. Some observers hope that Congress will provide large enough direct public subsidies to put every badly housed poor family in a high quality unit in the foreseeable future, or that the filtering process will work well enough to do so without huge direct subsidies. In my opinion, these hopes are largely wishful thinking.

Many poorer nations could also benefit from similarly accepting lower-than-optimal housing quality standards because they produce better results than unrealistically seeking higher standards. Some governments concentrate upon production of a small number of moderate quality subsidized units for the poor, while thousands more zero standard units are built in completely unregulated fashion. The net result would be superior if more public attention were focused upon trying to achieve even extremely low level standards regarding all housing, including shacks. For example, public funds might provide minimum-sized lots for shacks in selected locations, with streets, water and electricity available. This could help control the location of zero standard development so as to conform to urban planning, while allowing room on each lot for future upgrading and immediately providing minimal utilities for all residents.

Hopefully, other policy implications can be derived from the housing strategy model set forth above by examining the impacts of varying both key exogenous factors and the basic elements of each strategy.

Notes

[1] The recent surge of mobile home sales in the United States is in part a response to this need for lower quality housing. Mobile homes are much smaller than conventionally built housing, occupy less land, and are built with less durability. Yet their sales soared to 21 percent of all new housing units in 1969 precisely because so many households want new units, but either cannot afford conventional ones, or prefer to allocate more of their incomes to non-housing activities. Thus, the market is in effect sneaking lower quality standards "through the back door" on a growing scale.

7

The Law of Peak-Hour Expressway Congestion

Recent experience on expressways in large U.S. cities suggests that traffic congestion is here forever. Apparently, no matter how many new superroads are built connecting outlying areas with the downtown business district, auto-driving commuters still move at a crawl during the morning and evening rush hours.

To many a frustrated commuter, this result indicates abysmally bad foresight by highway planners. However, the real cause of peak-hour congestion is not poor planning, but the operation of traffic equilibrium. In fact, its results are so automatic we can even put them in the form of Downs's Law of Peak-Hour Traffic Congestion, or Parkinson's Second Law adapted to traffic: *On urban commuter expressways, peak-hour traffic congestion rises to meet maximum capacity.*[1]

Behind this law lies a complex set of forces which we can best analyze by constructing a model of commuter decision-making based on the following assumptions:

1. Every commuter seeks to minimize the total amount of time he spends en route to and from work, within four major constraints:

a. *Income.* This constraint limits the means of transportation available to the commuter. Helicopters are now the technically fastest means of movement available to most commuters, but only one in a million can afford them. Thus time-minimization means seeking the shortest time that is economically feasible.

b. *Money costs of transportation.* A marked change in these costs (such as doubling of the subway fare) may shift a commuter from one means of transit to another. For purposes of our analysis, however, we will assume that no changes occur in the money costs of various forms of transportation unless specifically mentioned.

c. *Place of residence.* Some residential areas are not served by public transportation. Others have very restricted parking for

Reprinted from *Traffic Quarterly*, Vol. 16, No. 3 (July, 1962), pp. 393–409, by permission of the Eno Foundation for Transportation, Inc.

automobiles.   Hence, each person's choice of where to live influences to some extent what means of transportation he will select in commuting. We will take everyone's place of residence as given for purposes of our analysis, even though the level of congestion may have definite feedbacks influencing long-run choices concerning job and residence location.

d. *Personal comfort.* Some auto-driving commuters could make faster time on public transportation, but the desire to avoid crowding and to be independent of time-scheduled trips undoubtedly makes comfort a factor in commuter patterns.

2. Most commuters follow the law of inertia. That is, once a commuter has selected a means of transportation and a specific route, he continues to follow it until some alteration in his environment pushes him across his route-decision threshold.

3. Route-changing alteration in a commuter's environment consists of some event which convinces the commuter that he could reduce his travel time by shifting his route (or his means of transportation.)

4. For convenience, we can classify all commuters into two basic categories: those with low thresholds (explorers) and those with high thresholds (sheep).

a. *Explorers* are imaginative, high-strung, aggressive drivers who constantly search for some new route that will save them one or two minutes' driving time.

b. *Sheep* are more placid, patient, and resigned than explorers. They tend to follow the leader and to travel the same route unless some significant change in their environment occurs.

Every weekday morning, thousands of commuters set out from their homes for work. Within the constraints described and through a process of trial and error, they choose means of transportation and specific routes calculated to minimize their time en route. Assume that there are two routes for auto-driving commuters from Natick, Massachusetts, to downtown Boston. Both routes carry commuters over roads also traversed by many more motorists driving to Boston from other suburbs, and by other motorists driving across the down-town-bound flow of traffic. Thus the congestion experienced by commuters from Natick is a result of the decisions made by residents of a great many other parts of the metropolitan area besides Natick. Out of these myriad individual decisions comes a "typical" time consumed going downtown from Natick on Route A and another "typical" time consumed by going on Route B.

Traffic Equilibrium

If these two times are about equal, then a balance is established for auto-driving Natick commuters. If they are not equal, imbalance exists. Explorers shifting from one route to the other, because of ephemeral obstacles on their usual path, will soon discover that one (say, Route A) takes less time; hence they will make Route A their normal path. Gradually word will filter around Natick and more driving commuters will shift from B to A. Similarly, commuters who live in other towns but also use routes A and B will be reacting in the same way. As the level of congestion on Route A rises and that on Route B falls, the total time required on Route A increases and that on Route B decreases. When the two travel times become equal, equilibrium has been established.

Normally, each such equilibrium is relatively stable because of the sheep, whose inertia keeps them grooved in the same route unless they receive decisive knowledge that another route is consistently faster. Since sheep outnumber explorers, the main streams of traffic on each major route remain the same day in and day out. On the margin, the explorers are ranging afield, testing other possibilities. If conditions change and they discover a faster route, they all vanish from the slower ones, and gradually some of the sheep follow. Ultimately, a new equilibrium is established.

In order to analyze the effect of a new expressway upon commuter congestion, let us assume that traffic equilibrium has been reached prior to the creation of the expressway. Then a new super-highway is opened connecting the downtown business district with outlying suburban areas. This road is a nonstop limited-access highway with multiple lanes in each direction. It has been cut through the city in such a way that its linear length is less than the length of any alternative combinations of existing streets. As a result, the no-traffic, nonstop driving time between the residential areas served by the new road and downtown is much less than on previously existing routes at any given automobile speed.

What happens to commuter congestion when such a new highway opens? To some extent, the answer depends upon what forms of public transportation are operating in the city concerned. Therefore we will consider three separate cases. We will also assume for the moment that both the total number of commuters and automobile ownership among them remain the same before and after the new expressway is opened.

Case A: A City with Auto-Driving Commuters Only

Where all commuters travel by automobile, the opening of a new expressway reduced peak-hour traffic congestion on many previously existing streets, because large numbers of commuters shift onto the new expressway. At first, they are able to make much better time on the expressway. However, word of this time disequilibrium soon spreads, and even more commuters shift from other routes onto the expressway. Gradually the time required for commuting on the expressway rises as peak-hour congestion increases; whereas the time required on alternate routes falls as traffic on them decreases. When these two times become identical, equilibrium is restored.

At the new equilibrium point, the rush-hour level of congestion on previously existing routes paralleling the expressway is considerably lower than it was earlier. Commuting on these routes therefore requires less time than before.

However, the rush-hour level of congestion on the expressway almost always exceeds its designed optimal capacity. For example, assume that the new road is designed to move 6,000 cars per hour past a given point at a speed of 50 miles per hour. When traffic volume at the peak-hour has risen to 6,000 cars per hour, these cars will still be moving at 50 miles per hour. Since this speed is probably faster than the speed attainable on previously existing city routes marked by cross streets and stoplights, equilibrium will not have been reached. More cars will move onto the expressway from other routes until the speeds on all routes are identical. However, even at this point, equilibrium will not have been reached. The expressway is shorter than the other routes; hence motorists traveling at the same average speeds over all routes will still arrive at their destinations faster on the expressway. Therefore route-shifting onto the expressway will continue until the average speed on the expressway is reduced to *below* the average speed on alternate routes. Clearly, the expressway was designed to handle traffic at *higher* speeds than previously existing roadways; yet, at equilibrium, traffic on the expressway is moving *more slowly* than traffic on the older routes. Therefore we can say that *congestion on the expressway has risen to surpass its optimal capacity*. This result is a necessary outcome of the forces of traffic equilibrium.

It should be pointed out that the maximum capacity of an expressway is not attained at the relatively high speed at which the designers of the expressway intended it to carry traffic. As the average speed of traffic along a major road increases, the average interval between cars rises, because drivers tend to allow themselves more room for braking. This reduces the total number of cars passing a given point in any period of time. In lower ranges of speed, such increases in interval are more than offset by the fact that more cars can pass a given point during one hour because the cars are moving faster. But above 35 to 40 miles per hour, the effect of larger average intervals between cars outweighs the effect of increased speed, so the total number of cars that can pass a given point in an hour declines. Therefore, as the number of cars entering an expressway per hour rises, a point is eventually reached at which all cars must slow down to accommodate the heavier traffic going by a given point in one hour.[2]

Since most modern expressways are designed to carry traffic at 50 miles per hour or faster, the number of vehicles they can carry past a given point per hour at this optimal speed is smaller than the maximum number which they can carry by this point in an hour. Therefore, when traffic volume rises markedly, the commuters' average speed is forced below this optimal speed, and congestion surpasses the optimal capacity of the expressway. As we pointed out above, this is exactly what happens in our theoretical model of commuter behavior.

The only way in which such heavy congestion could be avoided is through creation of a single expressway or system of expressways with such an enormous capacity that all the commuters formerly driving on parallel conventional streets could use the new facilities and still maintain optimal speeds. Furthermore, such facilities would have to be wide enough to carry most of these commuters *simultaneously*. Some auto-driving commuters attempt to avoid peak-hour congestion by leaving earlier or later than the period of greatest crowding. However, even if a new expressway were wide enough to carry *all* the peak-period traffic formerly moving on conventional streets, a telescoping of this "spreading out" over time would probably occur after the expressway opened. Drivers who previously left earlier or later than the peak moment to avoid maximum crowding would soon discover that they could depart closer to the peak moment, since the new expressway would reduce congestion at that moment. Therefore more and more commuters would tend to leave right at or around the moment of maximum convenience (assuming most government offices and businesses continued to open and let out at about the same time). This would tend to push the level of crowding at that moment back to where it was before the expressway was opened, although it would also make the total peak period of shorter duration. Thus convergences in commuters' *time schedules* as well as their *route schedules* tend to force the level of congestion on an expressway during peak hours upwards to the maximum capacity of the expressway. In pure theory, only a road or system of roads wide enough to carry every commuter simultaneously at an optimal speed would be sufficient to eliminate all peak-hour congestion. It is obvious that no such roads are practical unless we convert our metropolitan areas into giant cement slabs. Therefore Downs's Law still holds: congestion at the peak hour will rise until the commuters' average speed is forced below the optimal speed for which the expressway was designed.

In summary, a new expressway serving the downtown district of a city in which all commuters travel by car will have the following effects:

1. It will reduce traffic on existing streets, thereby decreasing the average journey time on those streets for the commuters who still use them.

2. It will carry very heavy traffic loads during rush hours, heavier than its optimal capacity; hence serious congestion will be created. Nevertheless, commuters using the expressway will have faster commuting trips than they did before it was opened.[3]

3. It will shorten the duration of the period of peak traffic congestion.

Whether the total time savings experienced in a city after a new expressway is opened—plus other benefits, such as greater safety—are sufficient to balance the cost of constructing the road depends upon the particular factors involved in each city; hence we cannot reach any conclusion about it here.

Case B: A City with Both Auto-Driving and Bus-Riding Commuters

A great many U. S. cities have extensive bus networks (some including fixed-rail streetcars) which carry thousands of commuters to work each day. How will the effects of a new suburbs-to-downtown expressway in such a city differ from its effects in a city with only auto-driving commuters?

Right after the expressway is introduced, congestion on all existing streets falls, as described in the first case above. This enables buses as well as cars to move faster at peak hours, thus providing better service to bus riders. However, in relative terms, bus service does not speed up as fast as commuting by automobile. Buses must stop and start to pick up and discharge passengers. Such delays take about the same time no matter how much traffic exists on the streets. The total amount of time thus consumed is a "fixed cost" of each bus route. For express buses which load in a few stops in outlying areas and run nonstop downtown (vice versa in the evening), this fixed cost constitutes a relatively small proportion of total trip time. But for local buses which stop every few blocks throughout their route, this fixed cost may consume a considerable portion of total trip time.

Therefore, even though the time cost of both bus and automobile commuting falls when the expressway opens, the time costs of bus commuting falls considerably less than that of automobile commuting. As a result, some commuters shift from buses to driving their own cars. This causes a rise in congestion that partially offsets the initial improvement in travel speed effected by the opening of the expressway.

The extent to which this feedback tends to return traffic congestion on city streets to its pre-expressway level depends upon such factors as (1) the percentage of commuters who traveled by bus on routes paralleling the expressway before the latter was opened; (2) the percentage of such bus commuters who used local as opposed to express bus service; (3) the incomes of bus commuters; and (4) the availability and cost of terminal parking facilities in the downtown area.

If any large number of commuters abandon buses and start driving to work, a second feedback occurs: the cost of bus travel per person rises. As passenger revenues fall, bus lines find themselves under increasing pressure to reduce service or to raise fares. Either move has the effect of driving more bus commuters to using their automobiles, thus worsening the bus revenue situation.

This second feedback has two possible outcomes. In the most drastic case, each attempt by the bus line to adjust to lower passenger revenues by raising fares or cutting service causes so many more passengers to switch to automobiles that another adjustment is required, which causes more passengers to quit riding, thus requiring another adjustment, etc., until the bus line goes bankrupt and ceases operation.[4] However, it is unlikely that construction of any one expressway in a city will cause its bus lines to go bankrupt. Each expressway serves only a part of the entire metropolitan area; whereas its bus routes usually serve a much larger portion of the area. Therefore a very slight fare increase over the whole bus system would probably compensate for a very large withdrawal of customers in the section competing with the expressway. For this reason, the shifts in modes of transportation caused by the opening of one new expressway are likely to bring about a new equilibrium at a point where most of the bus service extant before the expressway appeared is still in effect.

But completion of a whole series of new expressways in one city may produce a very serious cumulative effect upon the city's bus system. If all of these expressways together serve almost the entire area also served by the bus system, the total withdrawal of commuting bus passengers into private automobile commuting may be very large indeed. Hence the downward spiral into bankruptcy described above may actually occur. Because not many U. S. cities have whole networks of expressways serving commuters in all parts of their metropolitan areas, the results of this process are not yet clear. Of course, insofar as any revenue losses induced by new expressways are made up through subsidies to the bus lines, no spiral effect such as that described above will occur.

Assuming that some bus lines are still operating after a new equilibrium point is established, this equilibrium will have the following characteristics in relation to the pre-expressway situation:

1. Commuting time will be less than before the expressway opened for all commuters.

2. A smaller proportion of all commuters will ride buses to and from work, and a larger proportion will use automobiles.

3. Either the per person, per mile cost of providing bus service will have risen because of fewer passengers, or total bus service will have been curtailed, or both.

4. Because more automobiles will be used in commuting than formerly, a smaller improvement in traffic congestion (and hence a smaller reduction in commuting time) will have occurred than would have been the case if the same number of commuters used automobiles as before the expressway was opened.

Case C: A City with Segregated Track Public Transit and Auto-Driving Commuters

The third major type of commuter transportation (besides autos and buses) employed in the United States is transit with segregated tracks. That is, its rails or roadways are separated from other land uses and other forms of transportation (including streets) by elevation, depression, or fencing. Such transit includes subway trains, elevated trains, and steam and diesel-electric railroad trains. These forms of transportation all have one crucial characteristic in common: since their rights-of-way are completely separated from automobile traffic, the level of automobile congestion has no direct effect upon their speed or efficiency.

In a city served by such segregated track transit facilities, the effects of the opening of a new expressway are initially the same as those described in the two preceding sections. Traffic congestion falls on all city streets, and the expressway experiences heavy peak-hour congestion, but all street-using commuters (including those on buses and streetcars) spend less time en route than they did before the expressway opened. However, because the fall in traffic congestion on city streets has no effect whatsoever on the speed of vehicles using segregated tracks, commuters riding such vehicles experience no reduction in commuting time. *Thus there is a sharp change in the relative desirability of automobiles versus segregated track transit—a change favoring automobiles.* Consequently, many commuters who formerly used segregated track transit shift to automobiles.

Furthermore, the expressway cuts even more deeply into the segregated track system's noncommuter traffic. During rush hours, the expressway becomes extremely crowded, as indicated in previous sections of this analysis. But between rush periods, the expressway provides a relatively congestion-free, high-speed means for shoppers and other noncommuting travelers to move to and from the downtown area; hence it constitutes a dramatic improvement over pre-existing streets or other means of transit. This improvement creates a sharp disequilibrium in the previous distribution of noncommuting passengers among means of transportation—one proportionally much greater than the corresponding disequilibrium concerning commuters. Therefore a great many non-peak-hour travelers shift from fixed-rail transit to automobiles. As a result, the total passenger load of the fixed-rail, segregated track system becomes more and more concentrated in rush hours.

The New York subway system provides a striking illustration of this tendency. In the period from 1948 to 1956, the number of subway passengers entering the Manhattan business district on a typical business day during the morning rush hours (from 7:00 A.M. to 10:00 A.M.) fell 11.7 per cent. But during the other 21 hours of the day, inbound passenger loads dropped 20.8 per cent. These figures reflect both impacts of increased automobile usage upon segregated track transit: a decline in overall traffic, and a much heavier concentration of the remaining traffic in a few peak hours.[5]

These two impacts reduce both the total revenue accruing to the system and its efficiency in terms of cost per passenger per mile. As revenues fall and costs rise, the system finds itself in a perilous "squeeze." Its usual reactions are increases in fares and reductions in service or both. As with bus travel, these adjustments often cause further withdrawals of passengers from the system.

A dramatic example is provided by the Chicago and Northwestern Railway. Often cited in recent years as a model of commuter service modernization, the Chicago and Northwestern was making a small profit on its suburban passenger business before two new expressways opened in late 1960. Each of these superroads paralleled a set of existing Chicago and Northwestern tracks connecting downtown Chicago with outlying areas. Within three months after these two expressways opened, the railroad's suburban passenger traffic declined 9.6 per cent. Furthermore, this fall in traffic shifted the results of over-all suburban passenger operations from a profit to a loss.[6]

In any city where the number of nonautomobile commuters is relatively large, the shift from other means of commuting to automobiles may become extremely significant, especially if a whole network of expressways is built converging on the downtown areas. Some of our larger metropolises still have sizable pools of such potential "shifters" riding segregated track transit. In Chicago, about 45 percent of all persons entering the central business district on a typical day in 1959 used such transit.[7] In New York, 66 percent of all persons entering the Manhattan business district on a typical business day in 1956 traveled on segregated track facilities.[8] However, the number of persons using this type of transit is steadily declining as the automobile gains in popularity. Thus the percentage of persons entering Manhattan's central business district by auto and taxi rose from 15.7 in 1948 to 22.2 in 1956; whereas the percentage using segregated track transit fell from 72.4 to 66.4 during the same period.[9]

As more and more commuters start using their automobiles to reach work, the level of traffic congestion begins to return to the level existing before the expressway improved traffic conditions. Theoretically, such shifting could continue until the original automobile commuting time was re-established in spite of the added capacity introduced by the expressway.

Since the time required for commuting by rail is not changed by the introduction of the expressway, it would seem that the original equilibrium would reappear when the initial automobile commuting time was again required. But the original situation can never return. The new expressway has absorbed a great many former riders of segregated track transit, thereby permanently lowering the number of passengers using such transit. Therefore, even if congestion on the expressway rises so high that the original automobile commuting time is restored, the number of passengers riding segregated track transit at that point is much lower than it was before the expressway opened. Because of the high fixed costs in transit operations, such a fall in total traffic almost always raises the average cost per passenger. Thus when total passenger traffic falls, and that which remains becomes more concentrated during peak hours, segregated track transit firms are forced to raise fares or reduce service or both, as noted before. These changes diminish the attractiveness of their service compared to automobile transportation.

If a very large number of persons shift from segregated track transit to automobiles, the cost of such transit per passenger may rise so high that its attractiveness is drastically reduced. In such a case, congestion on the highways may have to become slightly worse than it was before the expressway was opened before automobile travel becomes just as undesirable as segregated track transit travel. But only the marginal equality of these two undesirabilities can establish a new equilibrium. We thus arrive at the paradoxical conclusion that the opening of an expressway could conceivably cause traffic congestion to become worse instead of better, and automobile commuting times to rise instead of fall!

In fact, this result is almost a certainty if the segregated track transit firms are caught in the kind of downward spiral into bankruptcy described in connection with buses. For if these firms actually go bankrupt and are forced to withdraw their services from the market altogether, all commuters formerly riding them will have to use automobiles or buses, and congestion on the streets will rise to record levels. The recent bankruptcy of the New York, New Haven and Hartford Railroad shows that this analysis is by no means purely theoretical. Of course, if government agencies or public receivers take over the bankrupt transit facilities and run them at a loss, this drastic outcome would be prevented.

However, it is probably likely that a new equilibrium will be established before highway traffic congestion has reached its pre-expressway level. But even in such cases, the expressway will be extremely crowded during peak hours—almost certainly loaded beyond its optimal capacity. Therefore the basic "Law" propounded at the beginning of this article—congestion rises to meet maximum capacity—will still hold true.

When a new equilibrium is finally established, it will have the following characteristics in relation to the pre-expressway situation:

1. A larger proportion of all commuters will use automobiles, and a significantly smaller proportion will use segregated track transit.

2. Passenger loads on segregated track transit will not only be smaller; they will also be more heavily concentrated during peak travel hours.

3. The aforementioned load changes will raise the per person, per mile cost of providing segregated track transit.

4. Segregated track transit facilities will have made a stable adjustment to their higher costs and lower revenues in one of the following ways:

a. By raising fares.

b. By reducing service.

c. By accepting lower profits (or greater losses), whether or not compensated by more subsidies.

d. By some combination of the above.

e. By going out of business.

5. Peak-hour congestion and average commuting time per trip on city streets other than the expressway may be less than, equal to, or greater than it was before the expressway opened, depending upon the shift of commuters from nonautomobile to automobile commuting.

6. Peak-hour congestion on the new expressway will surpass its optimal capacity; hence the average *speed* of commuters using it will probably be lower than the average speed of those using

alternative routes on older city streets (although the total commuting *time* for both will be the same), even if the average commuting *time* for all auto-driving commuters has fallen.

More People and More Cars

Throughout the preceding analysis, we have assumed that both the number of commuters and automobile ownership among them were the same before and after the expressway was opened. Removal of these two assumptions raises still further the probability that a new expressway will be overcongested during rush hours.

In spite of the explosive population growth in most U. S. metropolitan areas during the past twenty years, the number of persons in each major city commuting daily between outlying areas and the central business district has not always risen. In Chicago, for example, the total number of persons entering the central business district during a typical day in May declined from 1947 to 1959 by about 8 percent. However, the number of persons using automobiles to enter the same area during the same periods has risen about 15 percent.[10] Figures for New York City show similar trends.[11] This greater use of automobiles for commuting is only partly the result of new expressways. Actually, Chicago's two largest nonstop expressways for commuters were not opened until late in 1960; hence they have just begun to affect commuting patterns and are not reflected in the above statistics.

The primary causes of the shift to automobiles shown by these statistics are (1) higher automobile ownership and use and (2) the isolation of new areas of population growth from nonautomobile transit. From 1947 to 1959, automobile registration in the City of Chicago rose 67 percent; whereas total population did not rise at all. Within all of Cook and Du Page counties (including Chicago), automobile registration jumped 96 percent, whereas population increased only about 22 percent.[12] For the nation as a whole, motor vehicle registration from 1945 to 1959 rose by 130 percent to a total of 71.5 million vehicles, but population increased by only 33 percent.[13]

Thus, throughout the nation, the tremendous increase in ownership of automobiles during the postwar period has markedly raised the inclination of commuters to drive to work. Furthermore, low-density suburban housing has spread across the landscape into many areas quite distant from the nearest nonautomobile transportation. In such places, use of automobiles for getting at least part way to and from work is absolutely essential.

If we introduce into our model of commuting behavior analogous changes in (1) automobile ownership, (2) total population, and (3) population distribution, our conclusions regarding peak-hour overcrowding on expressways are strongly reinforced. Furthermore, automobile ownership is expected to continue rising rapidly, especially if real incomes continue to increase. The conclusion is inescapable that peak-hour traffic congestion on commuter expressways is likely to increase throughout the foreseeable future.

All of the preceding analysis is based upon the axioms concerning commuter behavior stated early in this article. If those axioms accurately describe the way commuters behave in the real world, our analysis leads to the following major conclusions:

1. Peak-hour traffic congestion on any expressway linking a central business district and outlying areas will almost always rise to surpass the optimal capacity of the expressway.

2. Therefore, in relatively large metropolitan areas, it is impossible to build expressways wide enough to carry rush-hour traffic at the speed and congestion levels normally considered optimal for such roads. The forces of traffic equilibrium will inevitably produce enough overcrowding to drive the actual average speed during peak hours to a level below the optimal speed.

3. Commuters driving on expressways should resign themselves to encountering heavy traffic congestion every day, even though they may spend less time commuting than they did before using expressways.

4. Since urban expressways cannot be designed large enough to eliminate rush-hour traffic congestion, other design goals must be employed to decide how large a capacity each such expressway should have. The only goal regarding commuting which is feasible is reduction of the average amount of time spent by commuters per trip. Low congestion and optimal speeds during nonpeak hours probably constitute much more practical goals for the design of urban expressways than any goal connected with rush-hour traffic movements.

5. Under certain conditions, the opening of an expressway may make rush-hour traffic congestion worse than before the expressway was built. This outcome can occur only in cities in

which a high proportion of commuter traffic is carried by segregated track transportation facilities before the expressway is opened.

6. Thus any program of expressway planning and construction must be integrated with similar programs concerning other forms of transit in the area if it is not to cause unforeseen and possible deleterious effects upon the level of automobile traffic congestion therein. In particular, marked improvement of roads without any improvement in segregated track transit may cause automobile traffic congestion to get worse instead of better. Since the U.S. has already launched a massive road improvement program, which includes construction of many urban expressways, continued failure to undertake an analogous program for other forms of urban commuter transit may result in a generally higher level of rush-hour automobile traffic congestion in those cities which now have extensive segregated track transit facilities serving commuters. Therefore such possibilities as the charging of direct tolls on expressways and the expenditure of auto toll collections or gasoline tax revenues on segregated track transit should be thoroughly explored as means of developing a *balanced* urban transportation system.

Notes

[1] C. Northcote Parkinson, *The Law and the Profits*, Houghton Mifflin, Boston, 1960. It should be noted that this article deals exclusively with expressways which do not require their users to pay any direct tolls in order to drive upon them. The possibility of limiting congestion on such roads by introducing high tolls has been extensively discussed in the literature of economics and highway planning. However, most of the commuter expressways currently being built do not levy any direct tolls on their users. Therefore the analysis presented in this paper is relevant to the majority of cities in which commuter expressways exist, are under construction, or are being planned. For a discussion of the toll problem, see James Buchanan, "Private Ownership and Common Usage: The Road Case Re-Examined," *Southern Economic Journal*, Vol. XXII, No. 3, January 1956, 305–316.

[2] For a discussion of relation between speed and hourly capacity, see Theodore M. Watson, Wilbur S. Smith, and Frederick W. Hurd, *Traffic Engineering*. McGraw-Hill Book Company, Inc., New York, 1955, p. 382. The table on the indicated page shows the following specific relationship for highways of four or more lanes:

Vehicles per lane per hour (maximum)	Speed
1,500	35-40 mph.
1,250	40-45 mph.
1,000	45-50 mph.

[3]For some evidence verifying this conclusion, see Paul T. McElhiney, "Evaluating Freeway Performance in Los Angeles," *Traffic Quarterly*, Vol. XIV, No. 3, July 1960, 296-312.

[4]The ultimate equilibrium point (even if it occurs only when the bus operator becomes bankrupt) is essentially determined by the immediate shift in the demand for bus service caused by the opening of the new expressway. If the demand curve for bus service shifts completely to the left of the average total cost curve of the bus company, bankruptcy will inevitably result eventually. If not, equilibrium will eventually be established with some buses still running. The spiral of repeated fare increases and psssenger losses which I have described is simply the process by which the bus company discovers the new equilibrium point (which may be bankruptcy). The spiral thus does not *cause* such an equilibrium to come into being. I am indebted to Professor Donald Bear of the University of Chicago for pointing out this relationship.

[5]Edgar M. Hoover and Raymond Vernon, (Cambridge, Mass.: *Anatomy of a Metropolis*, Harvard University Press, 1959), p. 218.

[6]Figures taken from a statement made by Mr. Larry S. Provo, Vice President and Comptroller, at a hearing before the Interstate Commerce Commission concerning the future of the Chicago and North Shore Railroad. Mr. Provo emphasized that the loss of passengers indicated was not a result of the general economic recession of 1960—1961, since the number of suburban passengers on the Chicago and Northwestern Railway had been rising in the recession months before the expressways opened, and also rose during the previous recessions of 1953-1954 and 1957-1958.

[7]*Chicago Area Transportation Study*, Volume II. Study conducted under the sponsorship of the State of Illinois, County of Cook, and City of Chicago in cooperation with the U.S. Department of Commerce. Chicago, 1961.

[8]Hoover and Vernon, *op. cit.*, 217.

[9]*Ibid.*

[10]*Cordon Count Data of the Central Business District*, Bureau of Street Traffic, City of Chicago, 1961. Table 3.

[11]Hoover and Vernon, *op. cit.*, 217.

[12]*Chicago Area Transportation Study, op. cit.*

[13]U.S. Bureau of the Census, *Statistical Abstract of the United States: 1960*. 81st edition. Washington, D.C., 1960, pp. 5, 560.

8

Losses Imposed on Urban Households by Uncompensated Highway and Renewal Costs

Urban highways and urban renewal are public outputs that impose many nonconstruction costs upon households living in the metropolitan areas where they are located. Yet present public policies ignore most of these costs by failing to take them into account when planning the improvements concerned, and failing to compensate the citizens who are compelled to bear them. This failure results in widespread injustice, and its heaviest burdens tend to fall upon citizens least able to bear them because of their low incomes and generally restricted opportunities.

This paper is aimed at remedying this imbalance concerning urban highways and urban renewal insofar as residential households are concerned.[1] It therefore seeks to (1) identify the nonconstruction costs which residential households are forced to bear by these two programs, (2) analyze which of these costs should be paid for by public authorities, (3) estimate the magnitude of certain key costs for which compensation should be paid but is not, and (4) indicate some policy implications of the analysis.

The Basic Principle of Compensation

People who are forced to move from their homes because of highways or urban renewal, or who suffer from environmental changes caused by these public outputs, sustain certain financial and other losses. These losses are essentially personal sacrifices which they are compelled to bear for the good of the public in

This paper is based on a study conducted under the auspices of the Baltimore Urban Design Concept Team and financed by several federal agencies. The opinions expressed are the author's and do not necessarily represent the views of Team members, the Maryland State Roads Commission, or any other local, state, or federal agency connected with the Baltimore Highway Project.

general, and of the beneficiaries of individual public projects in particular. It is therefore the duty of the public authorities concerned to compensate them for these sacrifices. Such compensation should place them in substantially the same status, in terms of economic and other well-being, that they occupied before being affected by the projects concerned.

Thus, the basic idea behind compensation consists of "making people whole" in relation to the injuries they sustain from public projects (other than paying their share of the input costs concerned, presumably through various taxes). Consequently, the losses imposed upon them should be identically offset by compensation provided to them, except to the extent that those losses are offset by the benefits provided by the project involved. In some cases, this basic principle must be substantially modified in practice. Nevertheless, it is the fundamental concept on which the law concerning compensation is based (insofar as a nonlawyer like me can determine), and upon which my analysis will build.

Types of Losses

The construction of major highways and urban renewal projects in urban areas imposes three basic types of losses upon residential households living in those areas, other than the losses resulting from paying for the costs of construction. In general they are losses caused by: (1) direct displacement, (2) uncertainty and delays connected with clearance and construction, and (3) other factors. Some of the individual losses listed are relatively self-explanatory, but others require considerable clarification. Twenty-two specific types are identified here and discussed in detail. They are listed for reference on pp. 224-25.

LOSSES RESULTING DIRECTLY FROM DISPLACEMENT

1. *Disruption of Established Relationships* Many households residing in any given neighborhood develop a number of well-established relationships with other persons, places, and firms in that area. These relationships include family ties and friendships with others living nearby, credit relationships with stores or banks, and habitual patterns of social and commercial intercourse. In some cases, particularly concerning elderly households, these

relationships represent the cumulative result of a large investment of time and energy in personal activity.

When these households are compelled to move, their relationships are often disrupted. The disruption can be minor, if the displaced household moves close by, or more serious or even fatal to the relationships concerned, if the household must relocate far away. The greatest hardship is likely for elderly people, since many no longer have the energy or the financial means to establish similar relationships elsewhere. To a great extent, these losses are psychological rather than economic.[2] Moreover, they are often encountered in the normal process of urban living. Therefore, displacement resulting from public projects sometimes merely speeds up moves and disruptions that would have occurred anyway. In such cases, losses accurately attributable to the public improvements are only those relating to the time period involved.

2. *Real Property Removal*   The creation of urban highways and renewal projects requires public acquisition of many parcels of land, both vacant and improved. The owners of these parcels and structures obviously suffer losses for which they are compensated by the government—normally, at "fair market" value. Fair market value is defined as the money price which a willing buyer would pay a willing seller under current market conditions if neither was under any compulsion to complete a transaction, both were fully informed about the nature of the property and its environment, and the property was exposed to the market for a reasonable length of time. In essence, fair market value is determined by establishing what the property concerned would have brought if sold on the free market at the time the legal proceeding is brought against the owner.

3. *Losses Due to Home Financing Arrangements*   Urban highways and renewal projects are frequently located in relatively low-income neighborhoods, where households may be purchasing homes through contract financing. Under this method, the occupant normally purchases the property at a contract price. This price, far above fair market value, has been inflated as a compensation to the seller for accepting a very low down payment (if any), and for dealing with a buyer whose credit standing is inadequate for obtaining a normal mortgage loan.

In contract sales, the seller often retains legal title to the property until the buyer has made a great many payments. When public authorities purchase the property they frequently pay the original seller, rather than the contract buyer, and the fair market value paid by the government is almost always less than the inflated price paid by the contract buyer. In such cases, the seller receives less from the government than the original buyer had agreed to pay him for the property. He may therefore hold that buyer liable for the difference. If so, the buyer may find himself paying for the property even after he has been ejected from it, and even though he himself did not receive any payment for it. This arrangement is clearly unjust, yet it is perfectly legal in many states.

On the other hand, the buyer can rarely be forced to pay the difference between fair market value and the sales price under these circumstances. Either he does not have enough money for a court judgment against him to be meaningful, or else the court will refuse to compel him to pay under the circumstances. When the authorities are aware of a contract purchase and know the name of the buyer, they often make both buyer and seller parties to the condemnation suit. This allows the court to wipe out all residual liability on the part of the buyer as part of the taking action. But the authorities do not always know contract sales are occurring, since there may be no legal record of the transaction until title actually passes.

When the government takes property obtained under a contract sale after the buyer has obtained title, the government's payment may be less than what he still owes on the property (which he has usually by then refinanced with a mortgage). However, this is less likely than the situation described above. In either circumstances, the government's taking causes an uncompensated loss to the contract buyer, who has been purchasing the property through monthly payments aimed at building up equity. When that property is taken by the government, the payment made for it is so small in comparison to his purchase price that all or nearly all of his equity is eliminated. This negates any efforts he has made in the well-established American tradition of saving money and investing it in the purchase of a home.

4. *Costs of Seeking Other Home* Persons displaced by highways must seek out alternative residential quarters, which requires investments of time and sometimes money. Some are compelled to perform this search during working hours, and to take on expenses they would not otherwise incur, such as travel costs.

5. *Costs of Paying for Other Home*   Anyone forced to move his residence must immediately find another residence elsewhere. In theory, if he initially lived in a residence worth $5,000, he should be able to move to another worth $5,000 and thereby find himself in substantially the same position he was before displacement. But in reality, it is almost always impossible for residents in low-income neighborhoods to find alternative housing elsewhere at the same low sum they received from the government (if they were owner-occupants) or at the same rent they formerly paid (if they were renters).

The fair market value of low-cost homes condemned for highway projects is normally lower than the current cost of similar dwellings elsewhere for several reasons. First, the units condemned are often run down and dilapidated. Second, they are usually old, and are obsolete in design, layout, and amenities. Third, they are often located in the most undesirable neighborhoods in the city (that is frequently why clearance is occurring there). Most housing units elsewhere are therefore worth more on the market. As a result, displaced owners cannot take the payments they receive and buy comparable housing elsewhere without additional cost, and displaced renters cannot find homes elsewhere at equally low rents.

An example of the plight of owners was recently revealed by a study of 112 displaced households in Baltimore. On the average, each white household involved had to pay $2,500 more for comparable housing elsewhere than it received from the government for its original home. Among nonwhite households, this excess relocation cost averaged $3,900 per household. Since the average original payments were $5,700 per household, the "excess relocation cost" of $3,000 represented an average 53 percent extra burden upon the households concerned.[3]

The degree of hardship resulting is greatest among low-income households, especially those comprised of older people. Persons owning expensive homes that are taken by the government can find comparable housing elsewhere much more easily. New units of similar quality and price are being constructed each year. Moreover, such persons are generally more competent and experienced in seeking alternative housing. It is true that construction costs have been rising so fast recently that even families in high-priced homes cannot easily take the fair market value of their older homes and buy new ones of comparable size, quality, and location. But it is certainly easier for them to come close to this objective than it is for low-income households. Little new low-priced housing (other-than mobile homes) is ever built in the United States except in public housing programs. And those programs fall far short of meeting the demand or the need for low-priced units. Consequently, there is a perpetual shortage of low-priced housing in most large urban areas.

The supply of such housing increases only through the relatively slow operation of "filtering down." This process involves a gradual decline in the price of older existing units until they are economically accessible to very low-income households. But large-scale migration of low-income households into a given city, or a slowdown in new construction such as that caused by high interest rates in the past few years, can cause the demand for existing older units to remain high. This keeps their prices and rents high too. Hence they remain beyond the economic reach of most low-income households. In such a situation, poor persons who have been given only the fair market value of their old homes find themselves unable to purchase comparable housing elsewhere—or any housing at all—for the same amount. For older persons no longer able to earn income, this can be a tragic hardship. Often they have worked hard to pay off all debt on the homes they were in so that those homes would provide them with shelter for life. Then the government forces them out of their homes, but pays them too little to buy any other housing elsewhere. They have neither the savings nor the earning capacity to pay the "excess relocation cost" necessary to find decent housing. Hence they may be driven into destitution through no fault of their own.

By failing to pay residential households enough compensation so that they can move into comparable housing elsewhere without loss to themselves, the government is essentially passing some of the true cost of the public improvement onto those whom it displaces. Moreover, this practice tends to injure most (severely) precisely the persons least able to bear any injury at all.[4]

To some extent, the higher cost of alternative housing accommodations results from the improved quality of those accommodations relative to the original units occupied by displaced households. Numerous surveys show that most such households relocate in dwelling units which would be classified as "standard" under criteria developed by the Department of Housing and Urban Development. Many of these households were displaced from dwelling units which would be considered "substandard" by the some criteria. To the extent that these displaced households live in better accommodations, it could be argued that the higher costs they pay do not constitute a loss imposed upon them by displacement.

On the other hand, this upgrading of housing quality is not necessarily the result of voluntary choice. Prior to displacement, they may have been living in relatively inexpensive substandard units because they chose to minimize the share of their incomes going to housing. After displacement, the share of their incomes devoted to housing almost always rises, whether they want it to or not. Insofar as improved housing quality is a result of involuntary restriction of their choice, it is not clear that this can be considered a pure benefit not requiring compensation. However, the improvement in housing quality which accompanies increased housing cost does constitute a complicating factor in any attempt to evaluate how much compensation should be provided in addition to fair market value.

This complicating factor is especially critical regarding renter households. Under present practices, displaced renters receive no compensation at all (except for moving costs in some states).[5] A study of real property acquisition in federally assisted programs made for the Congressional Committee on Public Works in 1964 indicated that about 58.8 percent of all displaced households and individuals were nonowner-occupants.[6] A study of over 2,100 relocated households conducted by the Census Bureau showed that a majority of rent paying households paid higher rents after displacement than before. Moreover, the fraction of their incomes devoted to rents rose, with the median shifting from 25.1 to 27.7 percent. The proportion of renter households paying over 20 percent of their incomes for rent rose from 67 to 76 percent.[7] Thus, there is no doubt that displacement generally forces renting households to pay more for rent, even though many are paying very high fractions of their income for housing already. (In the Census Bureau sample, over 35 percent of the nonwhites and over 24 percent of the whites were paying *more than 35 percent of their incomes for rent* both before and after displacement.)[8] Yet displacement also caused them to improve the quality of their housing, and even to occupy slightly larger units.[9] Deciding to what extent these households were compelled to bear "excess relocation costs" and to what extent they were merely upgrading their housing is certainly not easy. Yet there can hardly be any doubt that displacement forces these households to bear at least some uncompensated costs which they would avoid if they could.

6. *Moving Costs*   Clearly, transporting personal and other belongings from the dwelling acquired by highway authorities to the new dwelling costs resources. This fact is recognized by the law in most states. However, the Public Works Committee Report showed that only about 49.5 percent of the households and individuals displaced per year by all federally-related programs received payments for moving costs.[10] This study also estimated that only about 44 percent of the families and individuals likely to be displaced by federally related programs after 1964 would be eligible for moving-cost payments under the laws in force at that time. Thus, about 54 percent of the owners and 59 percent of the nonowners forced to move would not be eligible for such payments, although they would certainly incur moving costs.[11] The average size of payment made to displaced families or individuals for moving expenses was $119 under the highway program. This was larger than the average of $64 under the urban renewal program or $36 under the low-rent public housing program.[12]

7. *Higher Operating Costs at Other Home*   In many cases, living expenses other than housing costs are higher at the location to which displaced persons move than at their original location. This is particularly likely concerning commuting costs if they have had to move farther from their existing employment. The Census Bureau Relocation Study indicated that 37 percent of the displaced workers surveyed who had fixed places of employment stated that they had to spend much more time commuting to work than they did before relocation. Only 13 percent reported having to spend much less time; the remaining 50 percent spent about the same time commuting.[13] Moreover, households that have upgraded their housing involuntarily may encounter higher operating costs, such as greater heating bills and higher property taxes.

LOSSES DUE TO RELATED UNCERTAINTY AND DELAYS

In many cities, considerable time elapses between the first designation of a specific location for a highway or an urban renewal project and the actual taking of property in that area. Moreover, even before official designation, a long period of discussion about where each project might go often takes place. During the entire time from initial discussion to actual taking, the area concerned is strongly affected by both the possibility and then the actuality of future clearance. Owners of property in the area are extremely reluctant to make costly improvements because they believe their property will soon be demolished. Moreover, people outside the area are unwilling to purchase property in it because they could only use it for a short period of time. Thus, *the mere possibility that a highway or an urban renewal project will be created in a certain neighborhood produces a severe disruption of the normal processes of property turnover and maintenance in that neighborhood.* Furthermore, once it has become relatively certain that a highway or project will be constructed in an area, both commercial and residential tenants begin moving out. Few others can be found to replace them. This causes a decline in rates of occupancy in both residential and commercial property, and depresses the incomes of persons owning that property.

In many cases, all these consequences result from the mere discussion of a given neighborhood as a potential right-of-way or project site. But such discussion may last for several years before any specific area is officially designated. So these consequences may seriously affect a neighborhood which is not ultimately selected as the official location. The owners who suffer such losses are not eligible for any compensation from the government, even though it caused their losses. Specifically, property owners and residents in areas under discussion or actually designated as potential rights-of-way or project sites normally suffer the following losses due to delay:

8. *Deterioration of the Quality of Neighborhood Life*   This occurs because many store operators depart, reducing the variety of facilities available, and many residents depart, reducing the variety of persons living in the area. Furthermore, such departures create vacancies that encourage vandalism, crime, and physical dilapidation.

9. *Inability of Owners to Sell at Reasonable Prices*   Under normal circumstances, when a family head is transferred to another city, he sells his property on the market for its fair market value. But when a given neighborhood is under the cloud of impending demolition, few persons are willing to pay what was formerly the full fair market value for such property. Property owners are therefore confronted with a sharp depression in prices they are able to receive for their homes. They are either forced to sell at

these depressed prices because they must move, or forced to remain in the area because they are unable to get a price commensurate with their investment in the property. Persons who sell and move away also become ineligible for receiving any compensation when the highway authorities begin purchasing property. Thus, the financial losses they have been forced to endure by the highway are completely ignored under current legal processes.

10. *Interim Declines in Property Value*   For the reasons cited above, many properties decline in value once an area has been designated or even comes under discussion as a highway or urban renewal site. But in most states, the date at which fair market value is established is the date at which court action is taken by the government to purchase the property concerned. Many years may have elapsed from the time discussions of this site began to this legally established date. So the neighborhood may have sharply deteriorated through the mere "announcement effect" of the highway or project, as described above. Nevertheless, some sales probably have occurred in this area after such deterioration was far advanced. These sales then become the basis upon which appraisers establish fair market value, since appraisers use them to determine what willing buyers and willing sellers are actually paying for property in that area. Thus, property owners often receive from the government far less for their property than they paid for it, and certainly less than it was worth at the beginning of the process of discussion.

It is true that some owners of dilapidated and deteriorated residential property look forward to takings by the government. Such takings may "bail them out" of having to invest large sums in bringing their substandard properties up to conformance with local building and housing codes. For these owners, receiving even a relatively depressed price is a blessing in disguise. However, owners of code-violating properties are generally absentee landlords who are reasonably well-off economically, since owner-occupants generally maintain their property far better than absentee landlords. Thus, the small owner-occupants, particularly those possessing or buying single-family dwellings, suffer most from this.

11. *Losses of Rental Income*   Owners of residential income property are compelled to receive lower incomes than normal because many of their tenants depart, and others are unwilling to replace them unless rents are reduced drastically. Moreover, higher

maintenance costs caused by vandalism induced by the resulting vacancies further reduce the net income from such properties during the waiting period.

12. *Costs of Maintaining Property After Appraisal* The appraised value of the property is based upon its state of repair at the time of appraisal. But in some cases, several months may elapse between the appraisal and the legal action which finally takes the property. During this period, landlords may have to make certain vital repairs which do not appear in the appraised value and for which, therefore, they receive no compensation.

INDIRECT LOSSES IMPOSED UPON HOUSEHOLDS IN SURROUNDING AREAS

The impact of a major new expressway or urban renewal project is hardly confined to those persons directly displaced by its construction. Many other persons living or owning property nearby sustain losses because of the new improvement. The most significant of such losses can be described as follows:

13. *Higher Taxes Because of Greater Local Government Costs* The local government may incur added costs to prevent vandalism, increase police protection, and pick up additional debris caused by the deterioration of the neighborhood during the waiting period. These costs eventually cause a rise in property taxes or a reduction in other local government expenditures. They may fall on some of the displaced households themselves before they move, but their primary impact is upon the remainder of the households in the city.

14. *Disruption of Local Communications and Traffic* Unless a major highway is constructed on stilts, it normally blocks movement on a large number of the local streets formerly crossing its right-of-way. Urban renewal projects frequently involve the closing of local streets and the rerouting of traffic on more roundabout paths. Both these consequences decrease convenience of movement for local residents and others passing through.

15. *Reduction in Quantity and Quality of Local Services* Construction of a highway or an urban renewal project often adversely affects the quality of life in nearby neighborhoods by removing some of the facilities which served them. These can include commercial establishments such as stores and restaurants, recreational areas, aesthetic attractions such as trees, local transit service disrupted by the blocking of local streets, cultural facilities such as churches, and public education facilities. Not all of these

facilities are removed through demolition, but some lying outside the clearance area may abandon the neighborhood because of its reduced population, or may deteriorate in quality because of lower levels of patronage. In many cases, these facilities were located in deteriorating or dilapidated structures, and their removal may result in an upgrading of the physical condition of the remaining commercial establishments. Nevertheless, a reduction in the number of such establishments and their variety always decreases the choice available to remaining residents.

When the facilities eliminated are relatively unique (such as an excellent school or a park) their removal may constitute an irreparable loss to the community, greatly reducing its overall attractiveness. Under present legislation, no provisions are made for compensating the remaining community for losses of this kind.

16. *Reduction in Employment Opportunities and Increased Commuting Costs*   When industrial, commercial, governmental, or other employment-providing installations are displaced from an area, persons who formerly both lived and worked there are compelled to become unemployed or to travel farther for available jobs. Since most displaced establishments providing employment move somewhere else, loss of employment is usually not required. However, a relatively high proportion of small retail establishments in low-income areas forced to relocate are not reopened elsewhere. This proportion may run as high as 40 percent, and usually exceeds 20 percent.[14] The jobs formerly provided are completely removed from the market. Since such establishments normally employ local residents, the negative employment effects are concentrated in the surrounding area. More significant in terms of number of persons affected is the increase in travel costs to work imposed upon persons who formerly both lived and worked in the neighborhood.

17. *Spillover Impact Outside the Clearance Area*   As noted above, significant deterioration often occurs in the area where a highway or an urban renewal project will be located during the interval between initial announcement of its location and its final construction. The adverse impacts of such deterioration may spill over into surrounding blocks. This may reduce property values there, at least during the interim period until the new improvement is actually in being.

18. *Increased Competition for Low-Cost Housing*   When major public projects are constructed in relatively high-density low-income neighborhoods, they may require the destruction of

thousands of dwelling units within a given city. Such destruction causes a net decline in the number of housing units economically available to relatively low-income households elsewhere in the metropolitan area, the same number of such households as before will be competing for a reduced supply of housing units available in the price ranges they can afford. Theoretically, this will tend to raise the rents paid by *all* low-income households. The extent to which this theoretical effect is quantitatively significant in reality will depend upon the following factors:

The number of housing units destroyed by the public project in comparison with the total number of units available to low-income households in that area. Statistics concerning public projects in Baltimore illustrate the nature of this effect. In 1960, there were an estimated 95,000 housing units within the city limits of Baltimore occupied by low-income households (that is, those with incomes low enough to be eligible for public housing). About 64 percent of these were renter-occupied and 36 percent were owner-occupied.[15] In the period from 1951 to 1964, about 10,000 housing units in Baltimore were demolished because of various public programs, including highways and urban renewal.[16] Data concerning how many of the households displaced were low-income households are not available, although an informed but arbitrary estimate sets that figure at 75 percent. If so, about 7,500 low-income housing units were demolished in this 13-year period, or about 7.8 percent of the entire 1960 low-income housing inventory. This is slightly less than 1 percent per year. Consequently, such demolition would not seem likely to exert a very large upward pressure on rents in the remaining inventory.

The degree to which displaced households actually have access to low-income housing units elsewhere in the metropolitan area. In most large cities, racial segregation effectively prevents many Negro households from having access to relatively low-rent or low-cost units located in all-white neighborhoods. Yet a high proportion of the households displaced by public programs are Negroes. For example, the Census Relocation Survey selected a sample by getting the names of all families relocated by 163 Local Public Agencies in the United States from June 1 through August 31, 1964. Of the 2,300 families finally interviewed from this sample, 52.6 percent were nonwhite.[17] Since this sample includes Local Public Agencies in many smaller communities, the proportion of nonwhite is probably much higher in larger cities. This conclusion is borne out by Baltimore data. From 1951 through 1964, 89 percent of all households displaced by public projects in Baltimore were Negro households.[18] In 1960, the total inventory of housing in Baltimore occupied by low-income Negro (nonwhite) households amounted to about 43,000 units.[19] In the period from 1951 to 1964, about 8,900 Negro households were displaced by public programs. Assuming one housing unit was demolished for each displaced household, this means that such demolition equalled about 20.6 percent of the entire housing inventory occupied by low-income Negroes in 1960. The average of 890 units demolished each year equalled about 35 percent of the additional number of nonwhite households entering the Baltimore housing market each year because of net nonwhite population growth in the decade from 1950 to 1960.[20] Thus, when data for the *key segments* of the housing market are examined in isolation, the possibility that demolition connected with public programs might cause upward pressure on rents and prices in the remaining *relevant sections* of the housing inventory seems much greater than if data for the housing market as a whole are used.

The rate at which the supply of housing available to low-income households (and in particular, those being displaced) is being expanded through new construction or the "filtering down" process. The third factor in turn depends to a great extent upon whether the local housing market is in a relatively "loose" or "tight" condition. A "loose" housing market is one in which new units are being added to the total inventory faster than new households are entering or being formed in the area. As a result, the total available housing supply is increasing more rapidly than total demand, causing a downward pressure on both prices and occupancy rates. Under these circumstances, the filtering down process works relatively (but not absolutely) rapidly. Households in the middle- and upper-income ranges have many housing alternatives open to them. Therefore they more quickly upgrade their housing, thereby making a larger number of units available to lower-income families.

Conversely, a relatively "tight" housing market is one in which the demand for housing is rising faster than new supply is being created through construction (net of demolition). In such a market, increased competition for both the new housing units and the existing housing inventory creates an upward pressure on rents, prices and occupancy levels. Vacancies decline, and middle- and upper-income households find it more difficult to upgrade their housing. As a result, fewer existing units "filter down" to low-income households. Then, demolition of some of the housing units already available to such households because of a highway or a renewal project will have a far more serious impact upon rents for low-income households than when the market is "loose."

Low-income households are particularly vulnerable to shifts in the relative "tightness" of the housing market. They occupy the residual part of the housing inventory not claimed for use by higher income households. Since the latter have more money with which to bid for housing, their shelter needs are satisfied in the best part of the inventory. Moreover, new housing is almost always added to the upper-income end of the market, because cultural and other restrictions embodied in building codes and zoning regulations prevent the construction of new housing (other than mobile homes) at low enough cost so that low-income households can afford it.[21] These two considerations emphasize the dependence of low-income households upon the "filtering down" process as a source of additional available housing supply.

The housing situation of low-income households has become worse in the past few years because of a drop in the number of total new housing units started in the United States. In the period from 1962 through 1965, an average of 1.54 million new conventional housing units were started each year. But in 1966, only 1.20 million units were started, and in 1967 only 1.32 million units. This reduction in new housing starts occurred because of higher interest rates in the economy, rather than any reduction in the demand for new housing. In fact, the demand for housing has been stimulated by high-level prosperity. The resulting combination of rising demand and restricted additions to supply has created a very tight housing market in most metropolitan areas. This has caused declining vacancy and an upward pressure on rents at all levels of the market. *Consequently, the filtering down process has recently become a less efficient method of making new housing units available to low-income households.*[22]

The impact of a significant demolition of low-income housing units in a given neighborhood is magnified by the relatively restricted mobility of low-income households. Numerous studies have shown that members of many low-income households typically spend much of that part of their lives lived in the city within areas circumscribed by a very few blocks. As a result, they are relatively unfamiliar with housing alternatives available in distant parts of the metropolitan area. This is particularly true of Negroes because racial discrimination excludes them from many portions of the housing market. When such low-mobility households are displaced from their homes, they restrict their search for new housing to other areas nearby. Thus, *the increased competition for low-cost housing created by demolition for public projects does not spread itself out evenly across the entire housing market. Rather it becomes focused most sharply on other relatively low-income neighborhoods in the immediate vicinity of the clearance areas.* Consequently, demolition of what seems to be a relatively small number of housing units in comparison with the total number in the metropolitan area may still have a significant impact upon rents and occupancy in low-income neighborhoods surrounding the demolished houses. However, it is extremely difficult to measure this impact accurately. The effects of the pressure on rents and prices from this source cannot be separated from similar pressures from other sources (such as a general rise in the price level).

19. *Reduced Efficiency of Community Facilities Serving Surrounding Areas*   Schools, churches, stores, and other facilities near the clearance areas may be forced into less efficient operation by both the demolition of residences and the creation of the new projects. This can occur for either one of two opposite reasons. First, the reduction in their clientele or patronage may cause them to operate at an inefficiently low scale. This can adversely affect not only commercial establishments like retail stores, but also churches, social organizations, public schools, and medical facilities. This occurs when a significant proportion of the clientele of an organization is removed from the area, but the organization itself remains because it lies outside the clearance area, or the organization is cut off from convenient accessibility by its patrons. In contrast, if a public facility lies within the clearance area and is demolished, the diversion of its former load onto some nearby facility may overload that facility. An example would be removal of a public school and the diversion of its pupils to another already crowded school nearby. In either case, the reduced efficiency of the facilities concerned imposes a cost upon residents who live near but not within the clearance area.

20. *Changes in Relative Accessibility*   The purpose of the major highway is to improve the mobility of a large number of persons residing within the metropolitan area concerned. By altering the relative accessibility of different parts of the metropolitan area, such a highway has a dramatic impact on land values. The values of certain sites rise sharply (such as sites lying

near major interchanges and easily accessible to them). The values of other sites fall just as sharply (such as sites lying along former main arteries which lose traffic once the new highway is opened). These losses occur in all parts of the metropolitan area, not just in neighborhoods through which the highway itself passes. (This impact is caused by highways but not by urban renewal projects.)

21. *Losses Resulting from the Process of Construction*   Building a major public improvement often has a very disruptive effect upon the immediate vicinity. Local traffic is impeded both by added congestion and by the blocking of movement due to construction. The local government has to pay increased costs for traffic control and for the creation of alternative access paths. Businesses on surrounding streets lose sales because access to their property is diminished and heavy traffic congestion discourages patronage. Noise and vibration associated with construction may disrupt productive processes in nearby industries and generally lower the quality of the environment. Under present laws, no compensation is paid for all of these losses, even when they are substantial.

22. *Losses Resulting from Adverse Environmental Changes*   Public projects—particularly highways—often produce certain adverse changes in their immediate environment which reduce property values of adjacent parcels. For example, major expressways generate constant noise, higher levels of localized air pollution from exhaust fumes, the glare of lights at night, and increased congestion on some local streets near interchanges (but reduced congestion on others). Urban renewal projects may cause greater traffic congestion because of a higher proportion of car use among the new residents than the original ones and diversion of traffic. Even the sheer aesthetic effect of a major public improvement may influence nearby property values—usually downward in the case of major highways, and upward in the case of completed renewal projects (though perhaps downward during the waiting period before such projects are finished).

DISTINGUISHING BETWEEN REAL RESOURCE LOSSES AND REDISTRIBUTIONAL EFFECTS

Some of the nonconstruction costs cited above represent real absorptions of resources caused by highway and urban renewal projects. Examples are moving costs, losses caused by the process of construction, and costs generated by increased vandalism during periods of delay. Certain other costs do not involve resource absorption, but are redistributions of wealth from some households to others. Examples are higher rents or housing prices because of increased competition for housing among low-income households resulting from displacement, and losses in property values due to changes in the accessibility of various parts of the metropolitan area. For each household which suffers from these costs, other households gain corresponding (though not necessarily identical) benefits. Thus, when rents for low-income households rise, tenants suffer but landlords benefit. And when property values fall in some area where relative accessibility has been reduced, they rise in another area where such accessibility has been improved by the project concerned.

Welfare economists have long argued that these two kinds of costs must be distinguished from each other in making public decisions. Actions that absorb resources represent real costs that must be taken into account in deciding the allocative efficiency of undertaking some project. But actions that merely redistribute resources from one household or group to others represent distributional effects that are irrelevant to efficiency, as that term is used by welfare economists. Rather, such distributional effects are relevant to the *equity* of the project concerned.

All welfare economists agree that efficiency should be a key factor in determining public (and private) investment decisions. But whether such decisions should be based solely upon efficiency grounds, or upon both efficiency and equity grounds, is a matter of some dispute. In my opinion, equity effects are just as important as efficiency effects in deciding whether to undertake a project. However, exactly how these two types of effects should enter into particular decisions is an extremely complex subject which cannot be fully discussed in this paper.

In fact, this paper focuses exclusively upon the questions of equity and justice relevant to residential households which arise from the nonconstruction costs generated by highway and urban renewal projects. But the redistribution effects relevant to equity can result from *both* actions: those that absorb resources and those that merely shuffle them around among different households. Therefore, I have had to discuss both kinds of costs or losses, but, I have not distinguished between them insofar as their relationship to resource-allocation efficiency is concerned. This paper is not at all concerned with the allocative efficiency of highway or urban renewal projects, and will not discuss or refer to that important and complex subject any further.

Application and Modification of the Compensation Principle

WHY COMPENSATION SHOULD NOT BE PAID FOR ALL LOSSES

In reality, it is neither desirable nor possible to provide direct public compensation for all of the costs and losses discussed in the preceding section. In some cases, the positive impacts of the highway or urban renewal project tend to offset these negative losses insofar as individual households are concerned. Therefore, the public improvement inherently tends to "make people whole" even if no specific public compensation is paid to them. In other cases, there is no practical way of "making people whole" for the losses they suffer. Finally, there are a variety of losses which it is proper for the public to disregard for several different reasons. All these factors are discussed briefly below.

Some Losses Will Be Offset by Benefits As mentioned above, many land parcels gain greatly in value because of the increased accessibility provided by each new highway, or the local environmental improvement provided by most new urban renewal projects. This effect may offset some of the losses caused by the public improvement concerned. For example, increased ease of access to distant shopping centers may compensate automobile-driving local residents for the loss of some local community facilities. (Since most low-income residents do not own automobiles, this benefit has a relatively restricted distribution.) Similarly, if a completed urban renewal project greatly increases the number of high-income households in the neighborhood it may attract new and more diverse shops and improve the quality of services available in the area. Also, the elimination of low-cost residences and commercial facilities through clearance tends to reduce competition among those remaining, and may thereby enhance their value.

It is certainly true that the exact distribution of these benefits is not likely to be the same as the exact distribution of the costs and losses described earlier, even for a limited set of specific parcels (such as those near the project itself). Nevertheless, public authorities are legitimately entitled to take these benefits into account when trying to decide which types of losses for which to pay direct compensation.

Some Losses Must Be Considered Inescapable Risks of Property Ownership Dynamic change is one of the fundamental characteristics of a free enterprise economy. It inevitably produces unexpected and unforeseeable increases in the value of some properties, and equally unexpected and unforeseeable declines in the values of others. To some extent, such changes must be regarded as inherent in a successful free enterprise system. Hence there is no reason why the government or anyone else should guarantee continuance of existing property values as of any given moment.

It is true that governments adopt many policies specifically aimed at stabilizing values for whole classes of property, or entire areas. For example, zoning laws have this function. Yet even zoning laws do not protect the owners of every individual parcel from possible variations in value due to dynamic factors which influence the relative desirability of his neighborhood, or even of his parcel (such as the creation of a weird modern-design house across the street).

In reality, major public improvements constitute only one of the many factors that change property values. Others include purely private developments (such as new housing or industrial plants), natural events (such as hurricanes and earthquakes), changes in technology and overall economic demand (such as replacement of coal by petroleum for many uses, and the subsequent replacement of petroleum by nuclear energy), and social and cultural trends (such as the increased popularity of skiing).

Insofar as major urban highways and urban renewal projects are concerned, their impacts upon property values can be arbitrarily divided into *diffused* impacts upon properties in all parts of the metropolitan area, and *locally concentrated* impacts upon properties immediately adjacent to the improvements concerned, or almost that close. The diffused impacts can properly be considered as another of the many dynamic effects influencing property values which are inherent in a growing and changing economy. Therefore, the government need not compensate the myriad individual property owners who lose from this process, any more than it imposes special taxes upon those who gain. The losers can expect to pay lower property taxes if their property actually declines in value and this is reflected in assessments, just as the gainers can expect to pay higher property taxes for the opposite reason.

Locally concentrated impacts are far more likely to be both larger in proportion to total property value, and more easily traced to the specific public improvements concerned, than all other factors. Hence a reasonable case could be made, for example, for compensating property owners along a highway right-of-way for losses in value due to increased noise, ugliness, air pollution, and night-glare.

However, if such compensation is paid to locally concentrated losers, then it would be equally just for locally concentrated gainers to pay special taxes to offset their windfall capital gains. The absence of both these devices can be considered indirect evidence that the public affected prefers to risk suffering uncompensated losses in order to have a chance to benefit from unrecaptured gains. This is especially likely since total gains presumably outweigh total losses, or the improvements would not be made. Moreover, the difficulties and costs of computing precisely who gains and who loses from such property-value shifts, and by how much, are another strong argument for ignoring either positive or negative compensatory action, as is discussed below.

A dynamic economy similarly imposes certain psychological costs upon those living in it. Stable relationships are continually being disrupted or affected by the changes inherent in such an economy. A private apartment-house developer is not expected to pay for the psychological costs he imposes on previous tenants at a site where he buys some old tenement buildings, demolishes them, and puts up a new apartment project. Private developers are expected to pay the fair market price for the properties concerned, but not all of the other costs associated with change in any situation. Consequently, it would be unreasonable to expect the government to compensate every person who experiences a psychological loss because of the creation of a new public project, since it is part of the dynamic process of change inherent in social progress.

Some Losses Are Difficult to Measure   Some of the losses which have been described earlier cannot be accurately measured in such a way as to make compensation of the individual households concerned truly practical. Three specific difficulties connected with measurement can be delineated:

Nonmeasurability   There are no accurate methods of quantifying certain costs (or benefits), particularly psychological ones associated with the disruption of existing relationships. It is not possible, therefore, for the state to accurately assess the degree of such loss and compensate those concerned. This is particularly true because the only persons capable of assessing the loss—the persons affected—have a natural motive for exaggerating that loss if compensation is offered.

Nonseparability   Certain kinds of costs (and benefits) can be measured, but they embody composite effects of the public project and other forces at work in the economy. It is often not possible to discover how much of these effects can be accurately attributed to the project, and how much must be attributed to other forces. For example, increases in the value of any given land site can be caused by the impact of a project, by increases in population, by general inflation in the price level and by a host of other factors. Hence, it is extremely difficult even to estimate to what extent the public project is responsible for the change in land values that occurs in a given period.

Nonaccountability and wide individual variation   Certain types of costs are measurable and separable but difficult for public authorities to account for accurately, particularly because they are subject to wide individual variation. For example, the amount of time spent looking for alternative quarters can vary tremendously from individual to individual. It would be quite possible for each person to keep track of that time, and for authorities to place a value on each time unit. But excessive individual variations, plus a tendency toward over-reporting flowing from the natural interest of each person to maximize his compensation, would make complete compensation for every individual impractical and undesirable.

There are three basic methods of coping with the difficulties of measurement described above. The first is overlooking the costs concerned altogether. This is especially appropriate when the losses involved are probably not large for each individual concerned on the average. Second, standard estimates can be used as proxies for losses which are either nonaccountable or nonmeasurable. Third, public authorities can undertake actions aimed at providing benefits which tend to offset certain costs generated by the highway. For example, if public authorities created one new housing unit accessible to low-income households for every demolished unit occupied by a low-income household, and the new units were similar to the old in size and style and ownership, then no upward pressure on rents or occupancy levels would ge generated by the reduction in the supply of housing available to such households. Rather than attempt to measure the highly diffused losses caused by the highway, the authorities would nullify them by creating offsetting benefits. Such compensatory action is probably the only way to counteract costs which are diffused and probably small in each individual case, but occur over a great many cases.

SEVEN TESTS FOR COMPENSABILITY OF LOSSES

Any practical policies of compensation must take into account both the basic principle described in the first part of this report and the modifications set forth above. The result should be a set of practical policies designed to pay people direct compensation whenever the losses they sustain meet certain key tests. These tests can be summarized as follows:

1 *Attributability:* the loss concerned is in fact caused by the public project or the relocation generated by it, rather than by other economic or social forces.

2 *Significance:* the loss is relatively large both absolutely or in relation to the economic capabilities of those persons who suffer it.

3 *Noninherent Riskiness:* the loss cannot be considered an inescapable risk of property ownership, or an inevitable price of progress in a dynamic society.

4 *Identifiability:* the individuals or class of people who suffer the loss can be personally identified.

5 *Measurability:* the magnitude of the loss can be measured or estimated with reasonable accuracy, at least sufficient to design roughly offsetting beneficial actions.

6 *Deliverability:* compensation made for the loss by public authorities can be accurately directed at those who suffered that loss, whether they are individuals or an entire class of persons, and will not be received by others who did not suffer any such loss.

7 *Net Negative Impact:* the loss is not likely to be offset by benefits resulting from the public improvement and likely to be distributed in the same way as the loss itself.

It is clear that these tests represent the application of value judgments rather than purely scientific, economic, or legal principles. Hence, they are inescapably arbitrary. Yet, in my opinion, a compensation policy based upon both justice and practical feasibility will include compensation for all losses which pass the above tests. If losses do not pass these tests, I believe they are either not deserving of compensation, or else no practical means of providing it can be arrived at. However, my judgments are certainly open to argument and modification.

LOSSES THAT PASS THESE TESTS AND SHOULD BE COMPENSABLE

Table 1 lists all of the specific types of losses due to highways or urban renewal described earlier in this paper. It indicates which of

Table 1.   Compensability of Losses Imposed
Upon Residential Households

Kind of Loss	Does It Pass All 7 Tests?	If No, What Tests Does It Fail?	If Yes, Is Compensation Now Payable?
Losses Due to Direct Displacement			
1. Disruption of Relationships	No	5*	---
2. Real property removal	Yes	---	Yes
3. Losses on home financing	Yes†	---	No
4. Cost of seeking other home	No	2, 5	---
5. Cost to pay for other home	Yes	---	No
6. Cost to move to other home	Yes	---	Yes
7 Higher costs at other home	No	1	
Losses Due to Uncertainty, Delay			
8. Deteriorating neighborhood life	No	1, 3, 4, 5	---
9. Inability to sell home	No	1, 3, 5	---
10. Interim decline in property value	Yes	---	No
11. Losses of rental income	No	1, 3	---
12. Maintenance after appraisal	Yes	---	No
Indirect Losses in Surrounding Areas			
13. Higher taxes	No	1, 6	---
14. Disruption of traffic, etc.	No	3, 5	---
15. Deteriorating local services	No	5, 6	---
16. Reduced employment, etc.	No	1, 3, 5	---
17. Spillover effect outside area	No	1, 3, 5	---
18. Increased competition for low-cost housing	Yes	---	No
19. Reduced efficiency of community services in surrounding areas	Yes†	---	No
20. Changing relative accessibility	No	1, 3, 7	---
21. Losses from construction	Yes†	---	No
22. Losses from adverse environmental changes	Yes†	---	No

*Numbers refer to the classification of tests for compensability on page 214.
†Partially compensable.

these losses pass the seven tests mentioned above. The table also shows which tests are failed by those losses which do not pass all seven tests, and whether or not those which do pass are compensable under existing laws and regulations.

The subjective nature of the judgments expressed in this table should be emphasized. They are open to dispute on nonscientific grounds. Moreover, these judgments are not based upon the professional expertise of lawyers, but rather the inferences of economists. So they are certainly subject to further modification. However, they have been set forth here as a tentative start toward a more systematic development of public compensation policies than is embodied in present laws and regulations. Based upon the findings set forth in this table, six of the specific types of losses described earlier in this report are subject to full compensation, and four others to partial compensation. Eight of these ten losses are not now considered compensable under existing laws and regulations.[23] Hence, the analysis we have presented has led to conclusions quite divergent from existing compensation practices, as will be further explored below. The ten fully or partly compensable losses can be divided into four basic types, as follows:

1. Compensation paid directly to individuals displaced for nonwaiting costs, including: payment of the *fair market value* of real property taken as of the time of the taking; payment for some of the *losses of investment* resulting from specific financing arrangements not accounted for in the computation of fair market value; payment for the *"excess relocation costs"* of acquiring or renting alternative property; that is, the costs of such acquisition or renting in excess of fair market value or previous rentals paid; and payment for the *costs of moving.*

2. Compensation to owners of property for costs created by delays in the project including: estimated *losses of fair market value* occurring between the time a site is officially adopted and the time the legal proceedings are made against individual property owners; and estimated *costs of maintenance and repairs* made between the time of final appraisal and actual taking procedures.

3. Compensation to the housing market in general to offset the impact upon rents and prices of a reduced inventory of dwellings available to low-income households. This would consist of the provision of additional dwelling units by public authorities (whether built by them or paid for by them and built by private interests) so as to counteract the increasing "tightness" of the low-income household market caused by demolition of housing

units formerly available in that market. The number, size, and type of units that would be made available by public authorities in comparison to the number demolished would depend on particular housing conditions in the area concerned, including the degree to which racial segregation restricted the accessibility of the existing inventory to members of racial minority groups displaced.

4. Compensation to the neighborhood in general and the property owners in areas lying outside the clearance area, including: payments for *disruptions connected with construction* of the highway itself; provision of *additional public facilities and services* to offset facilities demolished in order to create the highway (such as public schools); and payments to adjacent or nearby owners to offset *losses due to increased noise, ugliness, air pollution, or other adverse environmental effects.*

Serious Injustice Results from Failure to Pay Compensation

The fact that governments fail to pay compensation for losses they inflict upon certain residential households does not in itself indicate that present compensation policies should be changed. No social institution perfectly conforms in practice to what it should do theoretically. In many cases, society endures such behavioral imperfections because their consequences are not serious. Those consequences neither constitute a great injustice for any sizable group, nor waste significant amounts of resources that could be more effectively used, nor threaten the rest of society with dire consequences. Correcting such imperfections is often not worth the cost in terms of legislative, administrative and general public attention, even if it might produce some net economic benefits or greater justice.

Therefore, in order to assess the policy implications of government's failure to pay compensation for the losses that I have indicated are properly compensable, it is necessary to roughly estimate the nature and magnitude of that failure's consequences.

CONCENTRATION OF LOSSES AMONG LOW-INCOME MINORITY-GROUP HOUSEHOLDS

The losses caused by urban highways and urban renewal for which no compensation is now paid are not spread evenly throughout the nation's population. By their very nature, they are concentrated upon the households which these public programs displace, and other households living close to the clearance areas involved. But these public programs tend to select locations where a high proportion of low-income, minority-group households reside.

This is true for four reasons. Three result from the fact that such households have a high proclivity for living in the oldest and most dilapidated housing in each metropolitan area, particularly within central cities. They do so because such housing is the least expensive available, and they are poor. Also, their choice of alternative locations—particularly in the suburbs—is restricted by ethnic discrimination in housing markets. Urban highways and urban renewal projects are concentrated in areas where such housing is found for four general reasons:

1. City planners often use these programs as a means of getting rid of the oldest and least desirable housing in the existing inventory. This is one of the explicit functions of urban renewal, which can only be done in relatively deteriorated areas.

2. The oldest housing is usually found in close proximity to central business districts, since U.S. cities, like most others, developed outward from the center. But major highways also focus on the area peripheral to central business districts because that is the optimal location for certain traffic arteries skirting or serving the downtown area.

3. Property in these areas is less expensive than elsewhere, since it is older and more dilapidated. Therefore, routing highways through such neighborhoods reduces total acquisition costs, especially since so many of the true costs of displacement are not borne by the government but by the households displaced.

4. Members of low-income ethnic minorities have not in the past been very well-organized politically to oppose the routing of highways through their neighborhoods, or the location of urban renewal projects there. In contrast, higher-income residents and owners of industrial and commercial property generally have the organizational and financial capability, and the political connections, to offer strenuous opposition to the location of these public improvements in their neighborhoods. This has happened in dozens of cities across the country, from Beverly Hills to Cambridge. To at least some extent, highway and urban renewal officials responsible for selecting routes and sites are naturally motivated to follow the geographic path of least political resistance. Until recently, that path has often run directly through the lowest-income neighborhoods.

As a result of these factors, almost all urban renewal projects, and a great many inner-city segments of federally-assisted highway systems, either have been constructed, or are planned for, sites and routes in low-income minority-group neighborhoods, particularly Negro areas. As the recent report of the National Advisory Commission on Civil Disorders clearly established, the residents of these neighborhoods include many of the poorest and most deprived citizens in the nation.[24] To concentrate the uncompensated losses resulting from urban highways and urban renewal upon them is triply unjust, as well as socially dangerous. It is triply unjust because these households are the least able to pay such costs, derive the least benefits from the projects concerned, and are already unfairly compelled by society to bear heavy burdens resulting from racial discrimination and segregation. It is socially dangerous because the residents of these areas have recently begun to react violently to their conditions of life, and may be stimulated to further violence by the injustices of society's failure to pay proper compensation for the losses described earlier.

In most cities, government officials are not likely to ameliorate the loading of these uncompensated losses upon low-income minority households by rerouting highways into wealthier areas. The "political heat" from such rerouting would be too great. Nor are they likely to shift urban renewal projects out of low-income neighborhoods, because the legal requirements for eligibility require concentrating them in such neighborhoods. Therefore, this kind of unjust concentration of losses can be avoided only by ceasing to construct such public projects altogether, or providing adequate compensation for the losses involved.

ROUGH ESTIMATES OF THE MAGNITUDE OF CERTAIN KEY UNCOMPENSATED LOSSES

But how large are these uncompensated losses? If they are relatively small, then perhaps they will not stimulate disorder. Nor will they create any more injustice than a thousand of the other essentially irremediable frictions that are inescapable in a large modern society. Thus, at least a rough quantitative analysis is crucial in assessing the policy implications of these losses.

The number of households likely to be displaced by all urban highways and urban renewal projects has been estimated by the Public Works Committee Report. About 96,400 households (including both families and individuals) will be displaced each year from 1964 through 1972. This includes all urban renewal displacement, and 82 percent of all highway displacement (since 18 percent of highway displacement in the past few years has been in rural areas).[25]

In past urban renewal displacement, about 27 percent of all displaced households were individuals, and 73 percent were families. The median sized displaced family contained 3.0 persons.[26] If these figures are applied to future urban displacement for both highways and urban renewal, then about 237,200 persons per year would be displaced by these programs. Moreover, it is reasonable to assume that at least an equal number of persons in surrounding areas are likely to be affected by some of the costs described earlier. Thus, in the eight years from 1964 to 1972, a total of about 3.8 million persons would be unfairly compelled to pay costs associated with displacement resulting from these two programs—including 1.9 million who would be directly displaced. Although this total constitutes less than 2 percent of the entire U.S. population, it is clearly a significant number. Estimating the magnitude of uncompensated costs imposed upon these persons is much more difficult than estimating the number of persons involved. However, a few rough calculations can be made as follows:

1. About 61,300 renter households will be displaced each year in urban areas by highways and urban renewal.[27] Displacement will compel most of these households to pay higher rents. The Census Bureau Relocation Study estimated that median rents for families (excluding individuals) were raised by relocation from $65 per month to $67 among nonwhites, and from $68 per month to $83 among whites.[28] The federal government has proposed compensating such renter families by means of a lump-sum equivalent to a monthly rent subsidy over a two-year period. The monthly subsidy would equal the difference between the family's rent after relocation in standard housing and 20 percent of its monthly income.[29] I am not familiar with the logical justification for this particular compensation formula. Perhaps a better one could be conceived. But for purposes of initial estimation, I have used it. Employing the median incomes of relocated families for 1964 reported in the Census Bureau Relocation Study, and assuming that 53 percent of all relocated families would be nonwhite, I calculated a weighted average total compensation of $221 for each renter family displaced. I further assumed that individuals should receive the same compensation as

families. (Even though individuals pay lower rent, they also have lower incomes.) Under these assumptions, the annual cost of compensating all displaced renter households for being compelled to pay higher rents would be $13.5 million.

2. About 35,100 owner-occupant households will be displaced each year in urban areas by highways and urban renewal.[30] In order to buy housing of quality comparable to that from which they were displaced (or somewhat superior), these households will have to pay a premium over the fair market values of their original homes. The Public Works Committee Report indicates the fair market values of a sample of 26,900 homes purchased by various government authorities in clearance operations were:[31] under $6,000, 29.0 percent; $6,000-$15,000, 51.5 percent; and over $15,000, 19.5 percent.

I assume that the average value of all homes under $6,000 was $4,000; the average value of those from $6,000 to $15,000 was $10,500; and the average value of those over $15,000 was $20,000. These assumptions yielded a weighted average fair market value of about $10,500. The relocation study in Baltimore cited earlier indicated that the average premium paid by home owners with relatively low-valued homes was about 53 percent.[32] But the premium for higher-value homes is likely to be a lower percentage. Therefore, I arbitrarily calculated the average premium for all future home-owner relocations at both 30 percent and 50 percent. To offset such premiums, the total compensation at 30 percent would be $110.6 million; at 50 percent, $184.3 million would be required.

3. The destruction of 96,400 housing units per year in urban areas by highways and urban renewal will reduce the supply of housing available there, especially for low-income households. This will tend to drive up the cost of both owned and rented housing for thousands of households who are not displaced, as well as for those who are displaced. Owners will gain from this effect, since the values of their properties will rise. But renters will suffer, since they will have to pay more. However, it is impossible to measure accurately the increase in rents which each individual nondisplaced household will have to pay because of this reduced supply. Therefore, I believe the only practical way to compensate them is to offset the drop in supply caused by displacement by building new housing available to low-income households. In "tight" housing markets, such an offset might require building one new unit for every one demolished. In "loose" housing markets, very

little new construction might be required. It is extremely difficult to estimate accurately the requirements for such an offset for the nation as a whole. A crude estimate is that one new unit should be constructed for every two units demolished. If the average unit so constructed cost $15,000, then the total capital cost of building 48,200 units would be $723.0 million per year.

However, it would be possible to provide incentives for private investors to put up all of this capital. The government would have to furnish subsidies that would virtually guarantee a successful market for such housing at a reasonable rate of return. Use of a below-market-interest-rate subsidy would not enable the very lowest-income households to afford such housing. But it would make it available to most displaced households. I have assumed the government would underwrite 6 percent interest by borrowing money with 6 percent bonds and lending it at zero percent interest. If 40-year financing is used, this form of subsidy would involve a cash outlay of $623 per unit per year. Therefore, creation of 48,200 units per year would require an annual subsidy of $30.0 million.

It is not certain, and may even be unlikely, that the cost of thus preventing non-displaced renters from suffering injuries from a reduction in housing supply would equal the size of the injuries they would sustain if no prevention occurred. Yet there is no simple way to estimate the size of these injuries; so I will arbitrarily assume they equal the cost of preventing them.

4. The Public Works Committee Report estimates that about 20,520 households per year to be displaced by highways will not be covered by programs providing compensation for moving costs.[33] (All households displaced by urban renewal will be covered by such programs.) The average payment for moving expenses made to those households displaced by highways who actually received such payments was about $119.[34] If this same average payment is extended to an additional 20,520 households per year, the annual cost will be $2.4 million.

These calculations do not cover all of the uncompensated costs likely to be imposed upon residential households in urban areas by highways and urban renewal. However, I believe they encompass the largest of those uncompensated costs. The total amount required to provide compensation for those discussed above would range from $156.5 to $230.2 million per year, depending upon the size of the premium which displaced owners would have to pay to obtain comparable housing elsewhere.

Thus, *present practices in urban areas regarding residential households displaced by highways and urban renewal projects will unfairly impose uncompensated costs of at least $156.5 to $230.2 million per year (in 1968 dollars) upon approximately 237,200 displaced persons and at least another 237,200 non-displaced persons.* In my opinion, this represents injustice on a massive scale. It amounts to an uncompensated loss averaging from $812 to $1,194 per household for each of the estimated 192,800 households involved. The median income of these households is probably around $4,000 per year.[35] Therefore, *the average uncompensated loss which each is compelled to suffer amounts to confiscation of from 20 to 30 percent of one year's income.* Admittedly, the calculations upon which these conclusions have been based are extremely crude. Yet I believe they are more likely to be too low than too high. How much proportionally would paying proper compensation for these costs add to the present nonconstruction costs of urban highways and urban renewal? Expected compensation for all real property—residential and nonresidential—to be acquired in urban areas under these two programs is estimated at $1.084 billion per year from 1964 to 1972 by the Public Works Committee Report.[36] This does not include moving and other relocation costs. But those costs are undoubtedly smaller than the costs of acquiring nonresidential property. So this figure is a high estimate of all costs which will be paid to displaced residential households under current compensation practices. Adding the estimated costs of paying compensation for the specific losses quantified above would increase this total by from 14 to 21 percent per year.

Conclusion

It is clear that present compensation practices related to residential households displaced by highways and urban renewal are grossly unfair. Those practices in effect shift a substantial part of the true costs of acquiring property for these improvements onto the residential households they displace and others nearby. These households are forced to bear from 14 to 21 percent of the real costs of acquiring urban residential land for such improvements. This injustice results in forcing relatively low-income families and individuals to bear heavy financial burdens which really ought to be paid by society as a whole or by the specific beneficiaries from the improvements concerned.

Public policies which clearly cause massive injustice should be changed as soon as possible. Therefore, I believe the authorities responsible for urban highways and urban renewal projects should immediately begin detailed exploration of practical methods for correcting these undesirable results of their past and present behavior. These methods should include finding means of calculating the magnitude of each presently uncompensated loss suffered by each household concerned, and means of either paying proper compensation for such losses, or taking actions which will offset their effects.

Some suggestions for achieving these objectives have been made in various parts of this paper. Yet the real purpose of this paper has been to indicate the nature of the problem, and to prove that it is large enough to demand immediate remedial action. If it has succeeded in this purpose, then the complex and difficult work of devising such action should soon begin.

The Kinds of Losses Imposed Upon Residential Households by Urban Highway and Urban Renewal Projects (Other Than Construction Costs)

A. *Losses imposed upon residential households by displacement itself*
1.   Disruption of established personal and other relationships
2.   Losses due to the taking of real property
3.   Losses due to home financing arrangements, especially contract buying
4.   Costs of seeking alternative housing elsewhere
5.   Costs of paying for alternative housing elsewhere
6.   Moving costs
7.   Higher operating costs of residing elsewhere

B. *Losses imposed upon residential households by uncertainties and delays*
8.   Deterioration in the quality of life during waiting periods
9.   Inability of property owners to sell property at reasonable prices during waiting periods
10. Declines in the value of properties during waiting periods because of neighborhood and individual property deterioration
11. Losses of income suffered by owners of rental property because of the departure of tenants before actual taking occurs

12. Costs of maintaining property after its fair market value has been established for purposes of litigation

C. *Losses imposed upon residential households not directly displaced but located in surrounding areas*

13. Higher taxes paid because of increased city costs to counteract vandalism and other deterioration in the area

14. Disruption of local communications through the blocking of streets

15. Reduction in the quantity and quality of commercial and other services available in the area because they have left or been displaced

16. Reduction in employment opportunities and increased costs of travelling to work because firms have been compelled to move elsewhere or have gone out of business

17. Spillover effects of deterioration in the clearance areas during the waiting periods

18. Higher rents or housing prices because of increased competition for housing among low-income households resulting from displacement

19. Reduction in the efficiency of community facilities through:

    a. Loss of patronage if displacement has removed customers

    b. Overcrowding if displacement has removed alternative sources of supply (such as a local school)

20. Losses in property values due to changes in the accessibility of various parts of the metropolitan area

21. Losses resulting from congestion, vibration, noise, street blockage, dust, and other negative factors involved in the process of constructing the new highway or urban renewal project

22. Losses in property values due to increased ugliness, noise, air pollution, or other adverse effects of the completed highway or urban renewal project

Notes

[1] Other similar losses are imposed upon commercial, industrial, and institutional establishments by urban highways and urban renewal. Although many of the principles discussed in this paper also apply to losses sustained by these establishments, we have not considered any such losses or proper public policies regarding them in this paper.

[2] A discussion of such losses is presented by Marc Fried in "Grieving for a Lost Home: Psychological Costs of Relocation," in James Q. Wilson, editor, *Urban Renewal: The Record and the Controversy* (Cambridge: M.I.T. Press, 1966), pp. 359–79.

[3] Unpublished letter describing the results of a survey conducted by the Baltimore Urban Renewal and Housing Agency.

[4] Not long after this article was written, Congress passed the Federal-Aid Highway Act of 1968, which contained measures specifically aimed at compensating households for "excess" costs of obtaining adequate housing after they had been displaced. Section 506 allows payment of up to $5,000 for "the amount, if any, which, when added to the acquisition payment, equals the average price required for a comparable dwelling determined, in accordance with standards established by the Secretary, to be a decent, safe, and sanitary dwelling adequate to accommodate the displaced owner, reasonably accessible to public services and places of employment and available on the private market." An earlier version of this article was submitted to a Congressional Committee conducting hearings on this Act, and therefore may have had at least a modest influence in helping to cause adoption of this improvement in federal compensation practices.

[5] The Federal-Aid Highway Act of 1968 also contained provision for payment of some compensation to renting families displaced by highways—thereby significantly remedying this condition. Specifically, Section 506 of the Act allows payment of up to $1,500 for displaced renter households "to enable such persons to lease or rent for a period not to exceed two years, or to make the down payment on the purchase of, a decent, safe, and sanitary dwelling of standards adequate to accommodate such individual or family in areas not generally less desirable in regard to public utilities and public and commercial facilities."

[6] Select Subcommittee on Real Property Acquisition, Committee on Public Works, U.S. House of Representatives, *Study of Compensation and Assistance for Persons Affected by Real Property Acquisition in Federal and Federally-Assisted Programs.* (Committee Print No. 31, 88th Congress, 2nd Session), (Washington: Government Printing Office, 1965), p. 21. Henceforth this document will be referred to in both the text and footnotes as the Public Works Committee Report.

[7] U.S. Housing and Home Finance Agency, "The Housing of Relocated Families: Summary of a Census Bureau Survey," in James Q. Wilson, *op. cit.*, p. 344. Henceforth this document will be referred to as the Census Bureau Relocation Study.

[8] *Ibid.*

[9] *Ibid.*, pp. 340–41, 347–48.

[10] Public Works Committee Report, p. 24.

[11] *Ibid.*, p. 25.

[12] *Ibid.*, p. 37.

[13] Census Bureau Relocation Study, p. 350.

[14] Public Works Committee Report, p. 30.

[15] U.S. Census Bureau.

[16] Baltimore Urban Renewal and Housing Agency, *Displacement and Relocation-Past and Future* (March 1965). Henceforth this document which described the period 1951 through 1964, will be referred to as the BURHA Report.

[17] Census Bureau Relocation Study, p. 337.

[18] BURHA Report.

[19] U.S. Census Bureau.

[20] U.S. Census Bureau.

[21]The only exception is public housing. It is just as expensive as private housing to build, but is subsidized sufficiently so that low-income households can afford it. But the supply of public housing in the United States is very small in comparison with the number of low-income households. Since 1937, about 780,000 low-rent dwelling units had been created by public housing programs through 1966. However, in 1966 there were over 11 million households classified as having incomes below the "poverty level" as defined by the Social Security Administration. Thus there were approximately 14 times as many poor households (including both families and individuals) as there were public housing units in 1966. The ratio of poor households to public housing units is considerably lower within certain central cities. Nevertheless, it still is fair to say that the number of public housing units in any major city in the United States is far below the number of households either eligible for such units, or desirous of living in them. This is confirmed by the long waiting lists for entry into public housing in most cities.

[22]Since 1967, conventional housing starts have risen back to the levels they had attained in the early 1960's. Thus, total conventional housing starts were 1.55 million in 1968, and about 1.50 million in 1969. Furthermore, rapid increases in the total output of mobile homes—which are not included in housing-start figures by the U.S. Commerce Department—made the actual total of new housing units even larger. Counting mobile homes, total housing starts were 1.87 million in 1968, and about 1.90 million in 1969. Nevertheless, this very large increase in annual housing output has not relieved tightness in most housing markets in the United States. Higher production has been offset by higher household-formation and expanding demand generated by continued economic prosperity. Therefore, the basic argument remains valid: Current housing market conditions impose high displacement costs on low-income households because "filtering" does not work well.

[23]As noted in preceding footnotes, two more of these ten losses became compensable in the Federal-Aid Highway Act of 1968. This leaves six that remain noncompensable at the time of this writing (early 1970).

[24]See especially Chapters 7 and 8 in the *Report of the National Advisory Commission on Civil Disorders*, Washington D.C., March 1968.

[25]Public Works Committee Report, pp. 260-61.

[26]William L. Slayton, "The Operations and Achievements of the Urban Renewal Program," in Wilson, editor, *op. cit.*, 212, and the Census Bureau Relocation Study, 339.

[27]Public Works Committee Report, pp. 260-61.

[28]Census Bureau Relation Study, p. 345.

[29]Public Works Committee Report, pp. 141-42.

[30]*Ibid.*, pp. 260-61.

[31]*Ibid.*, p. 22.

[32]See footnote 3.

[33]Public Works Committee Report, p. 26.

[34]*Ibid.*, p. 37.

[35]Census Bureau Relocation Study, p. 338.

[36]Public Works Committee Report, pp. 252-53.

9

The Land-Value Impacts of Transportation Arteries and How They Affect New-City Development

Major transportation arteries—particularly expressways and rapid transit lines—have powerful impacts upon land values in the areas they serve. Both the arteries themselves and their land-value impacts in turn play crucial roles in the development of planned "new cities" throughout the world. This article explores the nature of such land-value impacts, the roles they play in new-city development, and possible implications of those roles regarding public policy towards both major transportation arteries and new cities. As part of the analysis, the article also sets forth the basic economic strategy of new cities viewed as a form of land development. Many important aspects of new-city development and public policies toward it, however, especially aspects connected with non-economic policy objectives, are not considered herein.

How Major Transportation Arteries Affect Land Values

SIX STAGES OF DEVELOPMENT

Arterial expressways and transit lines are created in a process that has definite stages. Six of them can be arbitrarily defined for purposes of analysis; four occur before the artery is actually open for traffic and two after it is in operation:

Route Selection During this period, no one is sure exactly where the artery will be located, although a general corridor is under consideration. Hence a high degree of uncertainty exists concerning future land uses within that corridor. This causes significant price changes in nearby property. In inner-city areas, these changes are often negative and can be quite large if this time period lasts very long. In undeveloped outlying areas, price changes are positive, but are usually not very large at first.

Written for Institute of Public Administration workshop. "Transportation for New Towns and Communities," Dec. 15, 16, 1969.

Detailed   Planning   This   occurs   after   the   route   has   been chosen. No visible action takes place, but further land speculation may occur in the area concerned.

Clearance   and   Displacement   In   already   built-up   areas, especially   in   older   cities,   any   injuries   or   costs   imposed   by displacement now begin to affect those concerned. In new growth areas, where most land is vacant, this stage often does not occur at all.

Construction   A   major   arterial   route   usually   takes   several years for construction. While it is going on, transportation in the areas served may be worse than before because of disruptions caused by the movement of equipment and the tearing up of older roadways. This may generate severe losses of value for operating businesses dependent on local transportation. On the other hand, the fact that construction has begun confirms that the new artery will eventually exist. Hence, land-value impacts begin in earnest during the construction period.

Early   Operation   Right after the opening of the new artery, major adjustments in land use begin in adjacent and nearby areas because all the impacts described in the next section have suddenly come into being. The surrounding economy then goes through a period of transition while it adjusts itself to this fundamental shift in the environment. Very large changes in land values occur during this period.

Mature Operation   After a few years, surrounding land uses have already made the most dramatic adjustments to the traffic artery.   This   is   true   in   part   because   the   biggest   surge   in traffic—from nothing to its initial operating level—has already taken place.   Nevertheless,   certain   other   land-value   effects   can   occur during   the   mature   operating   period.   These   result   partly   from gradually rising traffic levels on the artery, but also from continual extension of urban development outward along the artery, and intensification of land uses in already built-up areas adjacent to it.

Many   land-value-impact   studies   indicate   that   the   biggest changes in value occur during the construction and early operation periods.   The   analysis   in   this   paper   is   based   mainly   upon   a comparison of land values before and after these periods. Hence it does   not   concentrate   on   the   dynamics   of   land-value   changes throughout   the   process   described   above,   though   these   will   be mentioned occasionally.

SPECIFIC FUNCTIONAL CHANGES

Land values are changed by major transportation arteries because those arteries have certain functional impacts upon the territories surrounding them. These impacts can be stated as alterations in the nature of the environment after the arteries are in operation as compared to before they were built. To summarize:

Rising general accessibility   By definition, a major traffic artery links each area it serves with other important settlement areas some distance away. Insofar as new cities are concerned, such arteries generally connect a relatively undeveloped territory with major urban centers nearby. Consequently, travel times from the previously undeveloped land to centers of employment, commerce, and residence in nearby metropolitan areas are greatly reduced. This affects not only land lying right along the right-of-way of the artery, but also nearly all land within several miles of it.

Increasing differences in relative accessibility   Certain specific parcels right along the new artery—particularly near interchanges if it is a highway, or station stops if it is a transit line—suddenly become much more accessible to distant areas. Relative accessibility to those areas rises much more than that of other parcels located somewhat farther from the artery itself, or from the major access points to it. Moreover, interchanges and station stops have powerful focusing effects upon traffic patterns that strongly influence land values of nearby parcels. These effects occur for the following reasons:

   As traffic moves away from these focal points, it tends to disperse over the landscape. Conversely, as traffic approaches the artery, it converges upon the small number of entry points. Hence, sites right near interchanges or station stops experience maximum visual and physical exposure to passing traffic both on the artery and entering or leaving it. This makes those sites extremely valuable to activities that can prosper from serving large numbers of customers, or at least from visual exposure to them.

   Rapid-transit station stops are points at which riders shift transportation modes. When they leave the rapid-transit line, they move on foot *to* private cars, buses, taxicabs, limousines, or further pedestrian journeys. When they enter it, they move on foot *from* these other modes onto it. In both cases, this *modal shift* creates a "natural break" in their journeys where they can conveniently patronize various types of commercial enterprises, especially convenience-goods stores. Hence modal-shift points have always been centers of retail and service commerce. In fact, most big cities originated where travelers had to shift modes from land to water (or vice versa). Many major in-city commercial districts sprang up where commuters habitually transferred from one streetcar line to another. Parcels of land near rapid-transit stations are well-situated to take advantage of this break in the journey to provide services to travelers, so their values will reflect this advantage.

Even users of automobile expressways experience a *quality-shift* in the nature of their driving when they enter or leave an expressway. This has some of the characteristics of the modal-shift described above concerning rapid-transit stations, but to a lesser degree. When traveling on an expressway (except during the most crowded moments in rush hours), a driver typically moves at from 50 to 70 miles per hour without stops, crossroads, or oncoming traffic to worry about. Once he leaves the expressway, he must move much more slowly, and be alert to frequent stops, crossroads, and oncoming traffic. This produces a different and less desirable *quality* of driving. The moment of shifting from one quality to the other involves a mental break in his journey, though he does not have to leave his private vehicle. The place where this break occurs is a good point at which to locate services for drivers, including convenience shopping centers and gas stations.

Interchanges are also the best location for services catering to users of expressways who are passing through the general area, but need to stop for gasoline, food, or lodging en route. The closer to the expressway itself such facilities can be located, the less lower-quality driving must be done off the expressway by those using these facilities. This causes operators of such facilities to cluster as close to interchanges as possible.

All of these focusing effects create unique accessibility and exposure advantages for sites located right near expressway interchanges or rapid-transit station stops. Naturally, such advantages reflect themselves in the values of those sites. Conversely, parcels of land located along former heavy-traffic arteries experience a sudden decline in their exposure to traffic, which has now shifted to the new artery. This can produce severe negative impacts on land values.

Visual exposure of adjacent sites   This visual exposure to passing traffic is much greater than for distant sites, and yields an advertising value for many kinds of concerns interested in creating a desirable public image. Their physical quarters in effect become advertisements for their existence, or even for their specific products. They can supplement this with signs or displays too. Sometimes the number of persons to whom these advertisements are exposed is enormous. If the ads are located along commuter expressways, they receive the kind of daily repetitive exposure so greatly desired by advertising experts. Therefore, the greater the traffic flow past a given point, and the more repetitious that flow, the greater the advertising value of visual exposure obtainable on adjacent sites.

Traffic nuisance suffered by adjacent sites   For an automobile expressway, nuisance effects include constant noise, exhaust fumes, night-glare from headlights, and an occasional physical hazard from a careening vehicle. Moreover, the expressway itself is considered an ugly blight on the landscape by many occupants of nearby property. The precise degree to which these nuisances impact adjacent property is greatly influenced by the physical design of the expressway concerned. A depressed right-of-way reduces noise, night-glare, and ugliness in comparison with either street-level or elevated rights-of-way. For rapid-transit arteries, the main nuisances include occasional noise whenever a train passes, swirling of dirt and dust into the air, some night-glare from train headlights, and the presence of an unattractive "scar" across the landscape. Again, the severity of these nuisances depends upon the physical design of the artery itself. Generally, however, the nuisance impacts of a mass transit facility on the surface are less powerful than those of an expressway. Naturally, when a mass transit facility is located underground, it has almost no nuisance effect on adjacent property except for increased traffic near station stops.

Barrier to local movement   In some parts of the area it serves, a major transportation artery creates a barrier to movement from one side to the other, thereby isolating certain areas along its route. This effect has a significant impact on land values only if efficient use of property on either side of the artery requires easy movement from one side to the other, or if habitual patterns of behavior in the area were based upon such movement. Since new communities are generally created in previously undeveloped areas, this impact is not very significant for them.

Removal of local facilities   Certain physical or other facilities formerly serving areas adjacent to the artery may have been destroyed or removed in order to make room for it. Their absence after the artery opens may affect land values nearby. For example, an expressway routed through a low-income residential area may cause thousands of housing units to be destroyed. This tends to increase demand for the housing in nearby areas still available to low-income households. The result is an upward pressure on land values on such parcels. Conversely, if the artery causes destruction of a shopping center, school, or other amenity which formerly enhanced land values in the neighborhood, this may have a negative impact on such values.

I believe it is fair to say that all impacts of new traffic arteries on land values are caused by one or a combination of the above functional effects. However, these effects sometimes exert opposite pressures on land values; so their net result cannot be forecast in advance without specific reference to concrete circumstances.

PRINCIPLES GOVERNING LAND-VALUE CHANGES

Dozens of empirical studies have measured the impact of major traffic arteries—principally automobile expressways—upon adjacent or nearby land values. Those used as a basis for this article are listed at the close of the article. Most of these studies compared land values before and after the artery was constructed and in operation. Some used "control areas" not adjacent to the expressway in order to isolate general land-value increases from those specifically caused by the expressway concerned. Careful analysis of many of these land-value studies has led me to formulate the following major conclusions about the way new traffic arteries affect land values:

Impact on adjacent land   A new traffic artery has no positive impact on the value of adjacent land unless other economic factors favoring urban growth are already present in the area. This rather surprising conclusion is confirmed by evidence from rural areas distant from metropolitan areas or even from small towns. Expressways passing through such relatively undeveloped rural areas have almost no impact on adjacent land values. Few, if any, users of land are interested in taking advantage of the potential effects described in the preceding section in such areas, since they are isolated from local population, employment sources, commercial activity, or repeated passing traffic. True, some development occurs at expressway interchanges in relatively isolated areas if they happen to be convenient stopping points for travelers between major population centers located on the expressway. But this example underlines the main conclusion rather than refuting it.

A crucial corollary of this principle is: The greater the dynamic strength of economic forces in an area served by a new traffic artery, the greater its potential positive impact upon land values. Thus, an expressway or transit artery extending outward from the center of a metropolitan area through outlying areas where rapid growth is occurring and beyond those areas will normally have the greatest potential impact on land values. Its effects "reverberate" with the dynamic growth factors already at work in the area to generate maximum further development. However, this corollary should be modified in light of the second conclusion stated below.

Intensity of local land use   The highest potential values for land adjacent to a major traffic artery exist where the greatest intensity of land-use is supported by the local economy. This conclusion has been derived from several different kinds of evidence. *First*, the highest land values lie nearest to expressway interchanges or transit station stops. Usually the most intensive land uses occur at these points because of the traffic-focusing impacts described earlier. *Second*, other things being equal, land abutting the artery generally has a higher value and more intensive use than land somewhat farther removed, because of the advantages of visual exposure and greater accessibility. *Third*, among nonabutting parcels, those closer to expressways and transit lines generally attain higher values than those farther away, other things being equal. *Fourth*, values of land adjacent to major arteries are much higher in areas of extremely intensive development (such as near big city downtowns) than in near-rural areas or those of much less intense development. *Fifth*, higher values exist in areas zoned for high-intensity uses than in those zoned for lower-intensity uses. For example, land zoned for industrial use along an expressway reaches a higher value than that zoned for single-family residential use.

All of these examples really illustrate the fundamental fact that high-intensity land uses generate higher land values than low-intensity uses, regardless of relationship to traffic arteries. It should be noted that this principle refers to the *potential level* of land-values, not to the *movement* of land-values from the period before to the period after the artery is opened.

Achievement of greatest positive net impact   The net impact of a major traffic artery upon nearby land values is greatest when the *movement* from actual intensity of pre-artery land-use to the highest potential intensity is at a maximum, subject to two constraints. First, the cost of conversion from initial use to highest potential use must be subtracted from the *gross* impact of the artery on values to get the *net* impact. Therefore, given the gross impact, the net impact is smaller as this conversion cost increases. Second, again given the gross impact, the longer the time required for such conversion, the lower the net impact of the artery on values. This principle has been derived from several types of experience. Three of these types can be stated as corollaries to it as follows:

> a. Vacant land (including that used for farming) will increase in value more and faster than improved land. It is easier and less expensive to shift land directly into its highest-intensity potential use when it is vacant than when it is already improved for a lower-intensity use. In the latter case, existing improvements must be cleared and replaced.

> b. Land which is already "ripe" for development will increase in value faster than that which is not. For example, if property along an expressway is already zoned industrial and has utilities, it will go up farther and faster in value than if those preparations for development must be made first.

> c. The closer to centers of urban development any land located along an artery lies, the greater its likely increase in value (abstracting from the local influence of interchanges or station stops). This results from the higher-intensity use normally possible on a close-in site as opposed to farther-out sites.

When negative impacts occur   The greatest negative impact of a new major artery on land values occur when there is a maximum decline in intensity of land-use on the parcel so affected. However, potential negative impacts on land values are generally not as great as potential positive impacts because every new artery has some positive effects on nearly all land near it. When a new expressway diverts traffic from a formerly major artery, this causes a sharp drop in potential intensity of land-use for some parcels along that older artery. However, this negative impact is at least partly offset by the positive impact upon values of the whole area's increased accessibility. Thus, expressways have usually not absolutely depressed any land values within metropolitan areas, even though they have diverted traffic away from older arteries therein. But in more isolated small towns, where no other dynamic factors are present to offset the loss of through traffic, expressways have had serious negative impacts on land values. Even there, however, reduced congestion makes it easier for the facilities concerned to serve local business adequately. So there is still some positive effect offsetting the negative impact of traffic loss.

Differing effects of different types of arteries   Automobile expressways affect values of adjacent land in ways significantly different from rapid-transit arteries. These differences are most marked when the rapid-transit artery concerned is a subway. Then it has none of the nuisance impacts of either a surface expressway or a surface rapid-transit line. In that case, high-intensity residential developments can be located right next to rapid-transit stations with minimal inconvenience to their occupants and maximum accessibility advantages. In contrast, the inescapable nuisances of an automobile expressway make residential uses on adjacent parcels almost always relatively undesirable. Hence, the land uses most compatible along an automobile expressway are industrial, office space, retail, and motel (though the latter also suffers somewhat from nuisance). There is one other important reason why residences are often conveniently located very close to a rapid-transit line (even when it is on the surface) but not to an automobile expressway. Automobile travelers can easily move some distance off the expressway without changing vehicles or suffering the inconvenience of walking. In contrast, rapid-transit travelers must change transportation modes when they leave the station. If they remain on foot, it is inconvenient for them to walk very far. If they shift modes, this imposes an added time and money cost which also makes it less convenient for them to go far from the station than it is for an automobile driver to move far from an interchange. Consequently, *rapid-transit facilities are more likely to generate high-intensity residential uses near their stations than automobile expressways are to generate similar uses near interchanges—or at all.* This same trait also indicates why the land-value impacts of a rapid-transit facility tend to be more sharply focused around its stations than the impacts of an expressway are around its interchanges. Thus, land adjacent to a rapid-transit line but distant from any station does not gain as greatly in relative accessibility to user of the rapid-transit line as does land similarly located along an expressway in relation to users of the expressway. In other words, the ability of auto drivers to move conveniently off the expressway and away from the interchange tends to diffuse land-value impacts more broadly around interchanges than is the case around rapid-transit stations. True, in areas where residents are relatively wealthy, they may drive cars to the rapid-transit station, park there, and use transit for the longer portions of their journeys. In such cases, land-value impacts of a station are diffused in approximately the same way as those of an expressway interchange. Nevertheless, there are always some rapid-transit passengers who do not drive cars to the station. Therefore, the preceding discussion of differences in intensity and type of land use around stations and interchanges usually retains at least some of its validity everywhere.

How Transportation Arteries Affect New-City Development

ECONOMIC PRINCIPLES OF NEW-CITY DEVELOPMENT

In order to understand how transportation arteries can be used to influence the nature of new cities, it is first necessary to explore some of the economic principles of new city development. The term *new city* has been used to denote many different kinds of communities. However, for purposes of this analysis, a new city can be defined as any urban development that (1) occupies a single large site under one ownership; (2) is planned and largely developed by a single organization (either public or private) in accordance with one comprehensive plan governing all land-use patterns in it; (3) contains several different land uses, including at least residential, commercial, industrial, institutional, and open space; and (4) contains some minimum planned total population, say 50,000. New cities of this type can be either *in-city* (within an already built-up area), *peripheral* (on the built-up edge of an existing metropolitan area), *satellite* (beyond the built-up portion of an existing metropolitan area but within commuting range), or *nonmetropolitan or autonomous* (beyond commuting range from any existing metropolitan area). Most privately built new cities have been either peripheral or satellite in nature.

Societies which have sponsored planned new cities have done so mainly for noneconomic reasons. For example, Brasilia, Canberra, and Washington, D.C. were all built as national capitals away from competing existing cities; Los Alamos and Oak Ridge were constructed to expedite national defense production or research programs; and Ciudad Guayana and many British new towns were built to divert growth from an existing capital city regarded as too dominant or crowded by national authorities. Moreover, essentially noneconomic factors—such as the desire to escape from environmental pollution and aesthetic ugliness—are key arguments used by the advocates of greater new-city development in the U.S.

Nevertheless, the basic economic strategy of creating new cities as a form of land development investment is a critical factor shaping their nature. This is true regardless of whether the new cities are created by public authorities, by private developers, or by some mixture of both. After all, the land they use and the capital needed to develop it are both scarce resources. And new cities require large amounts of such resources—especially if they are to accommodate any significant fraction of a nation's urban growth. Hence every society ought to create whatever new cities it allows or sponsors as economically as possible, within the constraints imposed by the key noneconomic objectives they are designed to achieve. Consequently, it is necessary to explore the basic economic stategy of new-city development in order to understand the way transportation arteries can be used to shape that development.

Initially, it is useful to view new cities in strictly economic terms as investments aimed at producing profits for their developers (whether public or private). As in every form of land development, the basic idea is to buy undeveloped land at a relatively low price, add amenities, and then sell or rent it at a relatively high price. Whether this proves profitable depends upon the spread between the buying and selling prices in relation to both the costs of development and the speed with which the price can be escalated. The more time elapses between initial purchase and final resale or rental, the less the profitability, other things being equal. This is true because more time means greater interest forgone on the money invested in both land and development. Speed is particularly crucial in new-city development because of the enormous initial investment in purchasing a very large site, and installing a completely new infrastructure and other facilities.

The huge liability created by this big "front-end" investment can in theory be offset by two advantages provided by that investment which are absent from smaller-scale developments. The first is the possibility of capturing within the boundaries of the site almost all the positive land-value impacts of key public and private investments. In normal small-scale urban development, specific investments like highways or shopping centers create "spillover" land-value effects on surrounding parcels that benefit other owners. But a single owner controls the entire new-city site; so such "spillovers" are converted from "external" impacts to "internal" ones. In fact, a key part of successful new-city strategy is planning major land uses so their spillover effects reverberate back and forth within the boundaries of the new city, thereby accelerating the process of escalating land values there.

The second advantage of large-scale development is the possibility of creating a uniquely attractive set of interrelated amenities on the site which makes it more desirable as a place to live, work, and play than competitive smaller-scale developments. The resulting superior attraction speeds up the process of urban development in the new city, as compared to other similar sized areas in the vicinity.

Thus, the basic *economic* objective of new-city development is to focus urban growth forces upon a relatively small undeveloped site (in relation to the entire metropolitan area) so as to speed up the process of urbanizing that site. The increased speed of development generates rapidly rising land values, particularly of industrial and commercial land. The resulting fast upsurge of land values provides the key economic payoff for new-city development. From the public point of view, it represents a more efficient use of scarce resources than slower and more scattered development. From the private point of view, it represents greater profitability. If development occurs fast enough, then land values will go up sufficiently faster than the carrying costs of the front-end investment to provide an adequate rate of return upon that investment (whether public or private) and upon subsequent infusions of capital. However, if development does not occur fast enough, the forgone returns on the initial investment (or the borrowing costs if the initial funds are not all equity capital) will accumulate faster than the profits from land appreciation. Thus, the speed of development and of rising land values is critical to the economic success of any new city.

For further clarity, I have broken down the overall strategy described above in the following specific tactics, which apply to both publicly and privately developed new cities:

A large site is assembled close enough to existing urban growth centers so that urban activity can be attracted from them, but far enough away so that initial land acquisition costs are relatively low. Selection of this site is the most critical step in the entire strategy of successful new-city development.

A comprehensive plan is developed for multiple land uses on the selected site. This plan has a crucial economic function in the overall strategy. It must enable the site to offer outstanding amenities and attractions to both potential residents and potential industrial occupants—amenities they cannot obtain in competitive developments being created through "normal urban sprawl." This quality difference is vital in attracting new residents and industrial or other economic-base firms to the site fast enough to greatly speed up the process of urbanization that would have occurred on the same land if no such plan was developed.

Initial investment of capital creating the minimal infrastructure is necessary to start attracting residents and economic-base activities. A key function of this front-end investment is to convince potential residents that the amenities promised by the plan will actually be realized. Hence, a sufficient basic core of urban amenities must be installed to make life tolerable for the initial residents, and to convince doubters that the developers have the capability as well as the intention of producing the planned new community.

Residential occupancy and economic-base activity is developed on the site on a large scale. The greater the number of residents who can be attracted to live on the site in a given period, the greater the potential market for commercial property serving them and the potential labor force for industrial and economic-base activities located in the community. Hence, it is to the developer's advantage to accelerate residential settlement as much as possible in order to generate faster increases in land values for commercial and industrial properties. It is also important for the developer to retain ownership of such properties as long as possible, although some industrial sites may have to be sold initially in order to attract employers to the area. Once commercial and industrial activities are in place on the site, this in turn stimulates further residential growth by providing more convenient amenities and potential jobs to people who move in. Thus, a "reverberation effect" occurs between speeded residential development and speeded commercial and industrial development. Hence the developer may be able to profit significantly from high residential land values towards the end of development cycle, as well as from higher commercial and industrial land values.

A relatively monopolistic advantage is maintained for the commercial and industrial land within the boundaries of the planned new city. As population accumulates on the site, the value of commercial land serving that site rises. But competitive facilities located outside the new city may also be attracted by the same population. Insofar as these competitive facilities are able to capture business from the households living in the new city, they reduce the potential value of commercial land therein. Yet maximizing that value is one of the keys to the economic success of the entire development. New industrial land near but outside the new city, and therefore competing with its industrial land, is not nearly as threatening. This is true because *any* industry or other economic-base activity that locates near the new city—whether inside its boundaries or not—increases the potential housing demand for units located within that city.

Therefore, from the developer's viewpoint, it is highly desirable for the commercial properties within the new city to maintain a relatively monopolistic position in serving its residents. In part, this can be done by designing the new city in such a way that residential traffic patterns "naturally" converge upon the commercial center within the city itself. However, it may also be desirable to block competitive commercial facilities from locating anywhere near the new residents by controlling the most accessible nearby sites. Many such sites would be adjacent to or near the major transportation arteries serving the new city. Thus, developer control of land uses along such arteries both within and outside the boundaries of any new city has very important effects on the economic success of that city. This is much easier to accomplish when the developer is a public agency than when it is a private firm, especially in countries with strong public land-use-control laws.

FOUR WAYS ARTERIES AID IN NEW-CITY GROWTH

Major traffic arteries serving new cities help them carry out the economic strategy described above in four basic ways. First, the *improved general access* of the new city to major metropolitan areas and other built-up areas nearby is vital. The more effectively a new city is linked to nearby sources of employment, potential housing demand, and urban services by a major traffic artery, the greater the impact of that artery in assisting the new city to develop rapidly. Thus, it is tremendously to the advantage of new-city developers either to influence the location of major arteries so they serve the new cities effectively, or to choose sites which are well-located in relation to planned arterial routes.

The second role of major arteries in new-city development results from the *highly specific focusing effect of access points* along such arteries upon the intensity of land uses near those points. Since high-intensity land uses tend to cluster around expressway interchanges and rapid transit stations, these access points can help a new-city developer stimulate rapid increases in land values within the community. In many European countries, each new city, explicitly designed around a rapid-transit station stop, contains major shopping center and clusters of high-rise apartments within walking distance of the station. Thus, *the traffic artery itself becomes a critical ingredient in both the economic success and the physical design of the entire new city.*

As noted above, the heart of the economic strategy of new-city development is stimulating rapid increases in land values, particularly for commercial land. Coordination of a rapid-transit station stop or an expressway interchange with the design of the community itself greatly assists the developer in achieving the steep increases in land values needed to make the project feasible. Formerly vacant land around these arterial nodes skyrockets in value because it can be shifted directly from nonuse or farming to very high-intensity uses. It is clear, therefore, that developers of new cities can reap substantial benefits from coordinating the location of station stops or interchanges with the basic layout and design of their cities—in fact, even building those cities around such focal points.

The third role of major traffic arteries also involves their influence on land-use patterns. Away from nodal points like station stops or interchanges, *land use along an artery ought to be compatible* with its particular traffic patterns. Land adjacent to an expressway might include open space, industrial parks, shopping centers, and office parks. If the artery is a rapid transit system, adjacent uses could include high- and low-rise residential where the artery is underground, some residential where it is elevated above ground, or the same uses as near an expressway where it is at ground level. Thus, the specific nature and location of the right-of-way within a new city will influence both the land-use plan for the community and its basic physical design. This influence will be greater in a typical new city development than in normal "urban sprawl" because a new city must incorporate superior land-use planning and physical design as one of its alluring amenities. The "pull" of this and its other amenities must be stronger than that exerted by "normal urban sprawl." Only if this is true can the creators of a new city speed up its development so as to achieve their general economic objectives. Proper incorporation of a major artery into the overall design of the new city is thus another way in which developers can capitalize on the artery to achieve their economic objectives.

A fourth impact of a major artery on new city development could arise from portions of the artery lying outside the boundaries of the new city. Insofar as land uses spring up along those portions in competition with those inside the new city, the artery may exert a negative influence on the ability of that city to achieve its goals. For example, if an important expressway interchange lies just outside the boundaries of a planned new city, private developers not connected with that city may create an attractive shopping center and general commercial node near the interchange. This facility could strongly compete with commercial property located within the new city itself. If so, it might reduce either the final property values attained by commercial property in the city, or the rate of speed with which those values moved upward. In either case, the result could be a serious economic blow to the new city developers. Therefore, it is extremely important from their point of view to prevent competitive facilities from springing up along major arteries either leading to their new cities or passing nearby. In our free-enterprise economy, new-city developers—whether public or private—can exert such influence only by (1) buying up potentially threatening land along the artery outside the boundaries of their new communities, or (2) having such land zoned for open space or other noncompetitive uses and rigorously enforcing that zoning. The first of these alternatives is very expensive. The second is fraught with political uncertainty and difficult to accomplish. Therefore, from the viewpoint of new-city developers, it is preferable to have any major artery near their city pass right through its boundaries, and to have all the major access points anywhere near the city located right in the heart of it. The first characteristic means the developers will own most of the nearby land along the artery anyway.   The second characteristic means opportunities for creating nodes of high-intensity use *competitive* with those inside the new community will be minimized in its vicinity.

All four of these impacts consist of ways new-city developers can use the functional effects of a major transportation artery to speed up the development process in their planned communities, and to accelerate the rise of certain key land values therein. Transportation arteries are vital in modern life, particularly for settlements on the fringes of metropolitan areas. Hence these impacts can be tremendously important to the economic success of new-city developers.

Public Policy Issues: Four Crucial Questions

In almost all countries, major transportation arteries are public investments paid for with taxpayers' money. Yet these arteries have tremendous impacts upon planned new cities (as well as upon older settlements). They affect the location, land-use patterns, physical design, and economic success of those cities. To what extent, and how, should public authorities planning and building major transportation arteries take these impacts upon new cities into account? To answer requires certain basic public policy decisions concerning urban growth in general. Four questions are crucial:

1. *Do we want a significant fraction of future urban growth to occur in the form of large-scale planned new cities, in contrast to alternative growth forms?* If so, then public authorities ought to view major traffic arteries as key instruments in the encouragement of new-city development. Such arteries should be located so they run through the centers of areas being developed as full-scale new cities. Major interchanges or rapid-transit stations should be located near central points in these new cities to stimulate high-intensity land uses. Finally, these nodes should be located quite far apart to prevent facilities competitive with planned new cities from appearing near them.

In practice, these objectives could probably not be attained without some overall planning of urban growth patterns in a given metropolitan area. Authorities charged with constructing transportation arteries cannot predict the location of potential new cities without some overall plan to assign sites to such communities well in advance of urban development in the area. In fact, the interstate highway system now runs through many areas where new cities might be built. Most of its routes and interchange locations are already set. Hence, coordinating new cities with existing facilities will require adapting the cities to the roads, rather than vice versa.

Moreover, such coordination implies that new-city developers will be able to assemble large sites around the existing nodal points on major arteries. Our fragmented landownership structure makes this impossible in most areas without creation of new public agencies specifically for this purpose. The agencies might be public development corporations similar to the ones that have built planned new cities in Great Britain and elsewhere. Or they might be strictly land-assembly organizations which would then resell large tracts to private developers for actual creation of planned new cities (something like existing urban renewal agencies, but dealing with larger areas and with vacant land). This structure involves some means of using eminent domain powers. Otherwise, we will probably not be able to create many planned new cities in or within commuting range of metropolitan areas that take maximum advantage of the land-value stimulating effects of major transportation arteries—especially existing ones.

If public policy does not favor development of planned new cities, then these tactics described are not needed. Major roads and other arteries can be located without regard to the potentials for developing large new cities around their nodal points. Such nodes can be created close together along major routes without regard to the subsequent difficulty of building quasimonopolistic commercial centers at any one node.

The above discussion seems to make this fact clear: *Continuation of existing transportation policies in the United States will make it virtually impossible in most metropolitan areas for either public or private developers to take maximum advantage of potential land-value-stimulation effects of major arteries in creating planned new cities.* A few new cities can be located so as to capitalize on at least some of the accessibility and other advantages provided by major arteries. But capturing the entire spectrum of potential benefits from such arteries so as to encourage planned new cities will probably not be possible, at least on any large scale. This finding reinforces a related but broader conclusion: *Only a very tiny fraction of future urban growth in the United States will occur in large-scale planned new cities unless major changes in existing institutions are developed specifically to encourage such communities.*

2. *Do we want to encourage non-automobile travel in metropolitan areas, as opposed to automobile or other highway-oriented travel?* Since 1960, the number of automotive vehicles registered in the United States has risen at an average rate of 3.4 million per year. This is 33 percent above the average annual increase in population of 2.56 million during the same period. To put it another way, the vehicular population of the United States rose 27 million from 1960 through 1968 (an increase of 38 percent); whereas the human population went up only 20.5 million (an increase of 11 percent). In view of these facts, it is not surprising that congestion on many streets and roads is increasing markedly. If we continue to add one-third more vehicles than people to the nation each year, it seems likely that congestion will continue to worsen. One way to lessen its future impacts would be to encourage nonautomobile forms of transportation within each metropolitan area. This could be done by building rail rapid-transit facilities between outlying new cities and the downtown center of each metropolitan area. In recent years, places of employment have become more and more scattered away from downtowns or from any small set of major nodes within the metropolitan area. But a deliberate, long-range policy of encouraging rapid-transit might partly reverse this trend. This could be accomplished by creating major radial rapid-transit lines in key directions outward from the central business district; deliberately encouraging large concentrations of employment at nodal points along those radials; and developing circular rapid-transit lines linking outlying nodal points in the same way that "belt" expressways do now. Similar tactics have worked in the past in those few major metropolitan areas in the United States served by rail commuter or rail rapid-transit lines, and they have worked in such European cities as London, Paris, Leningrad, Moscow, and Stockholm. It is probably impossible to stem the long-run tide towards greater use of individual vehicles by Americans. But the substitution of rapid-transit movements for a significant portion of present automobile movements—or of those which will arise in the future—is a potentially feasible objective worth considering in at least one major metropolitan area as a large-scale experiment. If public policy seeks to promote this general objective, then it would be wise to use rail rapid-transit stations as nuclear points for

new-city development. This would require the extension of new rail rapid-transit systems outward into presently vacant portions of metropolitan areas, or development of new rail commuter services serving such areas. It would also imply concentrating whatever planned new cities are developed around rail rapid-transit stations, rather than around expressway interchanges (though both kinds of nodes could be incorporated within each such community). It seems unlikely now that the United States will start using rail rapid-transit in this manner. For reasons of politics, economy, and efficiency, we are more likely to simply endure higher levels of roadway congestion.

3. *Do we want to recapture the "spillover" economic benefits generated by major publicly-financed transportation arteries directly into the public treasury, or do we want to continue allowing private landowners to enjoy these benefits? If the latter, do we want to exert more public control over how these owners use their land in return for providing them with such benefits?* A major stimulant to land values in all metropolitan areas has been public investment of funds in transportation arteries, particularly expressways and highways. Up to now, public authorities have made almost no attempt to directly recapture any of the economic benefits bestowed upon private landowners by the "spillover effects" of these transportation arteries. True, higher assessed values do lead to greater local property taxes on the parcels concerned. But an alternative would be excess condemnation of land along the arteries themselves—particularly near new interchanges or other nodes—and subsequent resale or development by public authorities. This would deprive private owners of the land served by these arteries of economic gains they would otherwise derive from proximity. Hence, direct recapture would significantly diminish the speed with which private land values rose in a planned new city, and would weaken the ability of major arteries to encourage private development of planned new cities, thus decreasing their economic feasibility. Such recapture, however, could encourage public development of planned new cities if the development organization, rather than the highway or transit authorities was the recapturing agency.

Therefore, to encourage the creation of planned new cities by either public corporations or private developers, transportation authorities should not be permitted to directly recapture the spillover benefits generated locally by transportation arteries. However, we might profitably alter our present almost completely laissez-faire policy by controlling who captures those benefits and how they use them. Public authorities responsible for creating major traffic arteries might require that new-city developers adapt their land-use plans for parcels along artery rights-of-way to compatible uses like those described earlier in this article. This additional public regulation of land use along major traffic arteries could also be obtained from public or private developers in return for cooperating with them in choosing the exact locations for rights-of-way and interchanges or station stops. It might not be necessary to bargain in order to get new-city developers to create proper comprehensive plans, since they need good plans to attract development. Moreover, similar goals can be achieved by other public agencies which also exercise surveillance over comprehensive new-city planning. Nevertheless, the bargaining power of all public authorities can be increased in relation to private developers if the former actually had the potential power of excess condemnation and public recapture. Then they could threaten to wield their power within new-city boundaries unless the developers' plans conformed to public objectives. Developers could profit further if this excess condemnation power were used extensively outside new-city boundaries to deprive potential competitors of much of the incentives to create competing facilities along the arteries. What specific tactics are used will depend heavily upon (a) which public objectives society chooses in regard to both new-city development and transportation planning, and (b) whether new cities are developed by public or private agencies.

4. *How extensively do we want to exercise public regulation and control over future urban growth?* If we wish to change past United States precedents and move towards a higher degree of public control over urban growth—as in most of Europe—then major transportation arteries should be used as key instruments in shaping urban settlement patterns. This might require extending expressways and rail arteries into presently vacant areas before high pressures for service arose there. The leverage thus created for public authorities would enable them to shape future growth, rather than simply reacting to it. On the other hand, to minimize public control of future growth, a largely reactive policy should be continued. This would involve locating major arteries where traffic patterns are already heavy and where urban improvement already exists. This tactic would continue to result in relatively high immediate traffic loading on the new arteries, requiring minimal "front-end" public investment in transportation arteries that do

not pay off at once. In contrast, extending arteries into unsettled areas would result in lower traffic loadings on the newest arteries and bigger "front-end" investments by public authorities. These alternatives are similar to other aspects of public cost involved in deciding what level of public regulation ought to be exercised over future urban growth. The greater the degree of public control chosen, the higher the initial public investment in all kinds of facilities, including highways, utilities, industrial land, and housing. Higher initial public costs may lead to lower long-run or total public costs or to much higher long-run benefits than the opposite tactic. But this conclusion has never been proved by any rigorous analysis, and remains largely a matter of speculation at present.

Major transportation arteries could potentially exert tremendous influence on the existence, location, design, nature, success, and speed of development of planned new cities. Whether they will do so depends upon fundamental policy choices regarding future urban growth which must be made by the governments and people of the United States. Up to now, there is little evidence that policies encouraging planned new cities will be chosen by Americans. If and when such evidence emerges, more detailed studies of the relationships between transportation arteries, land values, and new-city planning will then become appropriate.

References

Boyce, Byrl N., "Excess Acquisition Revisited: Control of Land Use at the Interstate Interchange," *Land Economics* 45 (August, 1969) 293-303.

Dodge, William H., *Influence of a Major Highway Improvement on an Agriculturally-based Economy; Case Study of the Impact of Interstate 94 in the Economy of Dunn & St. Croix Counties, Wisconsin*. Madison, Bureau of Business Research and Service, University of Wisconsin, 1967.

Florida State Road Department, *Severance Study—Rural*. Tallahassee, n.d.

Highway Research Board, *Community Consequences of Highway Improvement*. Washington, D.C., 1965. (National Cooperative Highway Research Program Report No. 18).

Highway Research Board, *Indirect and Sociological Effects of Highway Location and Improvement*. Washington, D.C., 1965. (Highway Research Record No. 75).

Highway Research Board, *Indirect Effects of Highway Location and Improvements*. Washington, D.C., 1965. (Highway Research Record No. 96).

McKain, Walter C., *The Connecticut Turnpike: Ribbon of Hope; the Social and Economic Effects of the Connecticut Turnpike in Eastern Connecticut.* Storrs, Conn., Agricultural Experiment Station, University of Connecticut, 1965.

O'Hare, Robert J. M., "Suburban Transportation: Its Impact on Persons and Property," *The Real Estate Appraiser* 33:12 (December, 1967) 7-8.

Oklahoma Center of Urban and Regional Studies, *The Relationship of the Highway Interchange and the Use of Land in the State of Oklahoma.* Norman, 1962, 1965, 2 pts.

Schmidt, Blaine G., *Delaware Highway Impact Study, Phase II Report (1959-1963).* Wilmington, 1967.

South Dakota Department of Highways, *U.S. Highway 81 Through Tankton, South Dakota.* Pierre, 1966.

Texas Transportation Institute. Its series of *Economic Impact Studies.*

U.S. Bureau of Public Roads, *Highways and Economic and Social Changes.* Washington, D.C., U.S. Government Printing Office, 1964.

University of Virginia, Bureau of Population and Economic Research, *The Socio-Economic Impact of the Capital Beltway on Northern Virginia.* Charlottesville, 1968.

Wallace, Richard S., and James H. Lemly, *Analysis of Economic Impact of Highway Change on Two Small Georgia Communities.* Atlanta, School of Business Administration, Georgia State College, 1969.

10

A Realistic Look at the Final Payoffs
From Urban Data Systems

The glamorous capabilities of computerized "urban information systems" appear so dazzling that no major city planning proposal is considered respectable unless it contains at least one section on EDP, ADP, or an urban data bank. Nevertheless, automated data systems are still regarded with uncertainty and uneasiness by many key urban decision-makers. How can anyone—even a trained data technician—judge whether these systems are really worth the huge costs involved? Even more significant, how will these systems affect the relative power and influence of various individual decision-makers?

Ultimately, the answers to these questions depend upon assessing the final payoffs from urban data systems. *Final payoffs* are actual *improvements in government or private action*, as distinguished from *improvements in the information* on which such action is based.

Up to now, most of the concern with urban data systems has not been focused upon final payoffs for three reasons. First, the technical design of these systems has seemed more exciting, more novel—and more amenable to analysis. Second, most detailed analyses of the decision process have been performed by members of computer hardware firms. Naturally, they have concentrated upon describing the impressive improvements in information they can undoubtedly deliver. Third, it appears obvious that better data in urban decision-making would have huge final payoffs, because it has hardly been doubted that better information would reduce both the frequency and the magnitude of planning mistakes.

This intuitively plausible but actually misleading assumption has caused us to deemphasize final payoffs. Therefore, this article will concentrate upon analyzing them.

All final payoffs from urban data systems consist of improvements in the effectiveness of decision-making. *Technical*

Reprinted from *Public Administration Review*, Vol. 27, No. 3, (Sept. 1967), by permission of the American Society for Public Administration.

payoffs are at least potentially beneficial to all participants in the decision-making process. They result from technical improvements in data inputs, processing, and outputs. Examples are greater speed of processing, greater consistency among outputs, and wider distribution of information. *Power payoffs* are gains in one persons's decision-making effectiveness made at the expense of another person's. They are *redistributions* of the benefits of decision-making.

In reality, every change in urban data-reporting or data-processing systems has both technical and power repercussions. Hence anyone analyzing the impact of automated data systems upon urban decision-making, or forecasting the attitudes of government officials towards such systems, must take both types of impacts into account. Yet in almost all studies of urban data systems, power payoffs are considered too political and too controversial to discuss. As a result, we get one-dimensional dialogues about problems which in reality have two or more dimensions.

It is time we faced this reality by taking a hard look at power payoffs. But first it is necessary to examine technical payoffs in more detail.

Technical Payoffs

A careful analysis shows that the technical payoffs from urban data systems are smaller than intuition would lead us to suppose. Also, they have certain characteristics which will strongly influence the forms of future urban data systems.

TECHNICAL IMPROVEMENTS IN DATA CAUSED BY URBAN DATA SYSTEMS

Computerized data systems could improve the data underlying current urban decisions by providing the following:

1. Lower operating costs of data processing.
2. Faster availability of information.
3. Wider distribution of information.
4. Generation of new information never before observed, recorded, or reported.

5. Greater consistency in reporting data.

6. Reduced distortion of data reported to top levels.

7. Eventual development of a giant data inventory. This could ultimately be used to formulate, test, and modify theories about causal relationships in the urban environment which we can now only guess at.

8. Greater freedom from routine recordkeeping.

On the other hand, the following technical costs are required to gain the above improvements:

1. Increased capital costs, including both hardware and software.

2. Demands for much more highly skilled personnel.

3. A tendency towards greater reliance upon quantifiable and measurable variables.

4. Increased narrowness of comprehension, particularly concerning incipient changes in the environment. Machine systems can respond only to stimuli they have been programmed to perceive, and in ways they have been programmed to react. Hence they are not sensitive to new types of data or to nuances in information that may signal changes in the entire situation.

5. Reduced sensitivity to the opinions and self-interest of intermediate-level officials in operating organizations. Information sent "straight through" from events to top-level administrators by automatic systems does not contain the interpretations of middle-level officials which often help place it in context, even though such interpretations always embody some biases.

These costs are often vastly outweighed by the improvements described above. Nevertheless, a balanced and impartial view of urban data systems must consider both.

ESTIMATES OF TECHNICAL PAYOFFS FROM TECHNICAL IMPROVEMENTS

The increased capabilities described above can greatly improve the data available to urban decision-makers. However, three factors make it hard to prove that these better data will lead to more effective decisions.

First, it is extremely difficult to measure the effectiveness of many decisions vital to urban affairs.[1] The errors of such measurement are often likely to exceed by a wide margin even the most generous estimates of possible increases in effectiveness caused by better data.

Second, even when the effects of decisions can be readily measured, variances in those effects may be due to factors other than data inputs. Whenever the same kind of decision is made over and over, it may be possible to test one set of decisions based upon "old fashioned" data vs. another set based upon all the same inputs except data from an automated system. However, it is difficult to do this before installing the automated system when such knowledge is critical to deciding whether the system is worth its cost. Moreover, it is impossible to set up adequate controls concerning unique or irreversible decisions to measure the degree of improvement in their effectiveness created by better data.

Third, many persons with different goals are affected by every decision. Whether given payoffs should be considered positive or negative—and to what extent—depends upon whose values are used in making the calculation.

All these major obstacles to measuring the technical payoffs of urban data systems become more severe the broader the decisions involved. For truly "sweeping" choices, (1) the relative effectiveness of alternative decisions is harder to estimate, (2) the number of factors considered other than quantitative information is much larger, (3) the decision is more likely to be unique and irrevocable, and (4) there is a higher probability that more groups with conflicting values will be affected. Consequently, *it is much easier to prove that urban data systems will provide positive technical payoffs concerning narrow operational decisions than concerning broad policy or operating choices.*

TECHNICAL PAYOFFS AND THE TYPE OF SYSTEM MOST LIKELY TO BE USED

Much of the academic and intellectual support for urban data systems has resulted from the seemingly enormous technical payoffs to be gained from truly comprehensive systems.[2] Such systems (1) service *all* government departments from a central data processing complex, (2) link these departments in a single information and report-printing network, (3) provide a single massive memory based upon a uniform coding system, and (4) allow instantaneous random access to this "joint memory" from remote stations in each department. In theory, such a comprehensive system should be able to bring together and analyze masses of data from all the various departments affected by even the broadest municipal government decisions.

But in reality, even if such huge systems existed, it would be tremendously difficult to *prove conclusively* that they provided significant technical payoffs concerning broad decisions. This is true for the reasons set forth previously. Yet comprehensive systems are immensely expensive. Much narrower data systems often provide the greatest *demonstrable technical payoffs* in decision-making—at least in relation to their costs, which are much lower. This implies that, in the near future, many urban politicians will buy narrowly designed data systems (such as those serving individual city departments) rather than comprehensive, "all-department" systems.[3]

In the long run, the biggest technical payoffs from improved urban data will probably arise from better knowledge of underlying causal relationships in the urban environment now shrouded by ignorance.[4] But developing theories about these causal relationships, and then testing those theories, requires an enormous stockpile of data about how each factor varies under a wide diversity of conditions. Hence this important technical payoff may not become available for something like a decade after massive urban data systems are installed and working.[5] This situation will further discourage many urban governments from initially purchasing comprehensive urban data systems.

The large extra costs of a comprehensive system must be borne immediately, or soon; whereas the extra payoffs it generates will not accrue for years. Even then, their appearance is by no means certain. Moreover human judgment can never be eliminated from the application of results derived from even the most sophisticated computer analysis. But when urban decision-makers realize that no data system, however comprehensive, will ever "give them all the answers," many will be reluctant to pay huge additional costs for what will probably seem like only marginal gains in final payoffs. After all, the bigger the role of judgment in the final decision, the greater the probability that a wise man will make the right choice without the help of a comprehensive computerized system.

For all these reasons connected with purely *technical* payoffs, it seems likely that many—though not all—cities will avoid early commitment to costly comprehensive data systems. As we shall see, consideration of *power* payoffs further strengthens this conclusion.

UPDATING AND ITS IMPACT UPON THE TYPE OF SYSTEM CHOSEN

Most of the technical payoffs promised by promoters of urban data systems require continuous data acquisition after the systems are installed. Such updating creates a major cost in any data system—in the long run, often the single largest cost, even exceeding the cost of hardware.[6] This huge on-going burden is tolerable only if the system itself is associated with an operating department which continuously procures the necessary data anyway as part of its normal behavior. This is another reason why many urban data systems are likely to start out as narrow departmental tools rather than as broad comprehensive ones.

Power Payoffs

Because of the uncertainties connected with the technical payoffs from urban data systems, power payoffs loom large in the minds of those who must decide whether such systems will actually be built and installed.[7]

HOW POWER PAYOFFS ARISE

Power payoffs arise because every change in organization, techniques, or decision processes shifts the relative power of at least some of the individuals involved. Invariably, these individuals place heavy weight upon such shifts in judging the desirability of proposed changes. True, in public they rarely if ever speak of these power shifts. Instead they usually refer only to the technical impacts of the changes being considered. But this does not fool anyone who really knows what is happening.

The power payoffs from urban data systems spring from four technical impacts of such systems. First, automated systems tend to transmit many data directly from events themselves to top-level officials, or at least to reduce the number of intermediate steps separating these two extremes. As a result, lower- and intermediate-level officials often have little or no opportunity of "filtering" important data before they reach top-level officials. "Filtering" can mean either distorting information by altering or leaving out parts of it, or adding personal interpretations to it, or both.[8]

Second, urban data systems inevitably shift some emphasis in decision-making towards more easily quantifiable factors and away from immeasurable ones. Third, such systems free lower-level officials from many routine reporting and recording chores. Fourth, they provide those officials capable of understanding and using them with much better information about certain aspects of urban affairs than those persons who do not use them.

The technical impacts of urban data systems described above tend to produce seven specific power shifts among the various "actors" in the urban decision-making process. The net power gainers from such shifts regard the data system causing them as having positive power payoffs; whereas the net power losers regard its power payoffs as negative. Any given person may gain from one power shift and lose from another. In fact, a single system might provide him with far more power regarding certain decisions or actions, and far less regarding others. Nevertheless, most well-informed people affected by a given data system will have definite opinions about whether it improves or worsens their overall power.

THE POWER SHIFTS CAUSED BY AUTOMATED DATA SYSTEMS

Automated data systems cause the following seven power shifts in urban decision-making—or in decision-making at state and federal levels when introduced there:

1. *Lower- and intermediate-level officials tend to lose power to higher-level officials and politicans.* The reduction in "filtering" of data at lower and intermediate levels of city hierarchies deprives officials there of some of their former influence, since machine systems often bypass them entirely.

2. *High-level staff officials gain power.* Since lower-level officials no longer condense data as it moves upward, and enormous amount of information flows directly to the "top of the heap." The politicians and line executives located there simply cannot cope with all this information unaided. So they rely on expanded staffs, or ever-more-overworked staffs, to provide the interpretation and filtering formerly done by lower-level officials.

Since the politicians and top-level executives concerned receive "filtered" information both before and after urban data systems are installed, it might seem that they are not net power gainers. However, this conclusion is false for three reasons. First, automated data systems often provide certain types of highly useful information never available before, or now available much faster. Second, staff advisors are likely to be more directly loyal to their top-level bosses than lower-level line operators, who have strong loyalties to their departments. Third, expanding one's staff creates additional channels of information which can be used to check up on the activities of operating departments. As every public and private executive knows, development of such seemingly redundant channels of information is crucial to keeping oneself well-informed about "what is really going on down there."

3. *City and state legislators tend to lose power to administrators and operating officials.* The latter are generally more sophisticated, have more technical training, are equipped with larger staffs, devote more time to their city jobs, can focus more intensively upon narrow specialties, are in a better position to control the design and operation of urban data systems, and are more likely to receive continuous reports from those systems by virtue of their positions.

4. *The government bureaucracy as a whole gains power at the expense of the general electorate and nongovernmental groups.* Government officials have continuous "inside access" to the data generated by automated systems, and they also control which data are built into those systems. No matter how idealistic they are, they will vigorously resist universal accessibility to these data. This occurs because accurate and detailed reporting of the behavior of any large organization—private or public—will inevitably reveal operating deficiencies that would be embarrassing if widely known. Moreover, the general electorate and most nongovernmental groups are not technically sophisticated when it comes to understanding and interpreting complex data.

5. *Well-organized and sophisticated groups of all kinds, including some government bureaus, gain power at the expense of less well-organized and less sophisticated groups.* The former are much better equipped than the latter to collect, analyze, understand, and react to the data outputs of automated systems. However, organization alone is not enough to counteract potential power shifts caused by urban data systems. Even well-organized groups may lose some power if their members are not technically sophisticated.

6. *Within city governments, those who actually control automated data systems gain in power at the expense of those who do not.* Most city officials are acutely aware of this potential

power shift. Each operating department naturally wants to retain as much power as possible over its own behavior and its traditional sphere of activity. Its members are especially anxious to prevent "outsiders" from having detailed knowledge about every aspect of the department's operations. Hence nearly every department with operations susceptible to computerized management will at least initially fight for its own computer and data system controlled by its own members.

At the other extreme, city planners and budgetary officials will both eventually espouse centralized data systems. They will view such systems at least in part as means of gaining control over the information channels vital to all operating departments—and thereby capturing some of the latter's power. Therefore, *much of the controversy which is sure to arise concerning the proper design and operation of urban data systems will reflect a power struggle for control of those systems.*

7. *Technically educated officials within city governments gain power at the expense of old-style political advisors.* The latter are the "wise old (or young) men" found clustered around the head of every local, state, and national government. Their function has always been to provide good judgment in the face of uncertainty. But urban data systems tend to substitute new types of uncertainty (such as that concerning statistical reliability) for old (such as that concerning the accuracy of individual insights). Well-educated data technicians will seem much more capable of coping with these new uncertainties than will the traditional "wise men."

However, politicians will soon discover that data technicians cannot really deliver on their promises to make accurate predictions of crucial variables. Our ignorance is still too profound for such accuracy. Hence a new advisory role will appear for men who possess *both* technical sophistication and wisdom. Although many men can learn sophisticated techniques, true wisdom is extremely scarce; so such advisors will acquire increasing power.

HOW POWER PAYOFFS INFLUENCE TYPES OF URBAN DATA SYSTEMS USED

The power shifts described above will markedly affect the attitudes of specific groups and individuals towards the use of automated data systems. However, not all power losers will oppose the system, and not all power gainers will support it. In the first place, most people who will be affected by a new system will be uncertain about whether they will gain or lose when it is introduced. Hence their attitudes will be ambivalent, unless they oppose it out of sheer inertia. Second, some power losers may accept the system because of its large technical payoffs, and some gainers may oppose it because its costs outweigh the technical payoffs they perceive. Third, some people who realize in advance how a new data system will affect their power will not attempt to influence the decision about whether to use it. Either they feel they cannot affect that decision, or they believe its impact will be slight. Therefore, only a minority of the persons whose power will in fact be affected by a new urban data system are likely to support or oppose it in advance because of their beliefs about its power impacts upon them.

Nevertheless, this minority will exert very significant influence for two reasons. First, a minority with strong opinions about highly technical matters almost always has great influence in our democratic society concerning those matters. The majority of persons are too ignorant or apathetic to express any technical views at all. Second, the only people likely to be in this particular minority are those who hold powerful positions in the urban decision-making structure—especially within the city government.

The officials in this minority will consist of two groups. On the one hand, city planners, administrative assistants to mayors and city managers, and other high-ranking staff members, plus some top politicians, will press for early introduction and widespread use of fairly comprehensive data systems. On the other hand, many officials in specific operating departments will drag their feet about introducing automated systems, restrict the use of such systems sharply, and insist upon allowing each department to set up and operate its own system.

In the long run, the former group will prevail. The higher technical payoffs of comprehensive systems will eventually become clear to everyone. But in the short run—which may last for a decade or even longer—the latter group will be more powerful in many cities in spite of its lower rank. In most city governments, the people who run the everyday affairs of each operating department invariably exert much greater influence over how those affairs are carried out than central staff members or even top-level elected officials. Introducing any automated data system into an ongoing department requires great changes in day-to-day procedures. Therefore, it necessitates overcoming the department's inherent inertia.

Few mayors or city managers, however powerful, are strong enough to fight such inertia in all departments simultaneously. Yet that is precisely what they would have to do in order to install a single comprehensive system covering all city operations, unless individual department heads become convinced that such a system would greatly aid their own shops. Furthermore, resistance to automated data systems within each department will be greatly reduced if its top-level officials have a strong incentive to use them. They would if those systems were designed specifically for their benefit and operated by them. Therefore, *perception of power payoffs by departmental officials is likely to cause many cities to adopt a highly piecemeal approach to the adoption and use of automated urban data systems.* Thus both piecemeal and comprehensive approaches will be followed by different cities in the next few years.[9]

It is quite likely that the total costs of eventually arriving at a single integrated data system in any city will be much greater via the piecemeal route than they would via initial adoption of a comprehensive system. The former approach will require gradually developing links between disparate individual systems not initially designed to function as a unit. The cost of such development will probably exceed that of providing such links right from the start in one integrated system. Moreover, some of the data necessary for development of basic theories about causal relationships in the urban scene can emerge only from an integrated system. But it will take much longer to create an integrated system through piecemeal construction. Hence technical payoffs based on knowledge of these causal relationships may be delayed for years. Similarly, under the piecemeal approach, those parts of government which receive automated systems last will not enjoy the technical payoffs thereof until much later.

In spite of these drawbacks, it is at least arguable that the piecemeal approach has sizable advantages for technical reasons as well as power payoff reasons. If cities refrained from installing any automated data systems until adequate research for fully comprehensive systems were completed, they would have to pass up sizable technical payoffs which can be achieved immediately in certain departments. Moreover, any attempt to install a comprehensive system in a large city might wind up as a piecemeal approach anyway. By the time the last "integrated" units were installed, technical changes might have made the first units obsolete.

Conclusions

It can hardly be doubted that automated data systems will soon have profound effects upon government and private decision-making in urban areas—and at state and federal levels too. Nor is it debatable that these revolutionary impacts will spring from the immense technical improvements in data which such systems make possible. Nevertheless, the future form and use of automated data systems will not depend solely upon improvements in data. Rather they will depend upon the ways in which data improvements increase the effectiveness of actions and change the power positions of the actors involved. These two outcomes constitute the *final payoffs* from using automated data systems.

Therefore, in order to forecast how automated data systems are likely to be designed and used in government, we must shift our attention from the dazzling technical capabilities of computer systems to the ways in which men apply those systems in the real world.

Three major conclusions emerge. First, significant technical payoffs from automated data systems are much more ambiguous and difficult to demonstrate than technical improvements in data. Second, the ways in which public (and private) officials use automated data systems will be determined just as much by their perceptions of the resulting shifts in personal power as by their desire to reap technical benefits for the public interest.

Third, the nature of both technical and power payoffs implies that many city governments—as well as state and national governments—will develop automated data systems in a piecemeal, department-by-department fashion. Hence the glamorous comprehensive urban systems we hear about from "computerphiles" are likely to be a long time in coming in many areas.

One final observation is warranted. Experts who set up urban and other automated data systems should pay more attention to power payoffs in designing those systems. Every data system serves real flesh-and-blood men. These men sorely need the help obtainable from automated data systems. But they will not accept or effectively use such help unless it is offered to them in a way that takes their own interests into account.

Notes

[1] Some of these difficulties are discussed in Robert Dorfman, ed., *Measuring Benefits of Government Investments* (Washington: The Brookings Institution, 1963).

[2] A summary of some of these benefits can be found in Edward F. R. Hearle and Raymond J. Mason, *A Data Processing System for State and Local Governments* (Englewood Cliffs, N.J.: Prentice-Hall, Inc., 1963), pp. 92–100.

[3] This same tendency, but in relation to the use of computers in business organizations, is discussed in George P. Shultz and Thomas L. Whisler, eds., *Management Organization and the Computer* (Glencoe: The Free Press, 1960), Chapter 1.

[4] See Melvin M. Webber, "The Roles of Intelligence Systems in Urban-Systems Planning," *Journal of the American Institute of Planners*, November 1965, p. 294.

[5] To some extent, this waiting period can be reduced by collecting comparable data simultaneously in a number of different places.

[6] Webber, *ibid.*

[7] Most analysts of urban data systems have ignored power payoffs. Exceptions are Webber, *ibid.*, and Shultz and Whisler, *op. cit.*

[8] Shultz and Whisler, *op. cit.*, p. 13.

[9] To a certain extent, this tendency of cities to adopt both approaches is corroborated in Don Rose, ed., *Automated Data Processing in Municipal Governments: Status, Problems and Prospects* (Chicago: Public Administration Service, 1966).

11

Competition and Community Schools

To an economist, many of the criticisms recently made against big-city public school systems have a familiar ring: they are identical with the complaints that consumers have leveled against monopolies for centuries. Since big-city school boards, administrations, and teachers' organizations are all essentially monopoly organizations, this similarity of discontent is no coincidence.

The classic antidote to monopoly is competition. By introducing alternative sources of supply, competition expands the choice available to consumers. Moreover, these alternative sources are likely to use different methods and approaches, or even to develop wholly new products, thus greater variety makes expanded choice really meaningful. Since consumers can shift their trade from suppliers who do not please them, suppliers have a strong incentive to provide what the consumers want. This attitude also means competitors regard innovations positively, as potential means of winning more business (if they can protect new ideas from instant duplication by competitors). In contrast, monopolists usually view innovations negatively, as a bother designed to upset established routines for no good reason. Clearly, if greater competition causes these results in general, it might produce some tremendous improvements in big-city school systems.

Community schools could represent a limited form of competitive influence within such systems if these new types of schools were organized, operated, and related to other schools in certain ways. The shifting of power in education from a single, monolithic administration to many decentralized boards would be quite similar to the breaking up of a monopoly into many competitors—that is, if consumers really had the power to choose among the competitors, and did not merely find themselves faced by many small monopolists rather than one big one. In this chapter, I will examine some of the possibilities, implications, and problems of introducing more competition into big-city public school systems, and show how they can be related to community schools.

Requirements for Effective Competition

In order to provide the major benefits of competition, any system of production must possess certain fundamental characteristics. It is not possible to explore all of these here. Instead, five key characteristics will be described and related to existing conditions in most big-city school systems.

MEANS FOR CONSUMERS TO EVALUATE OUTPUTS

If consumers cannot tell a good product from a bad one, they cannot exercise consumer sovereignty so as to pressure the production system into giving them what they want. In our highly technological society, it is often difficult for consumers to evaluate the quality of products offered them. Is a Ford station wagon better or worse than a Chevrolet station wagon of comparable size and cost? Few people are expert enough to determine the answer. However, since both Fords and Chevrolets are readily available, consumers can directly compare certain measureable traits, such as size, design, and accessories. They can even hire experts to make impartial tests of more complex things, such as acceleration, braking, speed, and stability under loads.

Similar comparisons of more abstract products—such as schooling—require the same basic ingredients. That is, there must be well-defined outputs from different producers; those outputs must be measurable in some way; such measurements must be made; and information about those measurements must be available to consumers. Unfortunately, none of these conditions prevail today in big-city public school systems. There are few agreed-upon definitions of what public school systems are supposed to produce; measuring those products that can be identified is extremely hard; they are rarely measured because doing so is expensive and potentially threatening to many teachers, administrators, and parents; and such rare information as does exist is usually a closely guarded secret.

Nevertheless, some information is available about the quality of education provided in different parts of the nation. It has generated strong discontent among many parents of children in low-income, big-city areas, especially those where ethnic minorities live, because it shows how poor are the results of public schools there as compared to other areas. But effective competition within, or outside, big-city public school systems can never be stimulated without vastly improving the quality and quantity of information evaluating the outputs of different schools and educational methods. How this can be done will be discussed later.

THE EXISTENCE OF ALTERNATIVE SUPPLIERS

Few "perfect" monopolies exist. Most consumers can usually find some alternative source of supply if they look hard enough, and users of big-city school systems are no exception. Parents living in big cities can send their children to private schools, buy entry into suburban schools without moving (in some cases), or actually move into the jurisdictional area of some other school within the big-city system or into a suburban system. But these alternatives are all far more expensive than using the neighborhood public school. Therefore, low-income households cannot employ such alternatives. And even middle-income nonwhite households are restricted from moving into many all-white areas where superior schools are found. Thus, for thousands of households in big cities, there are no educational choices available except sending their children to that public school which has a district encompassing their residence.

Creating realistic alternative choices for these households will not be easy. Even placing control over local schools in the hands of many decentralized school boards will not expand real choices if each family must still use the nearest public school. Consumers—including the lowest-income consumers—must be able to choose among several, at least two and preferably more, alternatives if competition is to have any real effects. Therefore, individual schools must have attendance areas that overlap to some degree. For example, consider an area containing five elementary schools run by a single board of education. Each of these schools exclusively serves an attendance area surrounding it; that is, all students living in that area must attend that school, whereas no one living outside the area can attend that school. Now assume that control of these schools is shifted from a single centralized board into five decentralized boards. This does not create any expansion of choice for individual families if the same attendance policy is retained. However, such an expansion could be achieved by merging all five attendance areas into a single inclusive area, in which any family could apply to attend any school. Or additional public schools (perhaps run by outside firms or agencies) could be introduced into the area and assigned attendance areas overlapping those of the original five schools. These expansions of choice would have to be accompanied by some scheme providing public payment of the extra transportation costs resulting from parents' sending their children to schools other than the ones closest to their homes. Otherwise, low-income families would be under economic pressure to continue using the nearest school, even if other options were theoretically available to them.

Inescapably, awarding consumers some freedom of choice creates uncertainty among producers concerning what "share of the market" each school will actually "capture." For example, if each of the five schools serve 20 percent of all students initially, allowing consumers free choice might result in 40 percent applying for entry into one school, and only 10 percent into another. Coping with such an outcome raises difficult administrative and capital-planning considerations relevant to the next two requirements for effective competition.

FREEDOM TO OFFER SIGNIFICANTLY VARYING PRODUCTS

Multiplicity of outlets does not guarantee true competition concerning a given product; it must be accompanied by freedom among several producers to vary the nature of the products they offer. If every car dealer sold only red Ford two-door sedans all with the same accessories and at the same price, vastly increasing the number of dealer outlets would not expand consumer choice. Similarly, providing parents with the ability to choose among several schools for their children would not really increase their freedom of choice if exactly the same subjects, approaches, types of teachers, and materials were used in all the schools. True, individual personality differences among principals and teachers always produce some differences among schools, even when they are all governed by identical regulations. But a meaningful range of variation in educational contents and quality can be offered to parents only if principals of individual schools, or supervisors of relatively small districts, have real freedom to vary the products they offer consumers. Thus, decentralization of control over a significant part of what goes on in individual schools is an essential prerequisite for effective competition in education. Moreover, such decentralization must cover most of the key elements of educational contents. It is a sham to announce that individual principals or district superintendents are free to innovate and then retain centralized and standardized control over hiring and firing of teachers, teachers' salary levels, selection of textbooks, allowable classroom sizes, a large part of the curriculum, most administrative procedures, and capital expenditures for new buildings and equipment.

This means that competition among several schools for students cannot be the force that generates decentralized control of those schools. Allowing parents to choose among different schools might set up much stronger pressures accentuating those limited product differentiations that could be developed within existing centralized rules and regulations. But those rules and regulations must be greatly relaxed to allow wide variation among individual schools before competition can exert its maximum impact. To create fully effective competition requires overcoming all the frustrating and difficult obstacles that have so far blocked significant decentralization of control in most big-city systems.

Nevertheless, I do not believe it is feasible to wait for complete decentralization before initiating major experiments in greater competition. At least a few competitive units in which the local board, the principal, or individual teacher had significant autonomy could initially be set up outside the existing public school system, or as special, additional units supplementing it in certain areas. Similarly, competition among units within the system could be started even though only marginal decentralization of control existed (though this is inferior to the proposal just mentioned). But to postpone using competition until "perfect" decentralization is achieved is to forgo using it forever—even though it could be an immediate force exerting at least some added pressure to create greater decentralization of control.

CONSUMER CONTROL OVER SIGNIFICANT RESOURCES

In a free enterprise economy, consumers vote with dollars for the products they like—and against those they dislike. They can do so because they have the power to allocate those dollars to whatever producers they prefer (except for a few monopolies like the telephone company). Since the income represented by consumers' dollars is vital to producers, consumer-spending choices tremendously influence producer behavior. Similarly, if competition is to have any meaningful impact upon big-city public school systems, the consumers must have control over at least some resources used in their operation.

Some control is already exercised by school consumers. As voters, they decide on bond issues and sometimes indirectly upon other tax increases affecting the total resources available to the system. When a family moves from one place to another to gain access to better schools, it shifts its taxable resources into the new area. This increases the tax base there, and perhaps decreases it in the original area. It also moves its children from one school to another, and children are significant educational resources in several ways. First, they influence the total attendance figures used by each school as part of its formula for obtaining state aid. Second, the quality of education in each school is markedly influenced by the nature of the students attending it. In general, students from middle-income, upper-income, or other homes with strong cultural environments represent an educational asset to any school. But students from culturally deprived homes may represent an educational liability—considered solely from this viewpoint. Thus when parents move a child from one school to another, they affect both the financial and non-financial resources available to the two schools concerned. Naturally, they also affect the demands placed upon those schools by their student loads.

But what about parents who cannot afford to move in pursuit of better schools, or are prevented from doing so by racial prejudice or some other force? If they are offered true choices among alternative schools, they can at least shift their children from one school to another instead of shifting their homes. However, this might result in a marked disparity between the number of students asking to attend each school, and its physical capacity to handle them. If 500 students apply to a school with a capacity for 100 students because it provides unusually desirable educational opportunities, how can the available places be rationed among the applicants?

At present, this problem is solved by setting boundaries so that the situation does not arise. But at the same time this eliminates any true choice among alternatives. Private schools often handle this problem by raising their tuition. But such price rationing discriminates against poor families and hence is inappropriate for public schools. The simple rule of first-come, first-served may be used, but this tends to favor students from the most intelligent and culturally-advanced families, since they are more likely to plan ahead. The only remaining methods of allocation I can think of are random selection and use of geographic quotas. The latter can be illustrated by a system which divides the total attendance area into five parts with equal student population; classifies all applicants by location into five groups corresponding with these zones; sets a quota of 20 percent of total enrollment for each zone; and fills that quota from the applicants for each zone through random selection among them. If the boundaries of the five areas are carefully drawn in relation to the socioeconomic and ethnic traits of the population, this system can result in a well-balanced student body providing both ethnic and social-class integration in combinations likely to remain stable (that is, parents of one group will not withdraw their children to avoid the resulting balance).

Nevertheless, as long as any such rationing system still allocates the same proportion of total resources to each school as an exclusive district system; consumer choices are not really affecting the distribution of resources in the system. The worst school would still get 20 percent of all students, state aid, and other resources. Furthermore, parents whose children were assigned to that school would not really be exercising the kind of free choice vital to a truly competitive system. Many would have perferred to send their children to some other school, but it was too crowded. This brings us to the final requirement for a truly competitive system.

FREEDOM FOR CONSUMER PREFERENCES TO INFLUENCE RESOURCE ALLOCATION

A key long-run advantage of competitive markets is that they cause the production of those goods consumers like to expand, and the production of those they dislike to contract or disappear. This same characteristic is essential to effective competition within big-city public school systems. Consumers must be able to use their power over resources to alter the long-range output of different types of education. At present, this is possible in theory when consumers move from one city to another. If most of the residents of City A were so repelled by its schools that they moved to much-preferred City B nearby, then the schools in City A would be forced to contract their operations—and those in City B would expand.

Unfortunately, the economic ability to shift locations in search of better schools is unevenly distributed in society. Wealthier people can and do move to areas where the schools are reputed to be excellent. Those schools consequently expand. They can do so partly because the arrival of more middle-income or upper-income families within their attendance areas gives them the taxable resources they need for expansion. Furthermore, most students from such homes are positively oriented to education and benefit from relatively cultured home environments. Hence, their very presence in classrooms improves the quality of education. In contrast, poor students whose families cannot afford to move are left in the schools considered relatively undesirable. The departure of middle-income and upper-income students from those classrooms cause a higher concentration of students from relatively deprived homes, thereby lowering the quality of education. Moreover, rising concentration of poor families within the attendance areas of such schools reduced the per-student taxable resources available to support them. Thus, making alternative choices available to the wealthier families in society but not to the poorer, and to middle-income whites more than to middle-income nonwhites, tends to create long-run effects beneficial to the wealthier—especially whites—and detrimental to the poorer—especially nonwhites. What other tactics might help public school consumers gain the long-run advantages of competition without this undesirable result?

We have already described a system for allowing parents to express choices among five elementary schools all serving the same merged attendance area. But if all the parents who wanted to send their children to the best-liked school actually were allowed to do so, it might become extremely overcrowded. At the same time, the worst-liked school would be nearly empty. This would result in an inefficient use of invested capital, and might significantly reduce the quality of education in both schools. Yet adopting any system of student rationing that ultimately allocates 20 percent of all resources to each school does not result in any expansion of the most-preferred school or contraction of the least-preferred one. However, such expansion and contraction could be encouraged by either or both of the following tactics:

The first tactic is the use of a certain amount of flexible classroom and other school capacity that could be moved from one place to another. For example, if a school system consisted of 60 percent permanent buildings and 40 percent mobile classrooms, then the latter could be shifted around each year to accommodate parents' preferences for specific schools. Teachers and other resources would also be shifted correspondingly. This kind of arrangement could be put into effect quickly in cities with rapidly growing populations and school enrollments. A high proportion of the new physical capacity they add each year could consist of portable facilities. In cities that already have fixed plants adequate for present and future enrollments, addition of such mobile capacity would represent a huge added expense and cause underutilization of existing capacity. However, in such cities, if some older facilities must be retired because of obsolescence, they could be replaced with portable units so as to arrive at the desired balance without added expense.

This tactic has two decided disadvantages. First, most parents—and many teachers—regard portable facilities as inferior per se and as stigmatizing to the schools concerned. Second, moving such facilities—and other resources—each year would be expensive and might be administratively disruptive.

The second tactic is that of shifting control over the nature of education in accordance with the expressed votes of parents' attendance choices while still using the same buildings and classrooms. For example, assume there are five equal-sized schools in an attendance area containing 1,000 students. If 500 of these students apply to attend School X because its approach is preferred, so well-liked (or for any other reasons), then the methods used in School X would be extended to at least one and perhaps one and a half other schools. This could be done either by expanding the administrative and curriculum jurisdiction of the principal of School X to these other schools or by putting pressure on the principals of the other schools to adopt the methods used in School X. Both of these tactics imply that some central agency exists within the system to perform these reallocations of resources or authority. They also imply that the methods used in School X can be extended almost instantaneously, or at least quite rapidly, to other schools without loss of quality. This is highly unrealistic, but it could be rendered more feasible if a longer period of adjustment were allowed.

Both of these tactics probably seem utterly impractical to the people who actually operate big-city school systems. Yet some version of them must be incorporated into those systems if competition is to have meaningful impact upon public education in large cities. Even now, there is an implicit assumption that each centralized school administration will somehow seek out and discover the most effective methods of education, and introduce them into the classrooms throughout its system. But it is precisely the failure to incorporate the most desired educational methods—and to reduce those least desired—that is one of the chief complaints against existing big-city systems. Moreover, a key response to this failure is continuing migration of middle-class families with children from big cities to their suburbs. Consequently, even if big-city school administrators believe the kinds of responsiveness to consumer preferences indicated by the above tactics are impossible, many consumers clearly believe they are both desirable and possible—and act accordingly.

The Need for a Comprehensive Evaluation System

The preceding analysis emphasized the critical need for accurate and easily available information which evaluates both the educational performance of public schools and the methods of education used in them. Without such information, consumers cannot tell whether their children are really getting proper training or to what extent certain parts of that training is fine, and others are terrible. Parents make such judgments now; but they do so only on the basis of personal impressions gained from comparing experiences in different schools with their friends and acquaintances or with the few national test scores that professionals release to them. Many parents in low-income neighborhoods do not even have these elements upon which to base accurate judgments. Therefore, it would be pointless to make the other institutional changes necessary to introduce competition into big-city public school systems without first creating an accurate and comprehensive educational evaluation system, putting it into operation throughout the system, and making the results known to parents.

Such a system might also create pressures on individual schools, principals, local boards, and teachers to adopt those methods that have proved most effective in training various specific kinds of students. Revelation of the success of certain approaches, and the failure of others, would generate both parental and professional pressure to expand the former and contract the latter. Hence, an accurate and widely publicized evaluation system could act as a substitute for the two tactics described in the previous section which seem both so necessary and so impractical.

Furthermore, an evaluation system of this type could greatly improve the efficiency of resource allocation within our enormous national education system. It is astounding that around $50 billion per year is spent on education in the United States, yet there is no systematic way of measuring the effectiveness of this giant expenditure. Few accurate measurements of relationships between costs and effectiveness are made anywhere in the system, and none are regularly applied, even to large parts, to measure comparative performance. As a result, widespread disparities in both effectiveness and efficiency appear and continue without any corrective action. It is widely believed that public schools in the South are generally inferior to those in the North. Many observers also believe that public schools in the East have higher academic standards than those in the West (especially in California). Yet even these conclusions are based mainly on a few national achievement tests in a narrow range of subjects, casual inspection of expenditure-per-pupil data, and personal observations. Admittedly, I am no expert on the nature of educational research, and I may be ill-informed about much pertinent analysis in this area. Yet I believe it is fair to conclude that existing methods of evaluating educational performance are grossly inadequate. They can neither identify nor encourage the adoption of many potentially huge gains in effectiveness from our current national spending on schools.

Accurate evaluation of educational effectiveness will be especially important if community schools become widespread in the United States. The shift of control over curricula to many decentralized school boards will probably lead to a wide variety of educational approaches in different cities, and even within each large city. Each school board will have a vested interest in claiming that its approach is successful. Unless there is some relatively objective way to evaluate these multiple approaches, neither parents, nor national educational policy makers, nor local taxpayers will know which methods are really working and which ones are failing. Admittedly, they do not know now either. Thus, the case for an accurate, comprehensively applied evaluation system will be no stronger under community schools than it is now. But this case is already overwhelmingly persuasive.

Problems in Performance Evaluation Systems

One of the main reasons why so few school systems have developed comprehensive and accurate means of evaluating their performances is the extreme difficulty of doing so. The need for good evaluation is desperate, but the need alone yields no clue as to how it can be met. In this section, I will identify some of the key problems involved, and suggest some potential approaches to solving them or at least coping with them.

MULTIPLE ASPECTS OF EDUCATION

It is widely agreed that children who go to school should learn how to read, write, and perform certain basic mathematical skills with at least minimal proficiency. Their ability to do these things can be objectively measured by means of tests and compared with the abilities of other children of the same age and background. But schooling is also designed to have many other impacts on the children it affects. These include creating or bolstering self-confidence; inculcating certain basic democratic values, encouraging positive attitudes toward work; providing minimal skills and disciplinary habits relevant to work; and teaching basic skills of interpersonal relations. Measuring these things—indeed, just defining them—is extraordinarily difficult; in some cases, it may be impossible. Yet few educators believe that these nonacademic aspects of schooling are unimportant, and many believe they are more important than basic reading, writing, and arithmetic.

Therefore, no evaluation system should evade trying to measure the capabilities and changes in capabilities, of students regarding these nonacademic aspects of education. Attempts should be made to develop clear difinitions of the traits concerned, and descriptions of various states of proficiency concerning them. These will differ from place to place, especially if community schools become widespread. Nevertheless, the different participants in the education system—including teachers, students, parents, and counselors—should be asked to evaluate students using these criteria. Admittedly, subjective judgments may be prominent in such measurements, but trying to meet this problem head on will provide many significant insights, even if really precise interpersonal or interschool comparisons prove elusive.

MULTIPLE DISTRIBUTION GOALS

Viewed as a whole, the nation's public school system (or that of any state, district, or city) expends certain resources in order to attain one or more of the following distributions of educational results:

1. The *minimum-citizenship goal*—there should be some basic minimum level of proficiency and capability for all students regarding the various aspects of education discussed above, especially those most relevant to democratic citizenship.

2. The *maximum-system-output goal*—the total capabilities of all students considered as a group (perhaps best measured by their total resulting productivity) should be made as large as possible within the constraints imposed by the total resources available to the system.

3. The *equal-opportunity goal*—all students emerging from the system (say, upon high-school graduation) should have approximately the same capabilities for entering into the post-school portions of their lives.

4. The *maximum-individual-advancement goal*—each student should be given as much development of his individual potential as possible, within the constraints imposed by total available resources.

Undoubtedly, other worthy goals could also be identified. But I believe these four express the major system-wide objectives of education that are most commonly discussed in the United States.

These goals imply widely differing distributions of publicly supplied educational resources among various types of students and various geographic areas. This is true mainly because such resources are only one of the four basic inputs affecting the educational performance of particular students, as will be discussed later. The degree to which individual students possess the other three inputs varies widely in a rather systematic fashion. This variance is related to such factors as their parents' income and socioeconomic status, their geographic location in the nation and within metropolitan areas, and their ethnic nature. Consequently, pursuing each of the goals exclusively, without regard to the others, would result in very different allocations of publicly supplied educational inputs. At one extreme, the equal-opportunity goal would require a heavy concentration of resources among the poorest and most culturally deprived students. They would receive much higher per student inputs than children from higher-income and more advantaged homes. The minimum-citizenship goal would also require concentrating more inputs per student among the most-deprived children. It might not result in quite as unequal a distribution, since the poorest-qualified children would not have to be brought up to the level of attainment with the best-qualified but only up to some minimum standard of basic achievement. In contrast, the maximum-system-output goal would concentrate publicly supplied inputs on the best-qualified students. This would result in the greatest total gain in technical proficiency per dollar invested.[1] The maximum-individual-advancement goal results in an indeterminate allocation pattern, since it really provides no precisely defined objective. If the goal is interpreted as equal advancement (in contrast to equal achievement), then this allocation would also probably favor the lowest-income and most-deprived students. It takes more dollars of publicly-supplied inputs to advance such students a given amount in achievement than it does students from more advantaged homes.

At present, the allocation of such inputs greatly favors children from middle- and upper-income homes, especially whites, and penalizes those from poorer homes, especially nonwhites. This most closely resembles the allocation appropriate for the maximum-system-output goal. It is so unlike the allocation appropriate for the equal-opportunity goal that any major public emphasis upon that goal would call for radical revisions in the existing distribution of educational resources.

The existence of multiple goals and their call for such widely varying resource allocation patterns for publicly supplied inputs pose a difficult problem for anyone trying to design an educational evaluation system. Such a system should tell its users how well existing education methods achieve some set of goals concerning the performance of the educational system as a whole, as well as the performance of each district, school, or classroom. But which of these system-wide objectives should be used in making this assessment? Since any educational system should probably serve several goals simultaneously, the question really becomes what relative emphasis should be placed on each goal? Different groups of consumers would undoubtedly provide widely varying answers to this question. Their answers would depend to a great extent upon how each type of emphasis would affect the total share of publicly supplied inputs going to their own children. Therefore, the evaluation system would probably have to be designed so that it could be used to assess the effectiveness of the system in attaining each of these four goals (and perhaps others) independently. This would allow each consumer group to arrive at its own conclusions concerning whether the system was allocating publicly supplied inputs properly.

MULTIPLE INPUTS AFFECTING EDUCATIONAL ACHIEVEMENT

Recent large-scale studies of educational performance in the nation's schools have dramatically shown that activities in those schools are only one of the basic factors influencing educational achievement.[2] In fact, it is useful to view the output of the educational process as resulting from at least four different inputs for each child: (1) genetically determined capabilities inherited from parents; (2) the child's home environment, both present and past (particularly during the first few years of life); (3) the school system and all its component parts (including teachers, buildings, other facilities, methods, systems of mixing students; and (4) the child's nonhome, nonschool environment, which will be referred to as the neighborhood environment. These causal factors could be broken down somewhat differently, but this classification is sufficient to illustrate the key points concerned here.

Educational achievement, however defined, is influenced by all four of these factors simultaneously. Thus, attributing it to only one factor is neither just nor accurate. For example, system-wide testing usually indicates that children in schools serving upper-income white neighborhoods score much better on most tests than those in schools serving low-income nonwhite neighborhoods. Yet it might still be false to conclude that the former schools were doing a better job than the latter. The superior achievement of the higher-scoring students might be entirely attributable to the three nonschool factors. The schools serving the lower-scoring students could conceivably be doing a much better job than those serving the higher-scoring students, thereby causing the achievement gap between these two groups to be smaller than it would have been if both schools had performed with equal effectiveness.

Clearly, any useful educational evaluation system must be able to measure the impacts of the school system itself separately from the impacts of these other factors. Moreover, it should be able to measure the specific effects of various parts of the school system (such as training of teachers, quality of facilities, system of mixing students, attitudes of teachers, methods of instruction, and types of curricula). Only if it exhibits such sensitivity can an evaluation system enable those using it to make effective decisions about what publicly supplied inputs to alter and in what ways. But this kind of analytic separation of causal contributions to a single result is extremely difficult to build into any educational evaluation system. The widespread controversy among statisticians over the meaning of the Coleman Report perfectly illustrates this problem. To cope with this problem will require any workable evaluation system to have the following characteristics:

First, it must be used throughout a large part of the entire American school system simultaneously and in the same manner. Only in this way can a sufficiently large and varied sample be obtained so that the impact of a wide variety of individual factors can be isolated through standard statistical techniques. An evaluation system adopted by a single city might be large enough if that city itself was a big one. But if it is used only in one small suburban area, with a relatively homogeneous population in terms of socioeconomic and ethnic traits, then the evaluations it provides may not be measuring the performance of schools at all. This means that entire states would be much better units for the definition and administration of educational evaluation than individual school districts, and the entire nation would probably be the best base. However, it will be extremely difficult to get statewide or nationwide agreement on any specific method of measuring educational achievement—especially concerning those elements not easily subjected to written performance tests (such as success in building student self-confidence or imparting basic democratic values).

Second, a key part of the system should be comparing the performance of each group of children at different points in time. This would provide before and after results that would isolate the impact of the school since—persumably—the other three factors will not have varied significantly between these testing points. In reality, children's capabilities change significantly merely because they get older and acquire better coordination and more general experience. But this could be largely offset by relatively frequent evaluation (at least once a year, and perhaps more), and by the next device described.

Third, major emphasis in evaluation should be placed upon comparisons among parts of the school system serving students from similar home and neighborhood environments. Thus, the performance of schools serving low-income neighborhoods should be compared with each other, rather than with the performances of other schools serving upper-income areas. (This should not preclude the latter kinds of comparison, however, since they are necessary to certain system-wide effectiveness evaluations.) This would be analogous to dividing sailboats into specific categories or classes for comparing the performances of their crews. Such categorization should at least intellectually—though perhaps not emotionally—counteract some of the resistance to evaluation from teachers and administrators who fear that unfair comparisons will be made in criticism of their performances. (Unfortunately, many are equally afraid of fair comparisons.)

Fourth, the specific contents and procedures used in evaluation tests must be adapted to the particular experiences of students with tremendously varying backgrounds. Negro children reared in low-income urban slums do not have the same mental images, vocabularies, sense experiences, or even world outlooks as children growing up in wealthy all-white suburbs, on isolated Appalachian farms, or in borderline barrios where English is seldom spoken. Therefore, the techniques used to evaluate children's educational skills, and the impact of schools upon them, must be adopted to the particular experiences of the various types of children concerned. This implies that a wide variety of evaluation techniques and vehicles must be developed. It also seems inconsistent with the first key trait for an effective evaluation system mentioned above: that it be used throughout a large part of the entire school system simultaneously and in the same manner. Admittedly, creating differently adapted evaluative techniques that still permit intergroup comparisons will not be easy. But reaching the moon was not easy either, yet sufficient national resources were applied to accomplish that task. And in my opinion the potential payoff for developing effective educational evaluation system is vastly greater than the payoff for reaching the moon. Hence, an effort much greater than our present one should be devoted to this task.

DEFINING SYSTEM BOUNDARIES

Selecting the area to be included in any evaluation system will have a crucial impact upon the ways in which that system might be used to influence the allocation of publicly supplied educational inputs. At least two of the other three basic educational inputs are unevenly distributed through space. Thus, each school attendance area, or school district, contains a set of consumers quite different from the average composition of students in the nation or state as a whole. Families with home environments conducive to relatively high-level educational achievement tend to live mainly in areas with other such families. Together, they create neighborhood environments equally conducive to high-level achievement. Conversely, families with home environments that discourage high-level educational achievement also tend to cluster together. This produces neighborhood environments with similarly discouraging effects. Moreover, since most school systems use the neighborhood school principle to establish student mixtures, such spatial clustering means that students of each type tend to encounter similar type students in their classes. But classroom environment is a key ingredient in any school system. Hence the operation of the school system in such a residentially clustered society tends to further aggravate the inequalities of educational achievement resulting from home and neighborhood environments.

Insofar as the equal-opportunity objective is relevant to public education, it calls for an allocation that uses publicly supplied inputs to compensate for the inequalities resulting from the other inputs affecting educational achievement. But the practical implications of this conclusion for any given school vary sharply. They depend on whether that "system" is considered to be the schools in just one small community, an entire metropolitan area, a state, or the whole nation. At present, states supply a significant part of all publicly supplied inputs to local public schools. But most states do not allocate those resources to any well defined and high priority goal (or set of goals). They largely leave the pursuit of such goals to individual school districts. The formula used to pass out state educational funds is based mainly (though not always exclusively) upon equal per-student distribution. Insofar as the sources of such state funds are regressive (as are property taxes and sales taxes), this approach aggravates income inequalities. But this aspect of the issue is too complex to explore here. However, it is clear that the basic duality of state funding for educational operations—collecting funds on a statewide basis but leaving the decision of their effects up to individual districts—has a profound impact upon the net inequalities of educational achievement in each state.

This result could either be reinforced or counteracted by future educational evaluation systems, depending upon what geographic areas they apply to. If a single evaluation system is used throughout an entire state, it will soon reveal profound inequalities in educational achievements. Experts know that these inequalities now exist. But there are few stark statistics that explicitly identify and measure them in the dramatic ways that a statewide evaluation system would. Political or legal pressure for much greater equality of results would be likely to emerge quickly from such a revelation. This might result in some effort to allocate state-supplied resources to compensate for the inequalities of distribution of the other causal factors described above. On the other hand, if all evaluation systems are strictly local in nature, they would use varying techniques that would obscure such statewide comparisons. The resulting pressures for greater equalization of educational opportunity would probably be much lower, as they are now.

In my opinion, every state should insist upon statewide evaluation of at least some key components of educational achievement. Since the state supplies a significant fraction of public school funds to all districts, it has the right—indeed, the obligation—to ask for some accounting of how effectively its funds are being used—not just whether they are being spent without fraud. Many states already require local schools to teach certain subjects or even use certain textbooks. Therefore, it is certainly reasonable for them to ask localities to appraise the effectiveness of their educational efforts by using certain standardized evaluation methods. As an added encouragement, the federal government should require every state that accepts any federal educational assistance to institute at least some statewide evaluation system on an annual basis, with results made public for each district and school.

LOCAL RESISTANCE

Most people do not like to have their activities scrutinized and evaluated by "outsiders." This seems especially repugnant if the results are to be made public and compared to similar examination of other people engaged in the same activities. Such "auditing" of behavior may be both within the rights of the community that pays the auditors and highly beneficial to it, but these truths do not usually diminish community resistance. After all, any competent evaluation of an activity carried out on a large scale, like teaching in elementary and secondary schools, is bound to reveal that only a minority of those evaluated are superior in effectiveness. By definition, most will be rated as either average or below average. Thus, the majority have little to gain in terms of their own status and prestige, and perhaps quite a bit to lose. Even many parents, who stand to benefit most from evaluating the effectiveness of teachers, are often reluctant to subject the achievement levels of their own children to rigorous comparison with those of other children for fear of losing prestige or status.

This nearly universal resistance to evaluation occurs in many forms. The most obvious is opposing any evaluation schemes at all. More subtle is limiting the scope of such schemes. A third is insuring that control over the design and operation of the schemes is maintained by members of the organizations to be evaluated, so they can exclude the most threatening forms of evaluation. A fourth form of resistance is insisting that the results of any evaluation be kept confidential, or disclosing them to the public in such diluted forms that no individuals or schools can be pinpointed as incompetent or ineffective. The last form is demanding that no remedial actions be based upon the results of evaluation systems—particularly that salaries and other types of compensation be entirely divorced from effectiveness of performance.

In my opinion, the basic motive for all these forms of resistance is the dual fear of being revealed as ineffective, or being pressured to change in ways that might increase individual effort. However, this fear is rarely mentioned by those who support such resistance. Instead, they contend that the particular form of resistance they support is in the public interest. For example, it is commonly argued that "outsiders" should neither design nor control evaluation systems since they are not familiar with local problems, techniques, or educational objectives. Even more frequent is the contention that evaluation schemes cost far more money than already hard-pressed school systems can afford to spend.

It is these forms of defensive resistance, rather than any technical difficulties of designing or operating evaluation systems, that are now and will continue to be the major obstacles to widespread adoption of evaluation systems. Moreover as teachers' unions become more widespread and more powerful, such resistance will greatly increase. Ironically, supporters of community schools, are likely to be just as defensive about subjecting themselves to "impartial evaluations" as are the supporters of established school systems who are now accused of ineffective performance—and for the same reasons.

How can such nearly universal—and intense—resistance to evaluation be overcome? I can only offer the following suggestions as possible tactics:

First, state and federal agencies responsible for providing funds to local school districts should insist upon use of evaluation systems with certain basic characteristics as a requirement for receiving such aid. This would provide a strong incentive for adoption.

Second, evaluation systems should be designed and operated by persons outside the district public school administration, but that administration should have some voice in selecting the evaluators. They could perhaps come from local universities or consulting firms in whom the administration has confidence, possibly because of previous experience.

Third, the analogy of public auditing done by outside accountants should be used to persuade congressmen, other officials, citizens, and major public media that evaluation systems not only make sense but are necessary to protect the public's legitimate interest in using its money wisely. The growing understanding and support for planning, programming, and budgeting systems provides further intellectual underpinning for effectiveness evaluation systems.

Fourth, proposed evaluation schemes should not be linked to mechanisms that would translate evaluation results into changes in school behavior. Deciding what to do in response to such results should be left up to the parents, educators, and politicians in each district. Thus emphasizing only the provision of accurate data may reduce the threatening image of evaluation systems in the minds of those who fear any loss of local control over public education.

Finally, evaluation schemes could initially be restricted to community schools. The diversity of approaches likely to appear in these schools makes the need for some means of measuring their performance seem plausible. Also, their experimental character fits in well with the need to innovate in the design of evaluation systems. Even more important, the majority of existing educators will not be involved in running community schools; thus they would not feel threatened by evaluation systems aimed only at those schools. Using evaluation systems only in community schools could even have a vindictive appeal to those educators who believe that community schools cannot work. Even if community schools did fail to improve educational effectiveness directly, they would still be making an important contribution to overall educational effectiveness by thus opening the door to widespread employment of accurate evaluation systems.

SCARCITY OF RESOURCES

Most big-city public school systems are desperately short of financial resources. Therefore, they regard any diversion of available funds from educational programs to other activities as too wasteful or luxurious to contemplate. The argument that diversion of 1/2 of 1 percent of all their funds into evaluation might result in a 10 percent or greater improvement in the effectiveness of the remaining 99.5 percent of all funds has so far failed to sway this resistance. However, I believe this is largely because there is so little evidence that effective evaluation systems can actually be designed. Once the possibility of creating and using such systems effectively has been demonstrated, school boards throughout the nation will be far more receptive to installing them. The initial, key task, then, is getting a few well-designed systems under way.

This is a "natural" situation for the use of foundation funding or federal experimental funding. Money for development of a large-scale evaluation system over a five-year period might be tied to money for some other kind of program a big-city system especially desires. This would "sweeten" the package so as to make acceptance of an evaluation system more likely. One such program, which could also be used as a testing ground for the evaluation system, might be the development of prototype community schools on an experimental basis. Once an evaluation system was placed in operation, its success (or failure) at stimulating improvements in the schools concerned would greatly increase (or further reduce) the incentive of other school boards to launch similar programs.

Alternative Ways to Introduce Competition into
Big-City Public School Systems

Assuming that greater competition in big-city public school systems is generally desirable, there are several specific ways to attain it. Some are mutually exclusive; but most could be used in combination.

WIDESPREAD AND WELL-PUBLICIZED USE OF EVALUATION SYSTEMS

The simplest way to create greater competition among public schools would be to design, install, and use educational effectiveness evaluation systems along the lines discussed earlier. Although such systems would probably encounter great initial resistance, their use would actually require no significant institutional or administrative changes in existing public school systems. They would generate greater competition solely by revealing to the consumers of education, and to all the professionals concerned, the relative effectiveness of each school, district, educational approach, or other element subject to any kind of measurement. Presumably, the persons in charge of those aspects that appeared to be least effective would receive heavy pressure from those they served, from their own professional pride, and from other educational professionals to adopt elements revealed as more effective.

Competition through better information would be most furthered by evaluation systems that measured: (1) the objective level of achievement of the students in each school (or even each classroom) related to analogous levels for all the other students in the system concerned, in the entire state, and in the whole nation, and particularly to other students in similar homes and neighborhood environments; (2) the contribution to that achievement of the school itself, and of specific elements within the school (such as teachers, methods, student mixture); (3) the contribution of the school to the attainment of nonacademic goals of education; and (4) the effectiveness of various specific educational techniques in relation to their costs (not just in relation to their results, as is typical of existing educational evaluations).

As noted earlier, formidable technical and political obstacles inhibit the early use of evaluation systems to stimulate competition in big-city school systems. Therefore, two types of compromises concerning evaluation systems appear necessary. First, any evaluation scheme that is at all sensible should be encouraged and initiated as soon as possible, even if it does not exhibit all or most of the desirable qualities described above. Second, there is no reason to wait until effective evaluation systems are designed before using the other forms of competition, as set forth below. It may be hard for parents to assess the quality of the alternative educational products offered them by competition without a good evaluation system. Nevertheless, any significant increase in competition is likely to produce desirable results and generate healthy pressures on present big-city school monopolies.

USE OF COMMUNITY SCHOOLS TO ENCOURAGE DIVERSITY

Community schools would also encourage a degree of competition within public school systems if they had at least two key attributes. The first is a diversity of educational approaches. This would presumably arise if a wide variety of communities actually had control over significant portions of the curricula in schools serving them. The second is an evaluation system that would measure the effectiveness of these different approaches and promulgate the results throughout the system. Both of these attributes would generate some of the benefits of competition even if students in each part of the city are compelled to attend the school serving their area of the city rather than being given a choice of several schools. Again, knowledge of what worked and what failed should generate at least some pressure on schools that are failing to adopt the successful approaches used in those that are succeeding—or at least doing better.

USE OF OVERLAPPING ATTENDANCE AREAS

There are several ways that overlapping attendance areas, discussed earlier, could be used to create greater competition within an existing public school system.

Expansion of existing attendance areas. If attendance areas for several schools located close to each other were merged, then students anywhere in the enlarged area could attend any school among those serving it. This would cause a concentration of applicants at the schools considered the best, and a shrinkage of applicants at those considered the worst. The approach would generate higher total transportation costs than the pure neighborhood school system. It might also require some form of student-rationing system other than geographic location. However, because simply merging attendance areas would not involve deliberately planned diversity, differences in quality within the system would result mainly from accidents of supervisory abilities. Most parents would probably continue to send their children to the school that was geographically most convenient, rather than encouraging them to go longer distances to find higher quality. Hence, the magnitude of the extra transportation costs involved, and the pressure to use nongeographic rationing, would probably not be great over the whole system; nor would the impact of the resulting competition become very significant.

Expansion of attendance areas plus creation of community schools. This approach is similar to the one above, but would involve more deliberately planned diversity among schools. Hence, the ability of students to choose from among several reasonably proximate schools would represent a more meaningful choice. This might result in a greater convergence of students on certain schools regarded as superior, and more avoidance of those regarded as inferior. Consequently, the whole system would not be so dominated by sheer geographic convenience (though I believe that would probably remain the single most significant factor in parental choice of schools). Transportation costs would rise significantly, and the pressure to adopt some kind of nongeographic student rationing system would also mount. Furthermore, the appearance of much greater diversity of educational approaches would create greater pressure to allow parents in any given area to send their children to schools located elsewhere, even though doing so would be less convenient. This would occur because some parents in each neighborhood would surely disagree with the particular educational approach or emphasis adopted by the community school serving that neighborhood. To insure proper freedom of choice, these parents would have to be allowed to send their children to some alternative schools. These alternatives could be either community schools elsewhere or schools still run by the centralized school administration, or both.

Community schools can be either entirely new structures (or at least structures newly used for schooling) added onto the existing system (in which case, the central authorities might still operate schools in almost every neighborhood), or conversions of existing schools into community-controlled schools (in which case, the central authorities would be running fewer schools). But in either case, use of enlarged attendance areas would be extremely important as a means of introducing and maintaining competition within the system.

Expansion of attendance areas plus creation of experimental schools. This approach is very similar to the one just described, except that the alternative schools would be run by innovation-oriented groups (such as private firms, universities, or local volunteers) rather than community-oriented groups—or perhaps in conjunction with the latter. For example, a community school board might select a basic approach to education, and then contract with a private firm to carry out that approach. This mixture of public control and private administration has already been endorsed by such educational experts as Theodore Sizer and Christopher Jencks.[3] It would provide many private firms interested in educational markets with a chance to show what they could do, thereby generating a new source of competition to existing public schools.

AWARDING PARENTS VOUCHERS TO BUY SCHOOLING

Milton Friedman has suggested that competition could be injected into public education by having educational services financed publicly but produced by a wide variety of private, profit-motivated firms. The parents of every child would receive a publicly financed voucher of a fixed sum per child. They could then use this voucher to buy educational services from any "approved" supplier they wanted to patronize.[4] As Henry Levin pointed out in his excellent analysis of this proposal, it would undoubtedly increase the variety of educational services offered to parents, thereby enabling them to find more easily the kinds of educational services they wanted.[5]

But this scheme would also have two less desirable effects. First, it is vital for society as a whole to insure that all citizens receive a minimum quality education regarding certain skills and knowledge necessary for effective citizenship. Yet experience with other forms of private consumption shows that ignorant, low-income consumers can be exploited by unscrupulous producers who persuade the consumers to pay exorbitant prices for inferior-quality goods. To prevent this outcome from occurring in education, it would be necessary for public authorities to exercise some form of regulation over all private producers of educational services. Such regulation might become nearly as extensive and standardized as existing public production of education.

Second, wealthier parents could add more funds to the voucher to buy better-quality services, but poor parents could not. Wealthier parents would evoke high-quality schools that would attract the best teachers and use the best facilities; poor parents would be compelled to give their children much lower-quality educations. Thus, direct price discrimination based on incomes would accomplish precisely the same result that geographic discrimination based on incomes now achieves. This would aggravate existing inequalities of educational opportunity rather than diminish them.

However, this second disadvantage could be offset by awarding a much larger voucher to low-income families than to higher-income families, as Levin points out. He describes two methods: a sliding scale with payments varying inversely with income, and provision of such aid only to the lowest-income families. He rejects the first as politically unrealistic, but regards the second as politically possible—perhaps because it is essentially a novel version of the aid provided under Title I of the Elementary and Secondary Education Act of 1965.

For purposes of this analysis, I will assume that some form of providing either full vouchers or bonus payments to students from low-income households, and allowing them to choose where to apply such grants, could be used to inject a significant degree of competition into big-city public school systems. Every such voucher or bonus should be at least large enough to pay for the extra inputs needed to offset the disadvantages imposed on the child's education by deficiencies in his nonschool environment. In fact, any voucher or bonus should be made large enough to convert each low-income child from a liability into an asset, as seen from the viewpoints of the suppliers of education and of the parents of other children in the schools involved. Then, the voucher or bonus would create a surplus over and above the marginal cost of educating the low-income child. That surplus could then be applied to improving the quality of the entire school which accepted such a child. This would provide a positive incentive for schools to accept or even seek out such children. However, it is unlikely that society will presently pay the relatively large "amounts" needed to accomplish this outcome.

A voucher or bonus arrangement favoring low-income students could be used in any one of the three basic forms describing the use of overlapping attendance areas. That is, it could be employed in conjunction with an expansion of existing attendance areas into large and overlapping zones, or with a similar expansion plus the development of community schools, or with a similar expansion plus the development of experimental schools (which might be related to community control). In the last case, special schools catering only to students with vouchers or bonus payments might be developed. They would be able to use very high levels of expenditure per student. In the first case, special schools with geographic quotas or bonus-student quotas could be developed. They could provide a socially integrated educational environment that would still take advantage of the added resources made possible by the bonus payments. But in all cases, the parents of low-income children would have to be allowed at least some discretion about where their children would use their bonuses if the benefits of true competition were to be generated.

Conclusion

Large bureaucratic organizations almost never make major changes in established behavior patterns unless strongly pressured by outside forces.[6] The most powerful form of such pressure is a direct threat to their continued existence, or to their current prequisites of office. This kind of threat can usually be created only by an alliance of all or most of the outside agents who support the bureaucracy. They must get together and demand that the bureaucracy change or else they will remove or drastically reduce their support. But when the bureaucracy produces some vital service, they can reduce their support only by creating a competitive institution to provide that service. Competition has the advantage of generating sustained, almost automatic, pressure upon the organizations involved to keep adapting their production to consumers' wants, without constant vigilance by the consumers themselves.

Big-city public school systems are huge bureaucracies. Therefore, one of the potentially most effective ways of getting them to change their unsatisfactory behavior is to introduce significant elements of competition into their operation. It would be totally unrealistic to assume that most, or even any large fraction, of the existing school systems in large cities could soon be replaced by competitive systems created or run by outsiders. There are simply not enough qualified—or even unqualified—teachers around to create truly parallel systems that could compete with existing public school systems across the board. Moreover, the additional capital investment required to build physical facilities for such an all-out system would be prohibitive.

Nevertheless, even a small dose of competition in certain forms could produce very important—even radical—changes in the nature and quality of education in big-city public schools. The first and most crucial step is developing and using effective ways of evaluating the educational performance of public schools. Other devices may also be employed to generate the benefits of competition, with varying requirements concerning the amount of basic institutional change involved.

Community schools are currently being advanced almost as a panacea that will create the clearly needed changes in big-city public school systems. But unless community schools are designed and operated so as to increase competitive pressures within those systems, I do not believe they will have the desired effects. The pressure of competition is the crucial ingredient needed to force big-city school systems to adapt their outputs to what consumers want and need. Without such pressure, those school systems will continue succumbing to the natural tendency of all monopolists: providing what is most convenient for them to produce regardless of its suitability to the true needs of those who must consume it.

Notes

[1] Henry Levin argues that the highest marginal payoff would come from applying added resources to students from the most deprived backgrounds. He assumes that there are constantly declining marginal returns to investment in education. Since deprived children have had fewer total resources applied to their education (by their parents as well as public school systems) than less-deprived children, the more-deprived children are not as "far out" on their marginal payoff curves as less-deprived children. However, I believe that the marginal returns from education are not constantly declining. Translating this jargon into English, it seems to me that children from affluent backgrounds who have already received considerable education can absorb a given additional amount of knowledge, or learn an additional amount of a skill, with less input from teachers or other publicly supplied resources than

deprived children can. Admittedly, this is a purely subjective judgment on my part. See Henry M. Levin, "The Failure of the Public Schools and the Free Market Remedy," *Urban Review*, Vol. 2 (June 1968), pp. 32–37 (Brookings Reprint 48).

[2]See James S. Coleman and others, *Equality of Educational Opportunity* (U.S. Office of Education, 1966), referred to as the Coleman report. See also U.S. Commission on Civil Rights *Racial Isolation in the Public Schools* (1967).

[3]See Christopher Jencks, "Is the Public School Obsolete?" *Public Interest*, No. 2 (Winter 1966), pp. 18–27, and Theodore Sizer, "Reform and the Control of Education" (processed; Harvard University, Graduate School of Education, 1967).

[4]Milton Friedman, "The Role of Government in Education," *Capitalism and Freedom* (University of Chicago Press, 1962), pp. 85–107.

[5]Levin, "The Failure of the Public Schools."

[6]This definitive generalization is taken from a source in which I have an unusually high degree of confidence. See Anthony Downs, *Inside Bureaucracy* (Little, Brown, 1967), Chapt. II and XVI.